THE

Rashid Maxwell is a poet, artist, environmentalist, writer of fiction and biography, designer and builder of buildings for meditation, carpenter, art therapist, ornithologist, gardener, landscape designer, lecturer in fine art, beekeeper, playmate of many grandchildren and agnostic as well.

In appreciation of the book

'It takes courage to be oneself—now more than ever there's a need to live with awareness and independence; with love and compassion. Osho's work is to bring awareness to all aspects of life. He has evolved new meditations for modern humanity. He values the heart and the head, the mundane and the mysterious, the sinners and the saints, male and female equally. Laxmi was an ordinary woman who led an extraordinary life. She is you and me. Like so many of us she wanted to make the world a kinder place but it was not until she met Osho that she could fulfil that intention. However, she had to pass through the fire of a master's transmission to become pure gold. That transmission flows through this book. I congratulate Rashid for this beautiful book. The readers will find inspiration to live life with awareness and celebration.'—Sushmita Sen (Actor)

'Congratulations, Rashid. This book helps give form to Osho's inspiration.'—A.R. Rahman (Composer, musician, singer, educationist, movie-maker)

'Osho led Laxmi to the edge of understanding the Ultimate Truth. She completed the journey herself. She appears to be a real and honest seeker of Truth.'—Sonu Nigam (Singer)

'Osho didn't just live amidst us: he changed the world he lived in and changed himself too. He wasn't a spiritualist but instead an intellectual messiah who held up the mirror for all to see. In many ways, he was the last of the philosophers we would embrace and be blessed to learn from. Yet again, he wasn't the quintessential teacher: he was in fact the essential shepherd. This book *The Only Life* is more than a book: it captures the essence of what Osho was and what his teachings are. Resonating long after he's left the body but never our souls.'—Suhel Seth (Author, marketing maven)

'Rashid has written a remarkable book. The story of Ma Yoga Laxmi is a story of self-discovery. It is a journey of the heart which goes through the dark night of the soul. The spiritual masters and mystics make such a journey to be free from fear and to discover their deep source of inner peace as well as peace in the world. By reading Ma Yoga Laxmi's story the readers will be able to resonate with their own struggles and blessings and realise that these are two sides of the same coin. I would like to congratulate Rashid for making this wonderful biography available to us. The story of Ma Yoga Laxmi is both heart wrenching and heart-warming at the same time. The book is a good companion on our own journey of enlightenment.'—Satish Kumar (Editor Emeritus, *Resurgence & Ecologist Magazine*)

'Ma Yoga Laxmi was to Osho what Anand was to Gautama Buddha with one major difference—there is no record or evidence that Anand's life with Gautama Buddha went through the number and kinds of twists and turns, ups and downs, deaths and rebirths that Ma Yoga Laxmi's life was so blessed to go through with Osho. She not only walked what Osho talked, she lived it and lived it joyfully. She had been a witness to the *sannyas* of thousands of us *sannyasins*. She had been our collective envy for her proximity to Osho as well as our collective tears for what she endured—being closest to Osho meant she received the maximum and the harshest hits from Osho's Zen stick! She was one of us and all of us. In Swami Dev Rashid's *The Only Life* she touches us once again and Osho's vision as well as our own hearts finds a lucid voice. A blessing for Osho lovers and a window for the uninitiated to Osho's vision and what it means to be a disciple of a master of masters.'—Kamlesh Pandey (Swami Anand Kamlesh) (Creative writer, media personality)

'From the very first sentence I was hooked. Writing with such elegance, passion and immediacy, Rashid has produced a beautiful, heartfelt memoir of a truly incredible woman, who exuded the sacred feminine throughout her humble life as well as being the very embodiment of the noble Self. *The Only Life* is a remarkable journey that will similarly transform all those who imbibe its profound and captivating prose.'—Paula Marvelly (Author, Editor, *The Culturium*)

'Laxmi's ongoing clear and constant transmission of Grace flows from this book of her life by Rashid Maxwell. I was lucky to have held a letter written by her in my hand, and was struck by the strength and peace within it. She was and still is an embodiment of service, devotion and humility, now alive and well as the luminous sober love that shepherds and supports all beings.'—Pamela Wilson (Sage)

'Listening to Osho is very refreshing. It enables deep reflection.'—Dr Kiran Bedi (IPS [Retd])

THE ONLY LIFE

Osho, Laxmi and a Journey of
the Heart

RASHID MAXWELL

**SIMON &
SCHUSTER**

London · New York · Sydney · Toronto · New Delhi

A CBS COMPANY

First published in India by Simon & Schuster India, 2017
A CBS company

1 3 5 7 9 10 8 6 4 2

Simon & Schuster India
818, Indraprakash Building,
21, Barakhamba Road,
New Delhi 110001

www.simonandschuster.co.in

PB ISBN: 978-93-86797-04-9
eBook ISBN: 978-93-86797-05-6

Typeset in India by SÜRYA, New Delhi

Printed and bound in India by Replika Press Pvt. Ltd.

MIX
Paper from
responsible sources
FSC
www.fsc.org FSC® C016779

Simon & Schuster India is committed to sourcing paper that is
made from wood grown in sustainable forests and
support the Forest Stewardship Council, the leading
international forest certification organisation.
Our books displaying the FSC logo are
printed on FSC certified paper.

CONTENTS

FOREWORD

I met Osho in 1988 with my senior film-maker friend Vijay
Anand. Since that time my understanding of the ways of
the world and of mankind has matured and evolved. Osho's
thoughts, discourses and books have greatly influenced my
movies, my sense of music, poetry, drama and aesthetics. In
1999 I wrote and directed the film *Taal*; it was both directly
and indirectly, consciously and unconsciously pervaded by
Osho's teachings; particularly the idea—'Rise in love, do
not fall in love.'

Osho takes you to a new horizon beyond traditional
beliefs. He nourishes the seeker in you and makes you
question, debate, explore the universal truth within you. It
is no wonder that so many of His people have been
transformed by the subtle alchemy of the master–disciple
relationship.

In *The Only Life*, we see how one of Osho's first disciples,
Ma Yoga Laxmi, embodies His vision of Zorba the Buddha,
the new man or woman who lives fully both the life of the
material world and the life of the spirit. Like all of us she
had to pass through dark valleys and strenuous times to
arrive at the sunlit summit. The author and disciple of
Osho, Swami Deva Rashid Maxwell shows how, through

meditation and engagement with life, harmony, wisdom and loving kindness arose in her, qualities the world needs urgently. This is a story for our times.

SUBHASH GHAI
(Film-maker)

Osho and his work—that is the only life that Laxmi has.

—Ma Yoga Laxmi

PROLOGUE

Biography is a branch of fiction. To find out facts we read the newspapers or click on Wikipedia. To hear the truth we go to an enlightened one, to poetry and works of art, or to a child.

This book dwells in the borderlands between history and myth. It was brought into being to retrace and remember the life of the late Ma Yoga Laxmi. She had to pass through dark valleys and rank swamps before reaching those high peaks in the sun to which we all aspire; she found that place of peace and kinship with all things.

Her story is a story for our troubled times. It is set in Devotion, the all but vanished land that lies beyond our customary horizons. She was the moon to Osho's sun. And Osho was, way back in the seventies and eighties, pointing to the cliff-edge where humanity now dithers. He was offering us then the remedies for now.

We know of all the problems piling up across the world; of global warming and extreme weather, of polluted environments and a flawed economic system, of war amongst nations, ethnicities and religions, of human rights and gender rights in jeopardy, of overpopulation and mass migrations, of the threats posed by Artificial Intelligence and bioengineering—the list grows everyday longer. And strangely, deep down in our hearts, we know the solutions too: Osho was proposing us a medicine for our malaise. He was showing us the way of balance and the threads that link us to each other and all things.

To change the world we must change ourselves. This is not esoteric—it is scientific. Nature has evolved as a myriad of species. With humankind, the natural, collective and unconscious process of evolution ends. With humankind, conscious evolution begins. Not as a species, but as individuals. This is twice as necessary now because we have evolved slower than our technology. Hence the saying, 'To change the world we must change ourselves.'

All our ills are in truth just one disease—unconsciousness, unawareness. This malady, of which we are not conscious, is cured by taking a simple medicine. A simple but by no means easy medicine—meditation. Meditation, self-enquiry, or what is now often called mindfulness is the fast track medicine that ushers in awareness; an awareness that solves or resolves all our problems.

The age of the expert is over; we stand at a door we can and must open ourselves. Like Laxmi, we need no beliefs, no ideology and no special knowledge. Such things have brought us to this dire extremity. Like her, we need to be open, open to changing our mind.

Laxmi takes the medicine; she inspires.

1. HIS ZEN STICK

She is one of many. She sits immobile, close to the podium, a marble buddha on a marble floor. In the silence of a thousand seekers, she is waiting in a timeless zone for the master to arrive. She listens for the glottal crunch of tyres on gravel, the master's slow approach. All anticipate his words, his silence and the fragrance of the evening meditation.

The wealth of India is memoried in the early summer heat and in the sounds and smells that carry on the warm night air. Trains shunt and clatter in a distant darkness, merchants mutter underneath the compound walls; the scent of jasmine and the fumes of diesel rickshaws hang suspended.

This night, the master who is never late, is late.

A ripple passes through the front few rows. Closed eyes are opened, ears pricked up. Someone in security half rises as two figures enter by the door beside the podium. They are the master's present secretary Ma Neelam, followed by the Ashram manager or 'Ashram-in-charge'. They tiptoe over to Ma Laxmi, a slight, bright songbird of a woman meditating in the reserved front row. She herself was Osho's first disciple and once his secretary and chief administrator. Neelam lays a gentle hand upon her shoulder, invites her with her eloquent eyes and elegant hands to stand and follow her. Laxmi, when she slowly rises, is diminutive. Neelam is tall. They glide, long black iridescent hair on snow-white robes, soundless through the curtained exit to the gravel drive behind. The guard sits back, alert but now relaxed.

Neelam whispers, 'Laxmi Ma, why are you here? You are not welcome in this commune. You are banned.'

There is a sharp intake of breath and then the hiss of Laxmi's outraged voice. 'How dare you say that to me! How dare you throw me out of my master's place! You have no authority to bar a disciple from listening to her master.' Laxmi's body shakes; blood has drained from her face.

'This message comes from Osho himself. Osho wants you to leave. At once.'

There is a long and loaded pause. Laxmi is fighting the turbulent flames of her recent past. The two who watch in silence see the struggle and its gradual resolution; the flames are starved of oxygen. With a shudder Laxmi's body softens, her anger dissipates. The two women now walk side by side, the tall and the short, towards the closed main gate; the Ashram-in-charge walks behind them.

'One's car is not here,' says Laxmi. 'One sent the driver home. What have people been saying about Laxmi?'

'Did you not receive the message earlier? That you are barred from entering?'

'No such message was received.'

Laxmi turns to watch the beam of headlights from the master's car, the car she used to drive. They flicker and move slowly through the silhouetted foliage. She feels her heart still thumping wildly. She slightly bows towards the lights and turns to face her escorts once again. Her large raven-dark eyes are unreadable. 'This is his Zen stick. *Lakdi lag gayi*. This is his blessing. I'm sorry I was angry with you.'

* * *

Laxmi is passing through a death. She, who was once Osho's hands, his voice, his everyday presence to hundreds of thousands of people; she, who once conversed with the high and the mighty, with prime ministers, superstars and global celebrities; she, who once was voted in the prestigious *India Today* magazine the third most powerful woman in India, is now, within fifteen years, cast out of the very Ashram that she herself had nursed into maturity.

This is not the first time such a blow has fallen on her. Seven years earlier she had been expelled penniless from Osho's pioneering commune in America by the very protégé she herself had trained and who had then usurped her position. Then his disciples, or *sannyasins*, around the world were instructed by that protégé—on pain of expulsion themselves—to give her neither shelter nor support. To add injury to insult she had been worked over by men from the United States Immigration and Naturalization Service and she had to have a cancerous tumour removed from her stomach.

How has it all come to this? To public disgrace and expulsion? When did it all begin to go wrong? How has such a dedicated and devoted woman become a pariah in the garden of her master? Or are things not what they seem?

* * *

Laxmi sits in the back of a car, trundling over the shiny, pot-holed roads of Poona, now re-named Pune. Her small frame jolts and shakes, her heart still pounds and she sees with unseeing eyes the buses and trucks and cars that constantly threaten collision. There is pain, a searing pain, between her breasts. The driver is asking her questions, expressing his own outrage. Words do not come to Laxmi's mouth; they are jammed below her throat. Darkness covers her heart. Yet somewhere, in some indeterminate corner of her being, there is light. Somewhere deep inside her is a sunrise waiting to dispel the darkness. Laxmi closes her eyes.

Some would call her a saint, some would call her a sinner. She is both and she is neither. She is you, she is me.

* * *

In the 1970s and '80s, a divided, caste-infested India was a nation in recovery from fratricidal wars with Pakistan, the assassination of its leader Mohandas Karamchand Gandhi, a murderous time of Partition, two hundred years of British rule, three hundred years of Mogul rule and an existential loss of confidence. It was impoverished, religious, unhygienic, proud and brightly coloured.

For as long as human beings have been conscious, India has explored the mysteries of life and death, the unseen worlds within each one of us. Now India was stumbling.

At the heart of Laxmi's story is the enlightened master Osho. He was formerly known as Acharya Rajneesh—a teacher by example—and later as *Bhagwan* Shree Rajneesh, the blessed one. Much has been written by him and about him. In this century he is all over the internet, the subject of hundreds of doctoral theses, a source and inspiration for every contemporary seeker of truth. He is a herald of the new India and a new humanity; of a new way of living on this earth. Osho combines and articulates the East's deep immersion in the spiritual with the Western world's material proficiency. During the 1970s his personal assistant, secretary and administrator and the president of his charitable foundation was Ma Yoga Laxmi. From around the world people were pouring into Osho's Ashram in suburban Poona. They came from every nation and religion, every age band, every field of education and achievement, every social stratum. Tens of thousands of visitors crowded into a few small acres.

They had come to attain wisdom, to grow up, to be healed and to be whole. They had come because their girlfriend or best friend had come. They had come because their world was on the skids. They had come because they had everything anyone could want in the affluent West and yet were lacking something. They had come to escape themselves or their family or the law and they had come to attain enlightenment. They took the leap into *sannyas*, which is Osho's gift conferring disciplehood on anyone who wants it.

In this crowded commune there were no commandments and no locks, no poverty, no rules; there was an ever-changing set of challenges and situations for each individual's growth. Correspondingly, there was an ever-higher high of meditation, love and creativity.

The thousands gathered each morning and each evening in an open-sided marble hall to hear the silence and the words of Osho; he left his room but twice a day to be with them for this.

Ma Laxmi was the one who made the cog-wheels of this massive enterprise run smoothly and efficiently. She was devoted to the vision of her master and, within that vision, the realisation of her own self-nature.

* * *

What exactly is a master? What exactly does devotion stand for?

The path we travel in this life, whether we know it or not, is one that a master or *guru* has travelled many times. He is a guide, a signpost, a catalyst, a doorway to the unseen world. He is an alarm call, a midwife and a wayside water seller. He is the still, small voice within each one of us. The master takes from us what we do not have and gives us what we already really are.

We are free to take this gift—or not to take it.

On this journey of self-discovery, which is the process of humanity's evolution, *guru–shishya,* disciplehood, is an age-old and effective procedure. It is the devotional relationship between a disciple and a master and a well-trodden path in the East. In the contemporary West, we have no such concept other than the faded memory of Jesus and his dozen. When happiness, peace, full awareness and freedom are the aim of life, then a guide who has already walked the way and is himself free of the clamour of ego is indeed helpful beyond price. He or she is one who has discovered the ultimate core of their being. This state brings tranquillity and clarity of vision. It does not bring infallibility but immense compassion and lucidity. In the East this enlightened being is recognised as worthy of devotion.

Devotion is a land grown hazy in our hard-nosed world. It is rare domain, rich with the flora of celebration yet innocent of artifice; a place where everything has value. Devotion is unflawed by poverty or riches, power or lack of power, success or failure. Its distant mountains, when approached, reveal to us the things we know but do not know we know.

Devotion has a bad press in the West; is thought of as something obsolete or sad; an ill-treated dog whose tail still wags with hope; or as something stupid, a married couple living out their days in mutual misery. And what is worse, these days, devotion is referred to as a place contaminated by religious extremism. Devotion in the East, by contrast, is often an over-fed pet, a chronic displacement activity, a smoke-screen hiding who we are. On both sides of the world, devotion is derided as a crutch for those who cannot stand on their own two feet.

Devotion in this story will have none of that. Here, devotion is a high road to freedom. It is freedom itself.

***

All stories have a dozen different versions; all lives have an infinite number of translations. Laxmi's life has many twists and turns, many ups and downs, many deaths and rebirths. Hers is an unorthodox journey...a journey of the heart.

***

Who was this woman, really? What were her guiding lights? Many people have commented on Laxmi's physical presence. She was short in stature; less than five foot, or one-and-a-half metres tall. And yet she seemed to be both large and luminous. Her eyes were bright as cat's eyes in headlights; her smile was the draught of some exhilarant. So full of energy was she during her time with her master, so fulfilled was every aspect of her life, she did not walk, she floated. This floating, be it following him to the podium, showing visitors a garden, or ascending the steps to her office was always somehow humble and ebullient too. The way Laxmi kneeled before Osho expressed not only love and gratitude but a pride in her responsibilities. The way she handed him his clipboard with the sutras or the questions for the morning's discourse was reminiscent of a sacred ceremonial. Laxmi glowed. Here below are a few thumbnail sketches of her.

All her thinking, everything, revolved around Osho. Her life was totally dedicated to him, to expanding his work. She *built* the Ashram in Koregaon Park, Poona. For her nothing was impossible. What he asked for had to be done! Period. If it looked farfetched or impossible to others, such words did not exist for her. [Ma Prem Isabel]

Laxmi was totally devoted to Osho and to doing anything which helped him and furthered his work. She never used his name, using only the words: HE, HIS and HIM. And, from the way she said these words, you knew that all the letters were written in capitals. [Ma Prem Veena]

I never saw her do anything like rehearse or make an effort to remember what she had to say, though she was often silent before a big meeting. So I was always astonished at her ability to express herself, at the fierce concentration and courage she exhibited when needing to reply to politicians whose agendas did not support her vision—or that of Osho. And there was never the slightest doubt that the mission that she was there to fulfil was his vision. She referred to him in these meetings as *Bhagwan Shree*, and she repeated these words often. She came from a position where it was self-evident that she was doing his work; his instructions to her were sacrosanct. And her elation when the meeting was over and some headway was made and we were back in the privacy of the car or the hotel room was infectious. She beamed and her eyes sparkled, and she always credited Osho. 'It is HIM, Swami'—HIM always with capital letters. [Swami Veetmoha]

She was in a different class from most of us. Laxmi had a real and noticeable spiritual presence. It was a very special time for me when she came out of his room. There was a blue light around her. She had, like Osho, an atmosphere of peace and beauty. I would not say that of any of the other powerful women who came after her. In spite of that tranquillity, I saw her get pretty tough with people if she had to. [Swami Christo]

It is a bewildered, bedazzled Krishna Prem they lead to Laxmi. I stand for a moment in the doorway of the new administration office, watching this woman I love, just savouring the sight of her. She sits in a high-back chair at the centre of a cyclone of activity, dealing, as she's always done, with everything at once. She's tinier than before, even more frail and bird-like, but still a vital energy emanates from her—mercurial and dynamic yet at the same time centred and alert.

She does not look at me right away—she's involved in something—yet I am aware she knows I'm here. And when our eyes do meet, seconds pass before anything transpires. Like old lovers reunited we simply look, saying nothing, as if the wordless gaze erases the time spent apart. Finally, with a sweep of one little arm, she indicates the stool beside her, patting it, inviting me to sit.

'So *Swamiji,*' she says, 'home-coming has happened!'

[Swami Krishna Prem, *Osho, India and Me: A Tale of Sexual and Spiritual Transformation*]

2. A GIRL GROWING UP

Laxmi was born at half past eight on the morning of 12 February 1933 in a well-to-do area of Mumbai, or Bombay as it was then called. That day the family textile business prospered so the baby girl was named after Laxmi, consort of Vishnu, the Indian goddess of material and spiritual wealth.

The maternal line of Laxmi's family had made a fortune during the First World War. Later the fortune was to vanish but the gene of pragmatic enterprise was firmly established in the bloodline. Laxmi's grandmother was an influential figure in the extended Kuruwa family so all the children were raised as independent-minded individuals who would face life on their own terms. In the words of a great granddaughter, 'It was thanks to her we all understood that what is here today may be gone tomorrow.'

The house, or rather mansion, Vatcha Villas, was jointly owned by her father and his elder brother, Laxmi's uncle. There was an extra bond in the Kuruwa family because the two brothers had married two sisters. Five children had already been born into the extended family and six more were to arrive over the next ten years. And that was before the grandchildren started to appear.

The family were Jains, one of the world's oldest religions, but they were not unduly orthodox. The young Laxmi growing up was attracted to pictures of Krishna—the colourful Hindu avatar. What must have seeped early into her bloodstream was the Jains' reverence for life in all its forms; a blade of grass and a grain of sand are as worthy of respect as a sparrow, a mountain and another human being.

Laxmi spoke with fondness of her early years; of caring adults and carefree holidays in the family country house, of fine clean clothes and fragrant gardens. She said she grew up free from want and largely free from petty restrictions.

But, of course, life throws up complications. The Jain tradition, as opposed to its core teaching, was patriarchal; it did not encourage girls going to school with boys. Laxmi's uncle, the titular head of the extended family, told her that she would not be attending school. Instead she would be educated at home in the domestic skills. Eight-year-old Laxmi promptly decided she would not talk or eat with the family. She locked herself in her room. Her mother, her father, her elder brother all at different times, came knocking on her door.

'Go away.'

'But what's wrong?'

'I'm not speaking to you.'

'Then how can we help?'

'You know what's wrong.'

'Girls don't need to go to school.'

'I hate you.'

'No you don't. Please unlock the door.'

A crashing sound came from inside the room.

'Are you all right? Laxmi! What has happened?'

Silence.

'If you don't unlock the door we'll have to break it down.'

Silence.

'You're an obstinate child...'

In the end Laxmi's father, Thakersey, who ran the family cloth business and was the main financial provider, persuaded his elder brother to relent.

The two brothers were of different personality types. Laxmi's father was a rebellious spirit; he supported the Indian Independence Movement, played with the children and often had a glass of beer after work. His brother by contrast was traditional and authoritarian, remote, teetotal, unbending.

Laxmi inherited from her father the tendency to rebel. This challenge to the family on the education of young girls revealed a fault-line that stayed untended in what otherwise appeared to be a happy and united family. Laxmi later described large extended families as pressure cookers where family members were constantly encountering each other. 'Day in day out relating becomes a useful therapy group for all,' she told a friend.

* * *

Laxmi, the eldest daughter and second born child of her parents, was always recognised as the most determined and single-minded of the family. Her niece Alpana remembers her childhood in that extended family. 'Once Laxmi had decided something, nothing would stop her and she would listen to no one.'

The significance of this observation weaves in and out of Laxmi's life.

* * *

The school to which the Kuruwa children were sent was co-educational, private and progressive, inspired by the great poet, polymath and Nobel Prize winner Rabindranath Tagore. The building itself had been a family house, now it smelled of cumin and crayons, Laxmi thought, as she clung to her brother's arm this first alarming day. Around them milled a herd of older children, jostling them, eyeing them, ignoring them.

'He pushed me,' Laxmi said to brother Kakubai.

'He didn't mean to.'

'Yes he did. He whispered something.'

'What?'

Tears welled up in Laxmi's eyes. 'He said, "Hullo Shorty."'

'Don't worry. He's an ignoramus.'

Laxmi swallowed back her rising sobs. 'What's an ignoramus?'

'Stop asking silly questions.'

'Why can't I...?' The headmaster's voice boomed across the high-pitched chatter of a hundred kids, calling them to the morning assembly.

* * *

By the end of her first term Laxmi began to feel somewhat free and at home in the school. She responded well to the challenges of learning, especially the practical crafts and sciences. She did not, however, make friends very easily and there were, anyway, few girls of her age in the school.

Each morning in the large hall, mats were laid out on the floor and the children sat in lines for assembly. One day Laxmi heard a prefect's voice call out, 'Laxmi please remove your shoes before you tread all over the mats.'

People everywhere turned to stare at her. 'Now go and clean them please.'

Laxmi bowed her head. She was blushing. It was with shame and sorrow that she cleaned the mat. Cleaning was her exculpation.

The following term, Laxmi was sitting silently before assembly. She had done her share of the daily laying out of the straw mats. She sat alone on one of them, hearing but not listening to the high-pitched chatter of the children's voices. She noticed how their babel filled the air. It seemed to bounce back off the rusty red, triangulated iron struts and concrete slabs that cluttered up the ceiling. She wondered if the gods, in particular Lord Krishna, listen in to every conversation. Or have they better things to do like advising kings and politicians how to win their battles?

A footfall on her mat brought her back to earth. The headmaster had just stepped on it on his way up to the podium. With his shoes on!

For a moment Laxmi sat in frozen disbelief. Then she jumped up to pursue him.

'Sir, Sir...'

'Yes Laxmi?'

'Sir, good morning. You walked on a mat.'

'I did?'

'Yes Sir. You have shoes on and you walked on the one I was sitting on. Now you have to clean it.'

'But my shoes are clean Laxmi. Perfectly clean.'

'But Sir, if we aren't allowed to walk on the mats, why should you be allowed to? It's not fair Sir.'

'That's true Laxmi.'

'So you have to clean it Sir.'

'Please go to the cupboard and get me a cloth.'

'Yes Sir. And Sir, does god come to Assembly every morning?'

'Errr...Laxmi...'

'Or is he busy doing wars and things?'

'The cloth, Laxmi. Fetch me a cloth.'

* * *

Cleaning and cleanliness always remained important to Laxmi; they distanced her from stress and the discomforts that life brought. Her older brother, Kakubai, for example. Kakubai was a big shape in her life; big and not entirely sympathetic. He was three years older and a bit too much of a tease. He had ingested the cultural illusion that men and boys are in some inalterable way superior to women and girls. Every day Laxmi had to go to school with him. They bickered in the back of the car, at mealtimes, in the playground and when they got home. He stole her pocket money or the chocolate she bought with it. She told tales on him to the grown-ups, elaborating his misdeeds. Uncle would take his side but when Laxmi's father was there, Kakubai would be more circumspect. Laxmi slowly learned to hold her ground, and to push back when required. Courage comes from trusting in one's heart she discovered, fear comes from ignoring one's inner voice.

Laxmi's class had swimming lessons once a week. For the first session, the children were lined up, squirming, giggling and joking at the pool's edge. None of them were swimmers yet. They were told to get into the water. They hesitated. But Laxmi just jumped. She, too, could not swim. The teacher said jump, so she jumped. Then only would she learn what

the teacher wanted to teach. By instinct her arms and legs
started flailing. Behold! Laxmi was swimming.

A group of boys were mocking her. 'Shorty wants to be
teacher's pet.'

'She floats because she's puffed up like a life-jacket.'

'Yeah, girls are more buoyant anyway.'

Laxmi stuck out her tongue at them.

* * *

One of Laxmi's cousins died of pneumonia and the ten-
year-old Laxmi was shocked by the thought of a burial.
'Kakubhai, what will happen to our cousin when it rains?
Will the ants and worms eat her body? Ugh! Do we all have
to die?'

'Give me fifty paise and you can have a bite of my Bounty
chocolate bar.'

'But what happens when you die?'

'All the lies you've told about me will come back and
torture you.'

'Liar, liar pants on fire. Hey don't push me. I'm telling
Mataji. But where do we go when we die?'

Kakubhai was not the only one to face her questions.

'Lar it is midnight. We are sleeping. Please go back to
bed.'

'But it's important.'

'What's important?'

'I need to know.'

'Can't it wait? What do you need to know?'

'*Mataji*, If the earth is round, why don't we fall off it?'

'Please Lar, not now. We need to sleep.'

'But I can't.'

'Then read a book for a while. Or count sheep.'

'But why doesn't everything fall off the earth?'

'Go to bed.'

'But I'm worrying.'

'Lar! I'm asking you one more time. Please go to bed.'

'You don't care about me. You don't care that I can't sleep. And I might not be here in the morning.'

'This is the third night in a week you've come asking questions. Even your daytime questions are becoming tiresome. "What makes thunder?" "Why don't people leave each other alone?" "Where is the moon in the day?" "How many hairs do you have in your head?" Lar, I am getting really fed up. And your father too.'

'But he will know. Please ask him. And no need to get angry just because you don't know the answer. Ask *Pitaji*.'

'He is asleep. He needs to work tomorrow.'

'How do you know he's not dead?'

'Come,' said *Mataji*, rising from her bed and taking hold of Laxmi's hand. 'I will tuck you up in bed and sing to you so you will sleep.'

Padding down the passage with their bare feet on the marble tiles, Laxmi suddenly stopped her mother short. 'But *Mataji*, I've just thought of something awful.'

'What is that? Not another question I hope.'

'*Mataji*! Why am I me and not someone else? What if I am someone else?'

'Whoever you are, you need a good night's sleep. That's it, come along and we can sort these questions out tomorrow. Okay lie down. That's right. Now this is a song that Mirabai used to sing to her lord Krishna...'

I want to give you all the beauty that my eyes can see,
and all the praise my mouth can sing,
I want to give you all the strength my body has,
and all the wonder that the musk parts of my—

'*Mataji,*' Laxmi interrupted. 'What are musk parts?'

* * *

One day during lunch hour at school, Laxmi was on her way
to pick up her *tiffin*. An older girl blocked her passage in the
locker room. Laxmi tried to move past her.

'Who are you pushing?'

'You're blocking the way,' said Laxmi extending her chin
defiantly.

'Do you know the word "please"? Or excuse me?'

'You don't need all that space.'

'Who's talking? You're the fat one! Look at you!'

'And you are an ignoramus,' Laxmi shouted up at her.

A crowd of curious children gathered around.

'Fatso! Fatso! Fatso!'

'Shut up ignoramus. You all are ignoramuses.'

Laxmi turned away mortified. She picked up her *tiffin*
and walked to the playground garden. It was true. She was
fat. She emptied her lunch down a hole by the wall in the
corner and watched as the crows competed with the rats. 'I
like eating. I like the feel of food inside my tummy. I hate
to look fat. I don't look fat. Do I look fat? Maybe a little.
Perhaps I do eat more than I need. Why shouldn't I?' said
ten-year-old Laxmi to herself. 'And they are ignoramuses.'

* * *

At the age of twelve, Laxmi suffered from a bout of smallpox, *variola minor*. Most of the family went down with it. Six weeks later she returned to school with a pock-marked face and short, lustreless hair. Her classmates shunned her. Laxmi was shocked and uncomprehending. She spoke to her father. 'Why are they pushing me away?'

'My little one, people pay too much attention to appearances. There is nothing wrong with you. You have not changed. A few things on the outside change but you are the same. You don't be worried. There will always be people who judge from appearances.'

'But I don't want to look funny and I don't want people to push me away.'

'It will pass. They will befriend you again.'

'I don't want their friendship. They are ignoramuses.'

'Dear one, they are not. Don't judge them.'

'Well, they are rude to me. And I want to be rude back.'

'Then how will you feel? Think about that. Anyway you will get your good looks back.'

Traditional ayurvedic medicine was highly regarded in the Kuruwa family. Shortly after Laxmi's birth, her mother had developed a severe and painful condition in one leg. Neighbours hearing her cries assumed the worst and called the police; a testament to how powerful the pain was. The local doctor saw no other option than to amputate. The family ayurved medical practitioner or *Vaid* was called in and restored her to health with a two-week regime of fasting, followed by a liquid diet. Laxmi kept a high regard for traditional medicine throughout her life.

Rejection and death are two of the great human disquiets. Laxmi remembered the story of Gautama Buddha, who, on seeing for the first time an old man, a sick woman and a corpse, had left home in search of truth and the meaning of life. She would do likewise. She packed a little bag with a hairbrush and a toothbrush, clean underwear and two *samosas* she found in the fridge. She wrote a note to her cousin saying she would be leaving the house in the middle of the night like the Buddha and begged her not to tell anyone. She went to bed at the normal time. When she awoke it was time for school.

But she had had a dream. She dreamed that Krishna rose up dancing from the barren, dried-up bed of a river. He sang to her:

When we search outside ourselves
For comfort or for meaning,
  We enter the great desert.
When we search inside ourselves,
Here is the sea of tranquillity,
  Here the feast awaits.

Laxmi wrote these words down in a notebook. A few days later, her father asked her, 'When will you be setting out in search of truth?'

Laxmi ran to him and hugged him. 'Oh *Bauji!*' Tears soaked his *kurta,* sobs shook her small body. 'Oh father I will never leave you. You are everything to me.'

'I have called in the *Vaid.* He will restore your looks. You are courageous, my little *gudiya.* You will come to know the truth and you will be happy. It is only lies that cause misery.'

Laxmi's friends forgot her vanished scars. She never forgot that just a few superficial marks had made her an outcast.

* * *

Laxmi's growing up was not much different from most girls of her age in India. She was conscious of her looks, mortified when teased by kids at school, shamed when they harried her for being fat. The family ayurvedic doctor had dealt with the facial scars, but Laxmi herself had to deal with over-eating. She swung the other way, ate very little and exercised every day.

'This is Laxmi. She is very total. She goes the whole nine yards,' declared her niece. From now on, despite her love of food, Laxmi would always live on a very restricted diet.

* * *

For the most part, they were golden years, the years of Laxmi's youth. She spent the long hot summers and holidays on the country estate in Gujarat. There, the space was generous enough for the serious political discussions of adults and the noise and turmoil of children. A war was happening in the outside world but most minds were concentrated on the long struggle for India's independence from Great Britain and the looming cloud of violence they feared that it might bring.

Laxmi valued the respect and freedom she, her siblings and cousins were shown by the adults. 'We were not heaped with expectations nor were we crammed with guilt. We were loved and taken lightly. And we had a lot of freedom.' In addition, Laxmi never forgot the order and cleanliness that permeated their house; the freshly washed, scented sheets and clothes, the wholesome food and the extended family meals.

At certain times of the year, itinerant singers, magicians, poets and storytellers came by their house. Like all children,

Laxmi knew there is another world hidden in this world. Her dreams and her imagination were fuelled and fired by tales of gods and kings, divine reprobates and devilish pranksters.

During Shivaratri, a festival that honours the god Shiva's union with Parvathi, there is a day of fasting. Laxmi's Jain family celebrated that event. A tribal shaman visited every year, offering *bhang*, an intoxicating drink. Laxmi's interest was aroused as she stood in the shade outside the family kitchen and watched the shaman crush the cannabis leaves in a pestle and mortar and flavour them with milk and cardamom, pistachio, saffron, nutmeg and dry rose petals. What was this irresistible drink to the young enquiring mind? Years later Laxmi was to say that happiness leads to boldness; only a dancing heart can take you into the uncharted. She sampled the *bhang*. With the arrogance of the young, she had hardly swallowed half her cup before she was complaining that it had no effect. The old shaman asked for a copper coin, rung it several times on the stone flag and dropped it into her drink. Laxmi drank again and took off into uncontrollable laughter. The family gathered round to enjoy the spectacle. When the other kids started mobbing her, she broke into uncontrollable sobbing. Her mother and an *ayah*, or governess, scooped her up and put her to bed where she dreamed more wild and woeful dreams. It took her three days to recover.

* * *

One morning after family breakfast Laxmi pulled her father aside.

'*Pitaji*,I want to learn how to drive.'

'Very good, Laxmi. It's a useful skill.'

'Which car shall I learn on? I think I like the Chevrolet. Or the Morris?'

'No need to decide. There are new models every year.'

'I want to learn now. Will you teach me?'

'Now?'

'Yes, now.'

'But you are only ten years old, my *gudiya*.'

'So?'

'And you can't see over the dashboard.'

'So? Do you have to be tall to drive? Please! I really want to know how to drive.'

'All right, all right! Don't stamp your foot like that. We'll use the old Austin of your cousin. And we have to get some cushions for you.'

Thus Laxmi's love of motor cars found early expression in the garage and the small roads of the family's country home. She, of all the children, boys included, was the one with an interest in machines. She was given some tools and a soldering kit. She learned to mend small household items like the broken iron, the clock that would not work and a grinder in the kitchen.

This is the advent of the practical Laxmi, the one who later kept the cog-wheels of a mighty Ashram commune turning smoothly.

* * *

Laxmi was still in school when her aunt died of tuberculosis following a short illness. Her mother too contracted the infection so it fell upon twelve-year-old Laxmi, as the oldest female of the coming generation, to take on the care of the children, one of them only two years old. At the same time, she had to become responsible for the upkeep of the mansion on three floors, and a full household complement of thirty-eight people, including a small army of servants. This was a huge responsibility for one so young.

Alpana, her niece, remembers that their clothes were always spotless, the house clean, and the children kept in order with a firm hand. 'She was a perfectionist. We used to call her Hitler, but not in a pejorative way.' When questioned more she responded, 'She was loving and fair but strict in a spinsterish sort of way. If you picked something up it had to be put back exactly in the same place. And once something was set in her vision she was deaf and blind to anything else. But she would play with us too. She managed to be both playmate and authority for us.'

It was never going to be easy acting mother to such a large extended family. One day Laxmi was so irritated by some administrative nuisance that she broke four glasses in the kitchen sink and did not even notice until someone warned her of the shards.

* * *

'What's that behind your back?' Laxmi ascending the curved marble stairs at their home met her father coming down.

'Nothing. Just a magazine,' said Laxmi reddening.

'May I see it?' asked her father

'Sure.'

'You are reading about religion?'

'No...umm...yes...umm...*Pitaji* why are there so many different religions? At school we have them all including kids with none. And we are no different from each other. What is the point of religions?'

'What do you think?'

'I don't know. Aren't they all trying to show us god? I think they are meant to teach us right and wrong, which we know already anyway. I mean we know when we've done good or bad, don't we *Pitaji*? But religions are all made by men. And mostly they give us fights and wars. I think they are made so we are not so scared of dying?'

'What an intelligent daughter I have! I think much of what you say is true. But where is god in all of this?'

'I don't know. Is there a god? Or gods? Why do we have to believe in god? Because our ancestors did? Because priests tell us to? *Pitaji*, everyone tells me different things and I don't know what to believe? I go to lots of temples. I like temples. Some of the priests are creepy. But I feel calm in temples. *Pitaji*, am I too fat?'

Her father laughed. 'La, you are perfect as you are. And we follow the Jain religion which is really more concerned with living your life with *ahimsa* or non-violence and awareness so your soul becomes free.'

'Umm perhaps I'm trying to find out what is my soul,' said Laxmi slightly lifting the hem of her skirt to continue up the stairs.

'Let me know if you do,' her father called as an afterthought up the echoing staircase.

'Okay. But you will know anyway.'

* * *

Mataji, as mothers are familiarly known, slowly recovered and Laxmi resumed her education for another six years until, once again, family demands and the conflicting need to extend her horizons and live out her Gandhian ideals caused eighteen-year-old Laxmi to drop out of college. Dropped too for now was the search for soul and god and the nature of religion.

She took to working part time with a voluntary organisation set up to help women move out of poverty. Wealthy Jains have a tradition of philanthropic work and the Kuruwa family were no exception. Before being diagnosed with cancer, Laxmi's father, apart from running the family cloth business, was involved in several welfare projects. He was also a trustee of a rich Jain temple and had the responsibility for building a charitable, low-income housing project.

Laxmi's father, unlike his elder brother, was a keen but clandestine supporter of Gandhi and the Indian Independence Movement. He practised and passed on to Laxmi its ideals of simplicity, non-violence and civil disobedience. He and his daughter chose to wear white homespun clothes, when not respectively at work or college. On one occasion, Laxmi's father took her to an open-air rally in Bombay (now Mumbai) where the Mahatma was speaking. Gandhi opened the proceedings with an appeal for everyone present to donate five rupees each. However, towards the end of his speech a detachment of mounted colonial police entered the arena firing shots into the air with the unsurprising intention of breaking up the meeting. In the tumult and confusion, the young Laxmi found her way to the podium on which Gandhi was sitting and pressed five rupees upon him. He laid his hand on her head in blessing. Within a year he visited the family's country home in Kutch in Western Gujarat and within a couple of more years he was assassinated.

***

As Laxmi blossomed into her late teens, her family's thoughts turned naturally to marriage. Not Laxmi's however. Doubtless she would be an attractive acquisition for any of the close-knit Jain families in Bombay; she was pretty, well-educated and her family was wealthy and highly respected.

With her father's loving support however, Laxmi—known forever in the family as La or Lar—fought off all contenders to the marriage bed.

* * *

'Laxmi,' said her mother one evening when Laxmi returned from college, 'You are nineteen years old. You have told us you don't want to marry. Are you sure you don't want us to arrange something?'

'I think for many lives I might have been a nun, a *brahmacharya*, a celibate. Or maybe in the last life I might have been a mother of fifteen children. Either way I have seen that marriage is a trap and a mis-sold insurance.'

'What do you want to do then?'

'*Mataji*, you have given us a lot of freedom in our lives. You have taught us money cannot buy security. Our great-grandparents made a fortune and it disappeared. We have learned from you not to look to others for our happiness. I don't know what I want to do.

'From father I have learned that change is the only thing that never changes; transformation is our destiny. Helping others is a part of our religion. I can do that and help out with the nephews and the nieces.

'I build castles out of air. I could start a catering business. I could be a fortune teller or a lady chauffeur. People look to me to get things done. When it works they call me great, when it doesn't why do they always want to kick me hard? I don't know what I want to do *Mataji*. You and father, unlike everyone else, do not pressure me. I am grateful for that.'

* * *

When Laxmi was at the market one day in late October of 1952 she bought a coloured print of the young Krishna. She had it framed and delivered to Vatcha Villas. Laxmi wrote that she had 'an uncanny feeling that, if the picture were damaged, then some ill-luck would befall the family.'

And so it happened. A young cousin did indeed damage the picture. Within days, Laxmi's beloved father was diagnosed with cancer of the throat. Hardly had the shock of that registered on the family before he passed away in early December.

At first Laxmi was in shock. She went about her days like a robot. She spoke to the family as if nothing was out of the ordinary; as if father was off on one of his business trips. Then the shock turned to an eruption of energy. Laxmi raged. Not at the family and not in public. She raged at herself, at the dirt in the house and the constant battle it took to keep the house clean. So she scrubbed and she scoured the floors, she deep-cleaned the bedrooms and threw out the sitting room curtains and cushions.

Then she retired to her room for days.

She blamed herself for his death. She blamed the family for making such large economic demands on her father. She blamed the British for starving her country of funds. And then she fell into sadness. It came in waves, in great wails of engulfing grief. She cried for hours at a time. She cried for days. She cried herself out into total exhaustion.

In the early days of the new year, the smallest shoot of new life appeared in her heart. One day she joined the family for lunch. First she hugged her mother and touched her feet, then she went round the table, caressing, touching, hugging everyone. She *namaste*d the family and said, '*Mataji* thank you. We've learned from you that everything in life is flow, is change. Nothing stays as it is. Whatever comes into form must one day return to formlessness. I have come to see that everything is perfect as it is.'

* * *

Laxmi developed an interest in the Ouija Board or planchette, a spiritualist device marked with the letters of the alphabet. Answers to questions are spelled out by a pointer held with the fingertips of the participants and are supposedly controlled by spirit forces.

Laxmi found that certain future events were foretold to her, including the death of both Gandhi and a psychologically disturbed cousin. On one occasion, while playing with the device on her own, Laxmi fell unconscious, hitting her head. This so frightened her that she abandoned the activity.

It is interesting how much weight Laxmi gave to the vaguely arcane and the downright superstitious. She mentioned too, that after meeting Osho, this leaning towards the arcane diminished. I think we can read it as a young person's unguided groping for some deeper meaning below the surface of appearances. It is interesting too that in the later notes Laxmi made of her life she gives very little mention of the death of her father, of what was a deeply affecting event for her.

* * *

Sex was a severely taboo subject in the Kuruwa household—as it was in most of India. When Laxmi had her first menstrual period, she was in school and had no idea what was causing her to bleed. On that occasion, her brother took the distraught girl out of class and brought her home for her mother's care and explanations. Even much later, at the age of thirty, Laxmi was somewhat shocked when she was called upon to assist at a birth in the family. She had, as a child, been led to believe that babies were a gift from god, somehow delivered to the door by a celestial postman. She wrote later that she herself never wanted to go through the experience of childbirth.

The basic thrust of life is to survive and reproduce itself. When we divert or pervert either of these primary impulses, their energy turns into unnatural and often problematic behaviour. Individuals become weak and submissive or frustrated and angry. Priests and politicians have long been known to foster sexual repression in order to manipulate and control people. The subcontinent of India, in spite of having pioneered the science of *tantra,* received a double whammy of sexual repression; in the first place from its early moralists and then later from its successive invaders, the Muslim Moguls and the Christian British. This is the terrible legacy and burden, along with the ensuing patriarchal attitudes, that all women of Laxmi's generation faced. Patriarchy says that men have the power and the rights. Women are there to support them. All women's opinions and feelings that counter this fact are wrong and irrational. Thus it is that women are robbed of their natural power and men of their natural tenderness. It will be Osho who comes to tackle these issues; to confront the establishment head to head.

For Laxmi to be single in India was difficult. Extremely difficult: more so than in most countries because of this extreme sexual repression. She did not need to read Freud to know that any natural impulse, if repressed in the name of religion or morality or even hygiene, proliferates in unhealthy ways. She grew up knowing all the social norms concerning women's roles, sensing all the pressures and the penalties of being single, yet quietly determined she would never marry, never submit.

When marriage was discussed, she felt a deep dread in her belly. She did not want to be a wife. She did not want to be a husband's property. She and all her siblings had felt cherished and respected as they grew up. Now, in early adulthood, the pressure to get married was ramped up by her cousins, friends and distant relatives, by neighbours and by casual acquaintances.

Laxmi at this time could not fully understand or fully articulate to herself that it was freedom that she really wanted. At that moment there was a barely stifled cry of 'NO' arising in her; an isolated confrontation with millennia of patriarchy.

This inchoate dismissal of marriage caused Laxmi many nights of turmoil. 'If I don't marry, everyone will think I've failed. Everyone will pity me. They think a husband is the justification of a woman's life. They ask me what will happen when I'm old, tell me that I am condemned to life without a godfather, a protector. I feel utterly lonely. I don't belong. Everywhere I look I see the sterile marriages around me. I don't see any married women with a life they call their own. Men seem to make a product of a woman, like they do of nature; an asset to exploit. Life should not have to be like this.' And thus the long hot nights continued. And thus women's long dark night of disempowerment continues to this day, only shifting slowly as the present situation grows ever less defendable.

* * *

Laxmi's father had loved and supported her above all the contrary and conventional family interests. Once he was gone she had to fight her own battles, hold out alone against the remorseless social and family pressures to marry and have children.

Laxmi had resisted the prohibition against her going to school. She had begun the slow process of establishing herself as an individual with natural rights and obligations. She was a participant in a long and arduous struggle that continues beyond the limits of her lifetime.

In the early 1950s, in the humid heat of Bombay's summer, Laxmi had a prolonged campaign on her hands. Her uncle arranged for a young man, recently returned from a university abroad, to pay a preliminary visit. Laxmi thought he was very handsome.

She asked him, 'What do you look for in a wife?'

'She should be good-looking, well-educated, healthy and wealthy.'

'And what if she should get smallpox and be disfigured?'

For a moment, anger flushed the young man's face. Laxmi said, 'If just the possibility of bad looks makes you angry, where is the love?'

The boy departed promptly.

On another occasion, her uncle found a likely bachelor for her to meet. A party was arranged, without Laxmi's knowledge, so that the two could be introduced. Laxmi was dressed with the help of cousins in a fine silk sari. She entered the hall looking beautiful, like a princess. When the young man was introduced, Laxmi immediately picked up the clues. If they try to fool me then I can out-fool them, she thought. By staring at the tip of her nose, Laxmi gave herself a fearsome squint. She added for good measure a slack jaw. Another poor young man was quickly in retreat.

Laxmi's uncle did not give up easily.

One day, in the heat of noon, he called her to his dark and shuttered study. 'If you do not marry, how do you think this reflects on the family? What do you think people think of us? It is shameful, I tell you. I am the head of the family and it is my obligation to see you married well. Are you going to see reason?'

'I see no reason to marry.'

'How can you be so blind and selfish? What? Have you no pride? And after all we have done for you!' Now Uncle rose behind his desk, his hand banging on the piles of paper, his face reddening. 'Yes, we even allowed you to go to school! And who is going to support you in your old age? Or your middle age? Come to your senses, girl! What do you think people will think of me, allowing you to be so headstrong? They will look at us...' Uncle paused in his tirade. He slumped back into the chair. 'Shame! You bring shame down upon my head by your conceits and wilfulness. How will I hold my head high in this neighbourhood? What would your poor father say?'

Laxmi stood speechless and perplexed. All her emotions were rejecting his words whilst her outward concern was for her uncle's distress. She felt the moments stand suddenly still. Above her whirled an obstinate fan. From the road outside, shouts of children ricocheted around the glossy walls of the shaded office. The silence and stillness in the room became menacing. Inside her was a swelling cry for her beloved father, a cry that she could not and would not release. *Pitaji* had been an educated man, a sensitive man. He valued women. He valued the freedom of people to live their lives how they wished.

An abrasive sound brought Laxmi back to the menace of the room. Her uncle had slid open a drawer and his hand was groping inside it. To Laxmi's horror, she saw it slowly emerge holding a revolver. She saw its gleaming blackness, envisioned its cold steel weight against her heart. Her inner voice was a silent scream, Shoot me! Shoot me yet I'll never marry.

The hand that held the gun was shaking; the muzzle was pressed against her uncle's temple.

'You bring me to this.' His look was fierce; accusing. Beads of sweat were running down his face and neck.

Now Laxmi must respond. Words erupted. She called his bluff. 'Go ahead! Shoot yourself! If you are destined to die like this, how can you escape it? And what sort of a messy, honour-killing would this be? You're a Jain.'

Again the awful silence, the fan, the children's cries. Suddenly the taste of fear in Laxmi's throat and an apology arising. But the hand was lowered, the gun replaced in the drawer.

'Get out of this room!'

Laxmi turned. She felt, between her shoulder blades, an inch of skin await its penetration and yet her feet maintained their steady gait towards the door. There she turned, bowed her head and closed the door behind her.

* * *

In an age and a culture such as ours where films, books, marketing and the media are ubiquitously sexualised, where even children are exposed to pornography and casual sex, Laxmi's rejection of marriage and her embrace of chastity may be hard to understand. India in the '50s and '60s was sexually repressive but Laxmi's condition need not be construed as a case of malignant virginity; she was just not drawn to sex. In this, paradoxically, she would be supported, by popular culture and morality.

* * *

Laxmi, inspired by her father and the pervading struggle for independence grew into adulthood wanting to change the world, to make it a better place. At the tender age of fourteen she had seen the mayhem and massacres of partition when Pakistan was formed. By 1961, at the age of twenty-eight, she was involved with the schooling and upbringing of her siblings' nine children at home. In addition, she had joined and become local secretary of the Gandhian All India Women's Congress in Bombay, *Mahilla Vibhag*. And there was another work that deeply engaged her. She became first a volunteer helper, then the secretary of a Jain women's welfare organisation. In this project a group of disadvantaged women were employed to prepare food as a source of income. Once Laxmi had been elected secretary, she took over the management of the project and sales doubled and redoubled. Within twelve months the workshop was repainted, air-conditioners were installed, and new refrigerators and ovens replaced the old ones. Laxmi said this experience taught her that currency should circulate and generate more currency. She also acknowledged in her later notes that she felt her ego became very puffed-up when she was praised for coming from a rich background and yet doing voluntary social work and wearing simple clothes.

* * *

Life was largely fulfilling for her but a tiny thorn snagged unrelenting in her breast. inside her chest. In between her work for charity, her duties with the Women's Congress Party, helping round the house and her sometimes-fraught excursions to the market, Laxmi often felt an irritation. It was all but unnoticeable. A worry? An omission? A presentiment? She did not yet give it a name or investigate it further. It might just go away.

But it did not. It got worse. There came upon her moods of deep frustration that would erupt as sadness, fear or anger. Night after night it niggled and itched. 'Things aren't quite right. This life is a meaningless struggle. The gods are not taking care. However busy I keep, I keep thinking something is wrong.'

For weeks she left the thorn untended in a corner of her consciousness.

One evening she lay in bed unsleeping. She asked herself, what is this feeling? Krishna! Mahavir! Help me please! I am adrift, uprooted, homeless. I don't know what I'm doing with my life. I have a loving, stable family and often-rewarding work, and yet...I feel I am an orphan of existence. Is this what I should be for the rest of my life?

But indeed her gods were taking care. Life would propel her to a meeting with her destiny, to a call for transformation.

* * *

In these charitable and political organisations, several friends were wives of members of the Indian Parliament. They were literate and socially progressive women. Dignitaries were often guests at their meetings. Laxmi was being groomed for a career in political and social work circles. But the thorn of a question festered, forever unattended to. 'What else is there? Is politics really the answer? I don't know. There must be something...something bigger, deeper. There's a longing in my heart...'

Laxmi stayed with this uncertainty for as long as she could. Then one morning she woke with a decision already formed and a lightness in her heart. I'll resign. I'll quit the charity work. If I clear out of that, maybe it will make space for something else to happen.

When she announced her resignation, the workers said they wanted her to stay and threatened to strike if she resigned. Laxmi told them that she needed to help with the family; something they all understood.

* * *

In February 1967, as the Ouija Board had foretold, one of Laxmi's cousins, who had serious mental health problems, jumped out of a window of the mental hospital while trying to escape. Laxmi had loved him deeply. She had sat by his bed for three days until he died of his injuries. As would be expected, this event had traumatic repercussions for Laxmi and the family.

'In your mid-thirties you will meet someone who will usher light into your life,' Laxmi's astrologer-cousin told her.

* * *

Let us now review Laxmi's life up to her mid-thirties:

- She was born into moderate wealth and a life of ease.
- She was tried and tested in the hotbed of extended family relationships.
- She was trusting and courageous enough to jump into a swimming pool without being able to swim. Also she had faced down her uncle with a gun.
- She had developed a political awareness through her father's affiliation with Gandhi and the Indian Independence Movement. She was the local secretary of the All India Women's Congress Party.
- She had an interest in the esoteric.
- She showed an organisational acumen when she had to run the Vatcha Villas household on occasions and when she helped a women's charity become profitable.
- She manifested an introspective nature when she noticed her ego swelling at the praise for her 'simplicity' in dress and service to the poor.
- She related easily with children.
- She was most particular about food and cleanliness.
- She had experienced a birth and the deaths of those close to her.
- She was open to something new happening in her life.

In all of this there was no hint of revolution but the possibility was always present.

It was 1967 and Laxmi, the 'spinsterish do-gooder' would have to change her life.

3. A SLAP IN THE FACE

For a brief, exciting moment in the 1960s, a bright light flared across the world. People everywhere were looking for a way of life that did not need recurrent wars, a rich and poor divide, the ruthless ruination of our rivers, oceans, air and forests and the ever present threat of 'Mutually Assured (nuclear) Destruction.'

M-A-D it certainly was.

The West had recovered from a debilitating and dispiriting world war, it had jobs for most of its workers, the shops were overflowing, the arts were thriving and the churches shrinking. It was affluent and powerful; but where was the promised happiness? The young and the young at heart, the liberals and the radical left and the truly eccentric thought life could be changed for the better through revolution; political revolution. During the Vietnam War that burst of light was brutally crushed. A new, post-modern order of ruthless military, industrial and agricultural capitalism was emerging and expanding into trans-national networks.

In India the rich and poor divide had grown ever steeper and deeper. The country oscillated between a resignation bordering on apathy and serial strikes and protests which were stamped on hard. Hindu–Muslim antagonism brought death and recurrent destruction. The British colonial yoke had been lifted but that only brought the sore disclosure that the nation had been burgled by its rulers. Its long awaited freedom would be slow to appear and then not manifest the sort of liberation that it promised.

In this decade of the 1960s Osho was a one-man ball of fire rolling through the states of poor old heartsick, over-populated India. He was calling for a real and total revolution.

Osho in the '60s challenged everyone and everything; the sacred cows, the great souls and the heads of state, the *Shankaracharyas* (the heads of Hindu religious orders) and all the institutions that supported the political, religious, social, economic and gender status quo. He disrupted their tired narratives, questioned the legitimacy of their functions. And he castigated the old beliefs that had served the people so ill.

All revolutions so far had failed so this would be an inner revolution. Osho's revolution was a revolution of consciousness. He was the visionary who saw that, for solutions to the world's problems, the first step must be through the individuals. Collective solutions come later.

* * *

For our present, post-national epoch too, half a century later, a revolution of consciousness is all that stands between humanity and global suicide. To change the world we too will have to change our selves, change our lives from the inside out. To find within what never changes.

This is a very great crisis. If we take the challenge, this is an opportunity to create the new. It has never been so ripe at any time in the past. You are living in one of the MOST beautiful ages—because the old is disappearing, or has disappeared, and a chaos is created. And it is only out of chaos that great stars are born.

You have the opportunity to create a cosmos again. This is an opportunity that comes only once in a while—very rare. You are fortunate to be alive in these critical times. Use the opportunity to create the new man.

[Osho, *Philosophia Perennis*, Vol. 2, Ch. 2, Q. 2]

* * *

'Love has happened!' exclaimed Laxmi to the male president of the local All India Women's Congress. He slapped her face. At the age of thirty-four, Laxmi has met her once and forever master—her *Satguru*. One slap is a trifling price to pay, she reflected later, for the greatest blessing life can offer.

She was the current secretary at the Congress Party Silver Jubilee Conference. The guest speaker was Acharya Rajneesh. She had agreed to propose a vote of thanks and close the meeting. But she forgot.

Her expectations for the speaker had been low. She knew Jain monks went barefoot, perhaps naked or near naked, with a begging bowl and wearing a mask to prevent ingestion of insects. She had seen them with their hand-brooms that they used to sweep away the bugs from underfoot.

This one was different. The first glimpse of him took away her breath. He wore a snow-white cotton *lungi* and a silk *chaddar*. She watched open-mouthed as he entered the hall. Such grace! Such beauty! Such a smile! Like the rising sun, it lit the dark penumbra of her soul. He moved like no one she had ever seen; effortlessly, powerfully and yet with so much delicacy. Laxmi felt her body come to full alert and her mind go very quiet as she watched him seat himself cross-legged on the podium.

Now a silence settled on the hall, a clear and ringing silence she had never heard before. It was not like the silence she remembered from nights in their country home, nor was it the silence when a long drive is done and at last the motor is switched off. This was a pregnant, momentous, revolutionary silence. Laxmi could not take her eyes off the man.

When finally he spoke, his words came softly as part of the silence; leaves floating on a limpid river to settle slowly in the humus of her heart. She received them with a sigh of recognition, was transported to another realm.

And when the time came for her small speech of thanks to the speaker, she forgot—forgot her role, her manners, her very self. Hence the words, 'love has happened' and hence the president's slap.

A smiling Osho was to tell her later that the journey towards self-realisation is a risky journey.

And it is a challenge too. That challenge is going to become a blessing to you. Those who will be able to accept the challenge and be with me, and those who will be so much in love with me that they can suffer for me, they will grow. They will grow to infinite heights. They will know something that is not ordinarily known by human beings. It is not available in the churches; it is not available in the temples. It becomes available only when a disciple allows him or herself to be so open to the master—that the master starts living in the disciple too. This is when the transfer of energy happens.

[Osho, *Take it Easy*, Vol. 2, Ch. 8, Q. 3]

* * *

The whole family were seated at the dinner table that evening. All eyes were on Laxmi. She had returned home from some meeting that afternoon brought by an irate gentleman. He had asked to speak directly to Laxmi's father or mother. Behind closed doors, he had reported to *Mataji* his observation of Laxmi's irrational and immature behaviour. Nephews and nieces listening at the door had heard the story. Soon the whole household knew.

'So you've fallen in love with a *babaji*?'

'Leave me alone.'

'You refused all those nice young men, what's so great about this one?'

'He's not a nice young man for a start.'

'Oh, so what does he have that they don't have?'

'You wouldn't understand.'

'See if we wouldn't!'

'I'd be wasting my breath.'

'We all want to hear.'

'Yes Lar, please tell us what makes him special?'

Laxmi pushed aside her hardly touched *thali* of rice, lentils and vegetables. 'Why are we here on earth? Where do we come from, where do we go to? You know how these questions wash around inside our brains from time to time? Well they do, at least, in mine. And then there are no answers so we let them drop unanswered. This man is not a *babaji*! He's beautiful and full of grace. He speaks from a place where all those questions have already been answered. Or dissolved. Listening to him I finally felt my life had a meaning, as if...'

She was cut short. 'As if it had no meaning before? Well then, why did you not kill yourself?'

'See? I said you wouldn't understand.'

'Don't listen to him, he's jealous.'

'The day I am jealous of her and a *baba* is the day I'll be crowned Queen of England.'

'Carry on Lar, please!'

'I've said enough. See for yourselves. Come and meet him when he's back again in Bombay. You'll see a man of love. You'll see what happens when the power of love is greater than the love of power. Okay?'

'You'll get over him.'

'Get lost silly boy.'

'You smell.'

'Thanks! You are almost right as well as being disrespectful. I am surrounded by his fragrance. I feel his presence still.'

* * *

Laxmi enjoyed the Congress work not just for the good causes it promoted but also for the opportunity to meet women of different ages and lifestyles. Now, as secretary, and with the agreement of her committee, she arranged for Osho to be the guest speaker at a later meeting. This time he would stay with the Kuruwa family.

In a hall bursting at full capacity, Laxmi heard him speak as if directly to her. He spoke of three levels of love and she drank in every word. He likened the first level to the lowest rung of a ladder. This love is physical, is demanding, often lustful and full of expectations. It is the only love that most of us know, she thought. The second rung of love is deep respect, is friendliness and intimate sharing. This love is physical and emotional and intellectual. The third rung manifests as profound compassion, as tender generosity. It is a love stripped of all demands; a love unaddressed, a love that falls like gentle rain on all and everything. 'Yes but how do we get to that?' said Laxmi to herself. A story Osho told of Meera stayed vividly in her memory. She was a queen who was born five thousand years after Krishna, yet her love, her devotion, for him was so great, so intense, that it burned her ego and she could face her family's murderous hostility with a smile and even gratitude.

With the talk concluding, this time Laxmi remembered her duties and rose to thank Osho on behalf of the Congress. Later she drove him to the family home. She said, 'I see love differently now. You have transformed my perceptions of it. Made sense of it. Perhaps I was a nun in former lives, or maybe had too much of sexual love. In this life I have no interest in the physical side of it. Sex is not a card that I've been dealt this round. But the way you describe it now I see it is but the first step of a divine process. That makes a big difference to me. It relieves me.'

* * *

This new perception of love Laxmi called a revelation, a comfort; a springboard to a new level of being. And over the following months, not only Laxmi but her mother, two uncles, a brother and a sister variously attended Osho's talks and were attracted to him and the intelligence of his vision. From the summer of 1967 he was invited to stay at Vatcha Villas whenever he was in or near Bombay.

His presence was especially valued when Laxmi's younger brother wanted to marry a Parsee girl. The entire Kuruwa family opposed the alliance. No one had ever been known to propose a marriage outside their Bombay-Gujarati Jain community. In the '60s, it was common to match the horoscopes of potential partners. In this case, the family would not even consider matching them. Osho was invited to help resolve the issue. He lightly pointed out to them their rigid ideas about religion and status and their underlying pride and fear: and they accepted his words. To the couple he said, 'Love is the art of being with another, meditation is the art of being alone. One needs both.' The family dropped their reservations and invited Osho to the couple's wedding.

When Osho returned to Bombay next, for three days Laxmi was all dance and delight. She said in her notes that he gave impromptu talks that were powerful, confrontational and fired with profound and radical insights. She said she herself often felt stunned and speechless listening to his lucid, poetic use of both Hindi and English. She took particular note when he spoke on love, on sex as a path to super-consciousness, on education and on women and the social structures. He challenged Gandhi's view of economics and the hand-loom philosophy so that Laxmi thought of giving up the plain white homespun fabrics that she wore. 'I am not trying to convert you,' Osho said. 'Only if what I say appeals to you, only then stop your weaving. With the time saved, you can work on your growth. Be more aware and meditative. Sit in silence, watch the sunrise, listen to the birds singing and enjoy the fragrance of flowers. These will enrich you and you will feel more energetic. In the moment of your death, neither social work nor family nor friends will be of any help. Only your awareness and meditation will be your light.'

One night Laxmi's brother asked Osho, 'What do you

enjoy most in life?' They were sitting in the lamp-lit drawing room, a circle of family members with a few close friends. Osho, seated cross-legged on a sofa replied, 'Everything that is beautiful.'

Laxmi was not expecting such an answer. Inside her head, a vista opened up. Her body was suddenly and inexplicably immobile. She saw coloured planets whirl and suns collide. *Everything that is beautiful!* For a moment she felt weightless, airborne, looking at the world through Osho's eyes. She saw all things connected, shining, pristine in their suchness. She saw the beauty of her family's faces, saw the turquoise light refracted from a circling fly, saw their house enclosing hope and love and striving in this sprawled-out, bountiful, filthy, over-crowded, grinding, and violent city. Now she knew, for a moment or forever, that everything *is* beautiful, that even ugliness has beauty, that ugliness is just the underside of beauty.

The new religion is going to be aesthetical, poetic. A man will be thought religious if he paints beauty, sings beauty, dances beauty. If he has grace, if his life is a joy...And not only joy in himself but an overflowing, a superabundance, of joy; not only that he is blissful, he shares bliss. That is the religion that is going to happen in the future. And the first hints of it have happened in Zen: it is only the Zen Masters who have been painting, and writing poetry. [...] The man who has a sense of beauty is bound to be good—and without any cultivation of good. The goodness will be just natural: it will follow his sense of beauty.

Let beauty be your God.

[Osho, *The Sun Rises in the Evening*, Ch. 5]

* * *

Laxmi realised her *khadi* cloth clothing was a pretentious statement just as much as the materials she scorned; silks and gold and ermine. She ordered new dresses in white and in colours of mill-made material. She found that her Gandhian idealism was slipping from her daily life.

One evening her mother spoke to her about the new love in her life, her *guru*. 'I see the changes in you. I see so much enthusiasm in you for this man. You always had a lot of energy, now you have a hundred times more of it. I feel something moving in me too. I want to know what drives you, what you feel.'

'I don't know what I feel. I'm out of my depth. Especially when I have to build a framework of words. All I do know is my heart and soul aren't mine any more. Everything is his. You are our mother. You gave us life. You know what love feels like. Part of you, your daughter, is now outside you, standing on her own two feet. I have never given birth but now I have a hint of what love is. *Pitaji's* love for us was generous and everlasting. What I feel from Osho is completely different. It's a kaleidoscopic love, brightly coloured and richly patterned. I want to care for him and be totally in service to him.

'Sometimes, when I'm getting in the car or walking in the market, I suddenly feel I'm lifted up, walking on a cloud. The sky above is boundless; anything is possible. It's silly trying to use these clumsy words...'

'What you say is beautiful, my dear. We all remember, deep down, how it was when we were children. Everything was possible. The world was a magical place awaiting us.'

'That's exactly what I'm feeling now,' continued Laxmi, jumping up and walking to and fro, barefoot on the marble-flagged floor. 'There are no limitations. Everything is boundless. Everything is part of everything else. I don't have a skin. Nor does this table. Or this wall. Look! We are just millions of atoms vibrating. Everything dissolves in love. And yet there remains something stable. Oh, one can't speak of these things! Osho is like the nucleus of every single cell, aware of everything. That's how it feels to me. He is everywhere, in everything. So it turns out that it is my love and my destiny to work for him. To work with him. It's the only life I can foresee right now.'

'But he's an ordinary man, isn't he?'

'*Mataji*! You have the knack of asking easy questions that are difficult to answer. Of course he's just an ordinary man. He eats, sleeps and defecates like us. But something has happened to him.'

'Has he told you? Do you know what?'

'He broke out of his conditioning. He escaped from the slow drip-drip of judgements and fears and carrots and sticks by which we are shaped to society's ends. He's arrived at a world of love and peace and truth and joy. Now he knows who he is. He can see to the heart of everything. He sees to the heart of me, I know. He answers our questions with such clarity—sometimes before we even ask them. And what's special, with his answers come no judgements. He seems to accept things as they are, and me for who I am. I don't know what I'm saying.'

Laxmi sat herself abruptly by her mother. *Mataji* took her daughter's hand and gently stroked it as Laxmi continued. 'Like you mentioned earlier, when we were children we knew that everything was possible. But now? We measure everything by money and utility. We live in worry and desire.

We die in fear and misery. He has somehow freed himself from all disorders. I sense that his experience of life is elemental, unedited, raw. Like he's a tree or a star or a great bird of the mountains. He sees to the heart of things. Isn't that what a *guru* does? I don't know *Mataji.*'

'Yes, my dear, for most of us in India, a *guru* or master is part of everyone's life. I have read that physicists say infinity is downwards as well as upwards. We can travel forever inwards into matter as much as we can travel outwards into space. Exploration inwards has been crucial to our Indian culture as far into the past as human history can travel. Guides are useful on the unmapped inner pathways. In India, the master who can give that guidance is immensely honoured. And it becomes an honour too to be his or her disciple. Of course, they themselves must have a grounding in the inner realms either through their own master or through a spontaneous experience of self-realisation. Most enlightened ones do not become teachers, and, of the few who do, most remain relatively little known.'

'I guess everyone says this about their *guru*, but Osho seems something different.'

'He does seem different. He is rooted in the modern world, the one pervading from the West. The one that's making *gurus* look redundant!'

The two women laughed and eyed each other tenderly. Laxmi continued, 'I agree. Most Westerners that I have met and read about would say they have done perfectly well for a thousand years without *gurus* and inner exploration, why should they waste time on them now?'

'They have done perfectly well? Yes, that's the joke. The irony. The world is haunted by wars, assorted strife and

"Darwinian" competition, nuclear weapons and polluted seas, shrinking rainforests, gender issues, patriarchal attitudes towards women, designer plagues, a nuclear winter and starving millions. Does it have to be like that? Why should fear and greed be our presiding faculties? That's not doing perfectly well.'

'So something has to change. We'd better start with ourselves.'

Mataji rose, put a gentle hand on her daughter's cheek. 'I trust you, La. Follow your feelings.'

* * *

That night, reading in bed, Laxmi came upon a myth about the Buddha.

The Devas came down to visit Gautama the Buddha after his enlightenment. They told him, 'Now you give the call. Now you tell all people far and wide your experience of bliss, of nirvana.'

'Who will listen?' replied the Buddha.

'Yes indeed,' said the Devas. 'Call a million and one thousand will hear. Of the one thousand, one hundred will listen. Of the one hundred, ten will understand. Of the ten, nine will be lost. One will arrive.'

* * *

Over the next years, more members of Laxmi's family were to become attracted to Osho, still known as Acharya Rajneesh. There was a maternal uncle, a compulsive gambler and proud sceptic whose life was transformed at his very first meeting with Osho. Laxmi herself devoted more and more of her time to Osho, his meditations and his care and now resigned from all her other commitments.

* * *

At first Laxmi was on the fringes of Osho's work, travelling with members of her family in Gujarat and Maharashtra to attend talks and retreats. As time passed, she took more and more responsibility to see that his rooms were clean, his transportation efficient and his food cooked exactly to his taste and dietary requirements. Osho was already a Type Two diabetic and highly allergic to certain smells and substances. Osho's cousin Kranti was one of his chief caretakers; she had been doing that continuously since his move to the university in Jabalpur. But she had her own career as a teacher to attend to.

Laxmi told her family, 'He gets offered such rubbishy food by people with the best intentions. And he often must sleep in unhygienic conditions. But the worst thing is people pressing round him to touch his feet with smells that trigger all his allergies. He accepts everyone and everything so someone has to step in and be a buffer for him and his sensitivities.'

4. NO ONE AT NARGOL

Osho, throughout his life, continually evolved his methods for sharing his vision. In the early days, he worked exclusively with individuals, tailoring his healing to particular spiritual needs. As his field of view widened out from Jabalpur, his insights became more subtle: he engaged with audiences both better educated and more sophisticated.

At the time Laxmi met him, after twenty years of travelling the length and breadth of India, frequently addressing crowds ranging from fifty to 100,000, he had collected a core of dedicated pioneers of the inner journey. At this stage he began to develop new methods of self-enquiry and meditation for the contemporary man and woman, those who live and work in an ever more stressful, ailing and confusing world.

The core of Osho's new techniques for exploring the inner self is to exaggerate and express the tensions of our body-minds so that when relaxation *is* allowed, it is a complete relaxation. Complete relaxation is the gateway to silence, to harmony and all that is creative and benign in humans. Osho tried and tested many of these new meditations on himself and his close friends.

* * *

Laxmi had seen Osho, she had heard Osho, she had sensed his magnitude and she had opened her heart to him. In Nargol, a small coastal town of palm-fringed, sandy beaches some hundred kilometres north of Bombay, in the month of May in the year 1970, she received one of the most beneficial and forceful gifts Osho has bequeathed to mankind— Dynamic Meditation. (This is described in the Appendix.)

Meditation has of course been around for many thousands of years. India is the home of meditation. Osho brought it, refreshed and updated, to the contemporary world. Before him, only Gautama Buddha, Patanjali and the great Mahavir presented their disciples with such a spread of useful techniques for the inner work. Since those days, the human mind has changed immensely. Osho renewed and reinvented techniques of meditation for an increasingly materialist, increasingly unconscious, increasingly desperate world.

His work back then was for our growth now.

The problem is our consciousness has not developed at the same rate as the technology we have conceived and created. These coming years will present us with a crash-course in developing this consciousness. Meditation, as mentioned earlier, is the fast track to awareness and a medication for all ills. The illness that this humanity scurries towards—which we see all around us—is the destruction of our global habitat and the mass extinction of species. We humans are the ones who currently carry the torch of consciousness; if we let it be snuffed out, we, and all living things suffer. The hardship that we, our children and their children are likely to undergo in the process is unthinkable.

Most environmental scientists and climatologists say

that we passed the tipping point for global warming in 2008. We cannot now avoid disastrous climate change. Humans have to learn new ways of facing unpredictability, disorder and paradox. Through the practice of meditation, we learn to respond, not react. We learn to open up to new improvisations, to drop old habits that cascade problems in all directions. Thus, meditation is a direct help in addressing climate change. And the battle for scarce resources. And the flooding of major cities. And skin cancer. And unbreathable air, overpopulation, massive uncontrollable migrations, rampant outbreaks of viruses and averting a nuclear winter.

Meditation is an enquiry within; it is the watching of the mind. It is a stepping back from the ego in order to see clearly who or what we human beings really are. It requires no equipment and no knowledge, no religion or belief; nothing but an interest in what is true. The human mind is a brilliant tool. It has taken us from the primeval forests into every corner of the earth and beyond. As an instrument of imagination and creation, the power of the human mind is seemingly unbounded. Exactly here lies the problem, the major existential problem of today.

Modern mind is a good servant but a poor master. Mind as conceptual thought has become the high chamberlain who displaces his king, the footman who supplants his master, the tool that controls the hand using it.

Mind equates with ego; it is who we think we are. Yet in truth we are not. Mind and ego are unreal. They are constructs of the past and the future. They are never of the present where reality abides. And they swing between desire and fear, hope and despair. It is guaranteed, therefore, wherever there is unrest and mayhem, distress and destruction on this planet, there will be found the human mind. It is the ego-mind that puts the earth in jeopardy.

Sports players often talk about being 'in the Zone' when they experience peak moments of consciousness. Sport demands of its players to be totally in the present moment. Sportsmen are competing and yet they must cooperate with flowing, unfolding events. They have all submitted to the discipline of their training and, at a certain point in the game, a new layer of consciousness emerges. The footballer then knows he can run through the wall of defence and place the ball in the goal, the tennis competitor finds that her arm itself knows where to put the racket for the winning shot, the racing driver feels the car is driving itself in an optimal line.

Sportsmen aren't the only ones who have such vivid moments. Dancers, poets, artists of all types are having them, expressing them, searching for them—and young children are mostly dwelling in them. All of us have had these peak moments at one time or another; in nature, during sex, listening to music; unexpected moments of utter calm and unity. We do not have to be kids, sportsmen, artists, or religious to arrive at this awareness—these fleeting moments can become our permanent state of being, thanks to meditation.

If we are not our ego-minds then the question must arise, who on earth are we?

The great teachers say 'Pure Consciousness'. However these words do not, in reality, answer the question. The answer must be an experience, not a concept. Meditation is the path to that direct experience of who we are.

Someone said we left the Stone Age, not because we ran out of stones, but because we just got more intelligent. Since the 1960s we have known that we cannot go on burning fossil fuels with impunity. But we have upped our carbon footprint by 50 per cent in just the last two decades. That is not intelligent.

Laxmi did not know then what physics, neurophysics and neurobiology tell us now—that there's no such thing as a 'thing'. All matter, including the body, is made of temporary, ever-moving, ever-changing molecules, atoms, and particles that have no actual location. Even less existent is the mind, with its thoughts that arrive from god knows where and over which we have no control. Nor did Laxmi know that later neurobiologists would confirm what Osho and the sages of the past have already described; that in deep meditation, a largely unused part of the brain comes into play. This part evolved, at its most primitive level, for sexual bonding. At its highest level, it is activated in meditation. This mental state perceives the interconnectedness of all things. It understands that what we do to others we do to ourselves. Scientists call the effect of the process 'Absolute Unitary Being'.

> 'Self blends with other, mind and matter are one
> and the same.'
>
> [Newberg and d'Aquili, *Why God Won't Go Away*]

This is the intelligence called for by the multiplying crises in our world today.

Laxmi was to devote her life to sharing the visionary insights of Osho for what he envisaged as the 'New Man and New Woman'; those who live at peace with themselves, their neighbour and with nature. In doing so she came to see for herself that there are no separate entities—that life is a network of inter-being. She walked the talk. She displayed intelligence.

* * *

Osho started the Nargol Meditation camp with a bang.

A new phase of my work begins with this camp. It is not only meditation, it is absolute ecstasy that I am going to teach to you. It is not only the first step, it is the last. Only no-mind on your part is needed and everything is ready. I am not a teacher. I give you the experience.

[Osho, *A Bird on the Wing*, Ch. 1]

Here in Nargol. Laxmi had her first exposure to these novel meditations,

There is an old Osho publication called *In Search of the Miraculous* that contains transcripts of his discourses he gave at that first camp. Strangely, it records the actual words of exhortation and encouragement that he uses during these early experiments in what is to become his hallmark Dynamic Meditation. He reminds the aspirant meditators that the sages of the past have all declared that we are not our bodies and we are not our minds. Then who are we? This was the theme of his meditation camp. The participants had to discover experientially and for themselves who they really were.

During the fifteen-minute third stage of Dynamic Meditation, now called the *Hoo* stage, Osho urged the meditators to keep asking themselves this root question: 'Who am I? *Main kaun hoon?*' no less than 182 times. Osho repeated the question for the meditators' most earnest enquiry.

'Let your every breath be filled with that question "Who am I?"'

'Stake your all on discovering "Who am I?"'

'Drown yourself in this pursuit, "Who am I?"'

Laxmi threw herself whole-heartedly into the process.

People have called her blinkered and obsessive. Laxmi turned these incipient features into positive qualities that fuelled her with an urgency to answer this paramount question. Slowly, with each questioning shaft, something solid in her belly began to respond. Just below her navel, some knot loosened; some long-locked energy began to move.

Laxmi kept this process under way even at meal times, even when cleaning her teeth, and even when going to sleep. Often the mind intruded. 'This is stupid! What are you playing at? Whatever will people think?'

* * *

Laxmi placed her mattress on the balcony of Osho's lodging. She lay sleepless in the warm dark starlit night. She asked herself the question, 'Who am I?' Again and again and again.

She noticed her breathing became vigorous and effortless. Then suddenly she seemed to separate from her body. She was aware and awake but she was not that person lying in the bed. She could see through its eyes but behind the eyes was an empty space. Through its eyes, she saw the panoply of stars, the silhouettes of trees and roofs in all their coal-black density. She could see Laxmi lying on the bed below her. Behind the eyes was no one and no thing but perfect symmetry. Great peace and happiness were there. She heard loud laughter coming from the body.

Her uncle, who was sleeping nearby, was awakened by the laughter. 'My niece has gone mad!' He panicked and rushed to awaken Osho. They came to the balcony where she lay. Osho stooped over her, laid a soothing hand on her forehead, then called her back into her body. As she returned he withdrew to his room.

Later next morning he confirmed that Laxmi had experienced an inner meditative awakening, also called *samadhi* or *satori*. This experience gave her the long-term understanding that she was not her body. As she said later to her family, '*Ghatna ghat gayi!*' which roughly and poetically translates to 'Happening has happened!' She had glimpsed the unreality of ego, its futile separation and its tragedy. She had glimpsed what the master lives in his day-to-day life, that there is no separate subject and object; there is only subjectivity.

Amid the cruel and difficult dramas that were to unfold in her life over the following years, this first lesson and her devotion to Osho would be her only guides, her unfailing support. As she said later, 'Laxmi as a physical entity died then and was reborn as a disciple.'

* * *

The following morning Laxmi was up at six as usual. She prepared Osho's bath for him. As she served him his tea he said, 'All of us are mad; the difference is only of degree. You experienced an awakening of the inner meditative energy last night. That is beautiful. But remember one thing. Your uncle suffers from a heart condition. We must all be aware of each other's situation. Let an awareness of others also be part of your meditation.' Laxmi bowed her head acknowledging Osho's compassion for all around him.

A few nights later, Laxmi again experienced intense laughter. This time she contained it. The following morning, she woke up acutely aware of each movement of her body; it felt light as though floating but her silk nightdress weighed heavy on her. She described the sensation to her uncle and asked him to lend her a *dhoti* (a five-metre strip of cotton commonly worn by Indian men at that time) which required no underwear.

'What are you going to do with my *dhoti*?' he roared. 'Do you wish to drop clothes and be naked during the camp?'

'Of course not. I'm asking to borrow it.'

'What nonsense! I've had enough. Go and pack your bags. We're going home immediately.'

'If you don't give me the *dhoti* you will be the first to see this body naked. Laxmi is dead and this is the beginning of a new life. I am grateful to my parents and to you, Uncle; but now I have no attachments.'

Her uncle looked into Laxmi's eyes, saw the light that burned in them and reluctantly loaned her a clean *dhoti*. When later she brought tea to Osho he laughed. 'I'll ask your uncle to buy you a *lungi* and *kurta* from the *bazaar*.'

For a while then Laxmi was able to witness her Self even whilst asleep. She began to wear lighter and simpler clothing and to eat more natural foods. She was becoming the hollow bamboo through which the master could later work.

***

A master comes into this world for the raising of human consciousness. His or her work is nothing less than the transformation of humanity. They are returning heaven to its proper place—here on earth.

They do not want to start a religion, nor to make people

good, nor create beliefs and belief systems, ⁄
of ethics; they do not want to endorse a g
one. Their only work is to pass on their un...
share their bliss and benevolence along with the tecнш...
means to bring paradise down to earth. What they lay before
us is the understanding that when we live in conscious
awareness, we unite with our true nature. We are in unity
with all that is.

A master is faced with an awesome task. We humans are
less than what we can be and ignorant of our potential. We
live in a region of slumber, in a state of achieved inability;
we move in a dream world of fear and desire, attachment
and mistrust, frenzy and inertia.

If we are ready to forgo our ego's demands and offer
ourselves to the master, they will use every device and every
opportunity to wake us up, restore our sight and stand us on
our own two feet. They will give us the means to accomplish
this. The master is a skilled craftsman, a psychologist, a
mother, an artist, a lover and a midwife. He or she lives in
an infinite now—available whether embodied or not.

* * *

Once home, Laxmi closed herself in her room for three days
without food. At first the family thought that she had had a
breakdown. Later they revised it to a breakthrough.

She had had an 'Out of Body Experience'; an *o.b.e.*

An Out of Body experience happens to one in ten of
the population, according to a recent survey. *O.b.e.* is the
generally accepted, non-sectarian term for astral or etheric
projection or travel.

Medical science is currently funding research into such
cases. As yet, there seems to be no clear theory of the hows

and whys of this phenomenon; what is clear however is that there is a similarity of experiences right across the world. Reports come from people of all or no religious beliefs in all cultures. They describe floating in space above their bodies; they experience feelings of calm, a pervasive sense of peace. They say that time and space cease to exist—or rather cease to be limiting factors. Often people describe a tunnel with radiant light at the end. Some describe meetings with a being of light or with relatives and ones they have loved. Often people go through some sort of life review.

The ability to have an *o.b.e.* can be learned or it can be induced by chemicals or by any number of intense activities such as mountaineering or long-distance running. Many have briefly experienced an *o.b.e* in the *Hoo* stage of Dynamic Meditation or on a long-distance hike. For some it is experienced spontaneously just before falling asleep. Enlightened ones live permanently in this condition. It is a master's work—part of his midwifery service—to sever the umbilical cord of the disciple from his ego.

To cut the physical cord between two bodies is not a very big thing, but to cut the cord between your consciousness and your body is certainly the biggest shock possible. It comes, finally—when the season is right, and the moment has arrived that you have to be taken out of your body, out of your imprisonment, and left totally alone in your tremendous freedom. This is called, in the mystic language, the second birth.

The first birth is from the mother's body. You become a personality.

The second birth is from your own body. You become a free individual.

[Osho, *The Hidden Splendour*, Ch. 1]

* * *

When the question 'Who am I?' is deeply explored and deeply lived, the seeker comes to *be* the answer. Or, as Osho puts it:

'Who am I?' is not really a question because it has no answer to it; it is unanswerable. It is a device, not a question. [...] Your mind will say, 'You are the essence of life. You are the eternal soul. You are divine,' and so on and so forth. All those answers have to be rejected: Neti Neti—one has to go on saying, 'Neither this nor that.

When you have denied all the possible answers that the mind can supply and devise, when the question remains absolutely unanswerable, a miracle happens: suddenly the question also disappears. [...] When the question has disappeared, then you know. But that knowing is not an answer: it is an existential experience. [...] The question 'Who am I?' is just a device to lead you into the unknown, to lead you into the uncharted, to lead you into that which is not available to the mind. It is a sword to cut the very roots of the mind, so only the silence of no-mind is left. In that silence there is no question, no answer, no knower, no known, but only knowing, only experiencing.

[Osho, *Ah This!*, Ch. 2, Q. 1]

At Nargol, as the camp drew to its close, Laxmi prostrated herself at Osho's feet. 'Whatever the consequences, you are my *Satguru*, my master, my *Bhagwan.*'

* * *

Osho does not have followers. He has disciples. The word 'disciple' comes from the Latin word meaning one who takes in, who learns, who receives. Osho has disciples, friends, fellow voyagers, a multitude of people who love him. He does not ask for followers. That word is demeaning. It implies a hierarchy that does not exist in Osho's field of play. In the '70s and '80s Osho's disciples or *sannyasins* came to be known in the international press as 'The Orange People'. We have Laxmi to thank for Osho's decision to magnify that colour.

* * *

Osho had returned to Jabalpur, leaving Laxmi in an altered state of consciousness, or, as she called it, 'dancing to a silent, ringing music'. He had reminded her that in this world everything changes except change itself. 'Do not cling to anything,' he had told her.

After such an unutterable experience of bliss, reaction was bound to set in. Over long weeks Laxmi became aware of a fearful subterranean rumbling, a shifting of tectonic plates within herself. At first she hardly heeded the disturbance and went about her days as usual. But she was irritable. She snapped at her brother, she complained to the *ayah* of all the young cousins' noise and disorder, she argued with her aunt. And it wasn't just irritation. Other unwelcome guests began turning up. Fear, resentment, grief, despair; they all appeared at unexpected and awkward times. At first Laxmi either ignored them or found good reasons for their presence in her life. She had a recurring dream when she found herself faced with an engulfing void. She thought she should re-enlist with the Gandhian movement—at least they had solid ground under their feet. But, and it was an enormous but, in a corner of her heart, she imputed to Osho some responsibility for sending these unwelcome visitors her way. After all, he had enabled for her a meeting with silence and bliss, so why not now with misery and anger?

One morning, preparing to dress for the day, she stood with her hand on the door of her almirah, the fine old cedar-lined wardrobe that had been in the family forever. She was looking at rows of white *kurtas* and *shalwar kameez*, the blouses and their matching baggy trousers. 'I have nothing to wear,' she said to herself.

That self-same day she went shopping with her mother. She bought half a dozen lengths of factory-printed cotton fabric to have made up into simple, classical Indian wear. That stilled the rumblings for a while.

Soon the calm was again disturbed. Whenever she closed her eyes in meditation, colours flooded in; fields of bright clear colours. 'Am I going mad?' she asked herself. 'The Nargol *o.b.e.* has changed everything; food, relationships, clothing, how one sees ones-self, everything!'

She told her mother to please give away the bulk of her clothes to a charity and go shopping again with her the next day. This time they bought cotton in plain prime colours; five metres of crimson and five each of yellow and orange and red and green and blue and violet. The rumblings were stilled again.

* * *

Laxmi stood one evening again staring into her mirror. The family were due to visit their cousins in a well-to-do district of Bombay. 'I'm too fat. And there's a spot on my cheek.' She said covering her face with her hands. 'This isn't how my life should be.' She did not go to supper with the family. 'I need a clean-out, I need to eat less rubbishy food. Why do I need to eat food at all?' Laxmi, from then on—and not for the first time in her life—began to eat extremely sparingly. She lost some weight and the drumming underground receded.

But not for long. The coloured fabrics were made up into loose-fitting clothes. She wore each coloured set of clothing for two days and watched the effect it had on her mood, her appetite, her sleep and how she related to people. When she came to wear the orange clothes, something strange occurred.

'Ah ha!' she exclaimed, smiling at her double in the mirror. 'This orange one suggests a new and different Laxmi. The brilliant colour makes her dance.'

And dance she did, before the mirror. A breeze from nowhere seemed to lift her limbs, swirl and sway her, move her body as a bough of spring-bright leaves high up in a tree. 'Oh, this colour, look how the body loves it, making arabesques and mudras and such gestures with the hands it's never made before.' And so, entranced, she watched her body dance. It danced for hours and hours. The passionate Meera, Queen of Rajasthan, was dancing for her Krishna. Laxmi's body was rejoicing in itself. Finally, it fell exhausted on the floor.

Her mother looked astonished when she entered later. They were due to leave for the railway station where Osho should arrive from Jabalpur that very afternoon. 'What is this colour that you wear! This orange is the colour of renunciation. You can't walk around this city dressed like a holy nun or mendicant!'

'*Mataji,* this body wants to wear it. What can one do?'

'But don't you understand, child, if you wear that colour it's committing you to a seeker's life of self-denial? To *sannyas.* You don't want that, do you?'

'No I don't. And I would not commit myself to self-torture in any way.'

'But Laxmi dear, I must tell you that if you did become a seeker of truth or god or whatever it is you are looking for, I will be right behind you; proud of you. Being without attachment to things and to people and to outcomes is beautiful. But remember, once you set your foot on the path there's no turning back.'

'Thank you, thank you. You have always been a support and wise counsel. I don't really know what's going on.'

'Well, we'll see what people think about this orange clothing? But now we have to go to meet his train.'

* * *

Many friends were at the magnificent old Victoria Terminus station to greet Osho. There must have been over a hundred of them spread up and down the platform. Laxmi, Uncle, *Mataji* and Kakubhai were nearly late as they pushed their way through the seething afternoon crowds. 'I can't see a thing from here,' said Laxmi and she dived between two white-clothed, talkative gentlemen and scurried up towards the approaching train behind a crimson turbaned porter.

When the hissing, steam-enshrouded engine drew majestically to a halt there was a shouting. A wave of bodies surged towards its gravitational centre. All had their hands pressed together in a greeting of respect. There, resplendent in white, framed by the dark brown doorway of the coach, stood the master himself. His hands too were raised in *namaste*, the master bowing to the divine that resides in all beings. A garland of orange marigolds was offered and he bent gracefully to receive it around his neck. After twenty hours on the train, he appeared as fresh as if he had spent

lazing in a hammock in his garden. People were
g around him wanting to touch his feet. Then he
noticed Laxmi in her brilliant sunrise orange. He beckoned
to her and she came running and touched his feet.

'Laxmi,' he said. 'What is the meaning of this colour?'

'Meaning, *Bhagwan*? It has no meaning. You tell me what
it means.' She was laughing now. 'It just happened. I don't
know why but I knew I had to wear these clothes.'

'Then existence is showing us something. This is
beautiful. This is how things will evolve. Today my Neo-
Sannyas begins. You, Laxmi, are the instrument of its birth.'

* * *

Some of Osho's supporters were angry with him and they
took it out on Laxmi as is so often the way. Anger cannot
be expressed towards an enlightened being but it can be
dumped on someone near him. Why the anger? Because,
for years, Osho has been demolishing the beliefs and the
trappings of the old religions. And now he was stealing
one of their emblems and presenting it again in a radical
new form.

As Osho later explained, traditional *sannyas* was life
negative. Neo-*Sannyas* is life-affirmative.

Celebration is the foundation of my sannyas—not renunciation
but rejoicing in all the beauties, all the joys, all that life offers,
because this whole life is a gift of God. [...] To me, life and God
are synonymous. In fact, life is a far better word than God
itself, because God is only a philosophical term, while life is
real, existential. [...] To me nothing is mundane and nothing is
sacred. To me all is sacred, from the lowest rung of the ladder
to the highest rung. It is the same ladder: from the body to the

soul, from the physical to the spiritual, from sex to samadhi—
everything is divine! My Neo-Sannyas lives this.

[Osho, *Come Come Yet again Come*, Ch. 2, Q. 1]

* * *

In the following days and weeks, in Bombay and in the
Himalayas, near Osho and away from him, with his words
and from his silence, Laxmi began to explore her inner
realm more consciously. Now she could catch glimpses
of the fearful, shifting tectonic plates inside her. Now
she understood that these impulses of disturbance and
dissatisfaction came from an unconscious need to remove
herself from her past beliefs and attitudes, her received ideas
and conditioning, even from her preferences. The ground
on which she had been standing for years needed to shift; it
needed to make way for the new. This had driven her to hate
her clothes and disdain her body. Losing weight and eating
less were her blind approaches to purification, wiping clean
a cluttered slate. Now with the deepening of her meditation
she felt a flooding of acceptance and harmony both within
and without.

* * *

Various friends and admirers, including Laxmi's brother
Kakubhai and a mutual friend of the family Himmatbhai,
invited Osho to come and live in Bombay. His response was
simple: his work was to help people bring more awareness
to their lives. Friends should understand that no one was
obliged to him, and conversely there must be no interference
in his work. It was up to the trustees of the *Jivan Jagruti
Kendra* (the registered charity for his work) to take care of

the material side. They could publish his books, charge entry fees for lectures, and charge for food and lodging. He was not, he emphasised, in need of money for personal expenses.

The trustees agreed to his proposals and Osho accepted their invitation. He moved into a fourth floor apartment in Cricket Club of India (CCI) Chambers on the select Marine Drive.

* * *

For Laxmi this was the dawning of her heart's desire. Now she could spend most of her days with and around Osho. Now, she could intensify her inner work and now, as more and more people came to visit, she could take up a role as his buffer, his secretary and occasional caretaker.

'Laxmi is excited.'

'You are like a kid,' her mother responded one morning at breakfast. 'You're always excited since you've found your *guru* and now work for him. For you each day is like a rock pool to explore, a tree to climb, a pure white page to draw on.'

'Yes. That is true. Laxmi Mark One is on the scrap heap and Laxmi Two is a six cylinder, surprisingly spacious, high performance roadster.'

'But how long will this one last?'

'With regular servicing, as long as it needs to.'

In these early days, it seemed, Laxmi had not acquired the people-skills characteristic of her time in Poona. She could be too protective, too dismissive, even downright devious. According to Ma Dharm Jyoti, there were two or three women who did not work full time and would often sit with or eat lunch with Osho when he was later living in Woodlands. This practice suddenly stopped. Kranti, Osho's cousin and caretaker, asked Jyoti, 'Did you say to Laxmi, "If they can eat lunch with him, why can't I?"' Jyoti replied, 'Of course I didn't say that. I'm always at work at that time.' Kranti supposed that Laxmi had made up the conversation not so much from jealousy but out of an impulse to protect the master from overzealous admirers.

* * *

One friend of Laxmi confessed that his first meeting with Laxmi was inauspicious, whereas the second a year later and all subsequent meetings were rewarding and enlivening. On that first occasion, Osho had called him, then an engineering student, to a camp in Dwarika, Gujarat in 1969. The meditations in that seaside town were all silent sitting meditations and it was possible to have individual *darshan* with Osho at noon. However, it was only on the last day that he, not being a Gujarati speaker, understood that he could have had a *darshan*. By then it was too late.

That night he was unable to sleep and, at four in the morning, he started walking to the distant lodge where Osho and his assistants were staying. Finding the watchman asleep in his booth, the young man entered the compound. He walked round the bungalow until he found an open glass door and stepped into an empty bedroom. He stood for a while bewildered and nervous. When he heard the sound of water splashing in a nearby bathroom, he sat down on the cold marble floor to wait.

He sat there for one hour. Behind him the grey of dawn became the cerulean blue of morning. Osho had been taking his bath. Now he entered wearing only his bath towel. 'And who are you?' he asked. The young man scrambled to his feet and bowed, apologised and explained his situation. Osho invited him to sit on the bed, which he did with great reluctance because, for him, a mystic's bed was a sacred place. Osho then gave him an hour-long *darshan*, laying out for him the parameters that his life would follow. 'You will turn Nepal orange as Padmasambhava turned Tibet blue.'

At seven o'clock, there was a knock on the door and three women entered—one of them, Laxmi, bearing a cup of tea. On seeing the situation, Laxmi burst out, 'How dare you enter the master's room? You have come so early without an appointment! You have disturbed his privacy!'

At this stage, Osho pacified Laxmi with introductions. 'These are my three deities. They are the extensions of my hands.' The young man looked at the small person with the big eyes and the fiery energy. He was scared.

* * *

Ma Neelam described Laxmi as being soft and yet firm in those days when she met her at a meditation camp in Manali. 'We girls were a bunch of *gopis* dancing day and night around Osho. Osho was speaking on Krishna and *gopis* are the cowherds who accompanied the young Krishna. We were so in love with Osho. I was running twenty times a day to the guesthouse to see him. Laxmi would tell me, "He is sleeping. Come back later." Or "He is eating. Come back tomorrow." One time I started crying. Osho was just coming out to give the evening talk. He put his hand on my shoulder. I said rudely, "Go and give your discourse. Your secretary does not want me to see you." Osho looked towards Laxmi who was standing there smiling and he said, "She was taking care of me. I was resting."

'Laxmi was unyielding but she was loving t[...]
I could always take my problems to her. If she could not
answer them, she asked Osho. I always trusted her as his
medium.'

* * *

Ma Dharm Jyoti is the author of an exquisite memoir of life
with Osho, *One Hundred Tales for Ten Thousand Buddhas*.
She told me, 'Laxmi was a good friend to me. We met when
she was still a social worker wearing white. That was before
Osho moved to Mumbai. When he lived in CCI Chambers
in Bombay I used to visit him almost every day. Laxmi
always sat near the door of his room behind a table. I came
to know that she had been appointed as his secretary and
we needed her permission to meet Osho. I felt funny at first
taking permission from her to meet him. She had, I guess,
instructions about this and everything else she did.

'We used to do Dynamic Meditation in one room there
before Laxmi arrived at around eight o'clock in the morning.
I managed to tell Osho about needing her permission to
meet him and he laughed. Osho said, "This is not a big
problem; you come and meet me before Laxmi arrives." I
was happy, so I often used to go to Osho's room before eight.
However, she was just doing her job under Osho's guidance.'

* * *

One day Laxmi and a friend called Ankit were waiting
outside the CCI Chambers for a car to take them to their
respective homes for lunch. An acquaintance of Ankit
passed by and they greeted each other. The acquaintance
then noticed Laxmi's orange clothing and bowed deeply to

her. Spontaneously Ankit said, 'This is Ma Yoga Laxmi. We have been visiting the Acharya Rajneesh.' Ankit then turned abruptly and rushed up the stairs to Osho's apartment. Laxmi followed, protesting that Osho would be sleeping now, and anyway, the car had arrived. Ankit did indeed disturb Osho, telling him he had surprised himself by introducing Laxmi by the invented name and title 'Ma Yoga Laxmi'.

Osho sat up in bed and on a fresh sheet of paper wrote: 'Ma Yoga Laxmi, Secretary to Acharya Rajneesh'. He said, 'Laxmi, you are reborn. Let the old identity die. A new name will remind you to disconnect yourself from the past and to live a new life. Now I will begin to initiate people into my Neo-*Sannyas* with the title *Ma* (Mother) for the women. That word denotes the feminine attributes of warmth, love, softness and care. And for the men I will use the prefix *Swami,* one who is a master of his self, one who has overcome his unconsciousness.'

It was at this time that Laxmi and others conceived the idea of wearing a necklace or *mala* with a locket containing Osho's photograph. Osho gave his approval.

5. A NEW ERA

Laxmi stood ready for the final *Kundalini* meditation. The retreat was drawing to a close. The air was chill and she hugged her thin bare arms. She looked around. Somewhere nearby, amongst the fifty or so other meditators, were her brother, sister and uncle. People were preparing themselves by stretching their limbs, removing and folding outer garments, bending their bodies in elegant yoga postures or standing silently with closed eyes. After just ten days there was already an easy intimacy amongst the participants.

They were again in Manali, a small town in the foothills of the Himalayas where on this day, 26 September 1970, a new era was to begin. The meditations took place in a sandy field of sparse grasses, now bedraggled by many feet. The main buildings and the scattered residential cabins were behind them, partly hidden by the oaks and pines that fringed the field. Before them rose the mountains.

Laxmi let her eyes rise to the brilliant peaks, let them wander through the pristine intricacies of snow and rock, light and shade, sky and cloud.

'Ahhh! These mountains! Their spaciousness! Their silence!' She felt a subtle current of electricity rising through her feet up to her navel and her heart. 'Mankind fights endless wars, involves itself with trivia, while here in these eternal snows people have found peace. Sages have explored the inner reaches of consciousness and passed their understandings to succeeding generations. These mountains inspire me to devote this life to the exploration of who I am and what death holds for me.' A shiver ran through her frame. 'We are blessed to be here.'

On the stroke of five o'clock, with the sun slowly descending behind the loom of mountains, Osho arrived to lead the meditation. He said, 'Friends, those of you who wish to become Neo-*Sannyasin*s may meet me outside my lodge at eight o'clock. All are welcome.' Laxmi again felt the tingle of electricity. 'Another veil is lifted: yet still the mystery expands.'

* * *

Osho initiated into his *Sannyas* Laxmi and eleven others, including one Westerner and one Japanese woman. He placed a *mala* round the neck of each person and told them, 'The hundred and eight beads are strung on one thread: likewise, all the paths of spirituality lead to one absolute and ultimate truth.'

This valley of Kulu–Manali in the mountains would, fifteen years later, be the setting of another critical event in Laxmi's life.

* * *

More and more people heard of Osho and came wanting *darshan,* an audience, or literally translated, 'to see a Seer'. His words and reputation began to spread beyond the boundaries of India. Gradually the practicalities of living in CCI Chambers became insuperable. For a start, the main room onto which the front door opened would only hold about twenty-five or thirty people. It was here that the discourse series 'I am the Gate' was delivered. Neighbours complained of the crowds and of the lift being overused, overloaded and breaking down. The last straw came when the owner of the block forced his way into Osho's rooms, injuring Laxmi and saying to her, 'I don't need your permission to see Osho in my own building.' Another change was imminent.

* * *

Osho's discourses are a history of the world. They are not the usual bloody history of kings and presidents and generals. They are the history of mankind's most precious beings, those who enhanced the evolution of our species. He spoke on scores of enlightened masters great and small, well-known and obscure; on Buddha, Krishna, LaoTsu and Jesus as well as on Ikkyu, Ko'Hsuan, Totapuri and Meister Eckhart. His underlying message was, 'If so many people can do it, why not you? Then the world can look forward to a life we all want.'

At the beginning of 1970, Osho moved into a spacious three-bedroom apartment on the first floor of a block overlooking well-kept gardens. This was Woodlands on Peddar Road, where his work would begin its massive expansion, as too would Laxmi's responsibilities. The front door opened onto the very large sitting room that could just about contain a hundred people. Part of Osho's large library of books was set out on shelves here. Osho's room was simply furnished with a large bed, a small bookcase, a desk and a chair. There was a door in the wall to his clothes cupboard that was sometimes mistaken by confounded visitors for the exit door.

One of Laxmi's main, and probably self-imposed, functions now evolved as Osho's 'protector'. Her prominently positioned desk in front of Osho's room was an endorsement of her secretarial role and now that Osho had decided to charge five rupees for entry to his discourses, she was his treasurer too. One man objected to the entry fee. He stood at the doorway demanding an explanation. 'Okay,' said Laxmi, 'but an explanation will cost you ten rupees.' The man paid five and came out later, satisfied. 'First class. Very fine. Now I understand the need for money to support this work.'

A young English girl, Aranya, on first arriving, asked Laxmi why she was not allowed to walk right in and see Osho then and there. 'He will never tell you "no"; he always says "yes". So that's Laxmi's job—to say "no".'

Osho, at this time, held many meditation camps in Gujarat, Rajasthan and Himachal. Those who saw Laxmi there described her as being wholly engrossed in her meditations, unmoving, undisturbed. 'She was an inspiration to us,' recalls one friend. 'And if one had messages for Osho or questions one always felt she was good at conveying them in both directions. She was clear and quiet. We trusted her.' As an afterthought she added, 'She always had so much work on hand yet she was always centred, never stressed. We thought she was enlightened.'

* * *

One day a disciple invited Osho to come in her Mercedes to look at some land that might be suitable for purchase as an Ashram. Laxmi was not invited and not happy. Throughout the afternoon she was restless and uneasy. Come the evening and the time for Osho's scheduled discourse, she was patently alarmed when he did not show up. Friends sallied forth in all directions to look for him but to no avail.

Much later Osho arrived, his usual serene and smiling self. He told the friends there had been an accident and the disciple's car was totally wrecked. No one was hurt. Laxmi, confirming herself as his protector, asked Osho not to travel in other people's cars any more.

* * *

A number of people have described this small woman with big eyes sitting behind a desk near the entrance of the Woodlands apartment as forbidding. Swami Chaitanya Keerti, later an editor and the community press officer, described his first meeting with Laxmi in *From Allah to Zen*.

I arrived in Bombay on the morning of 4 September 1971. I had five rupees in my pocket. I had been told how to get to Woodlands Apartments. I had arrived too late for the morning meeting, so I waited till 2.30 p.m. for my first meeting with the master.

I introduced myself to his secretary, Ma Yoga Laxmi. There were a few cheerful *sannyasins* sitting nearby laughing and having fun. I asked Laxmi if she would arrange a time for me to meet Osho.

"Have you heard His discourses?" she asked.

"I have been reading His books,"

"Then it would be better," she said, "if you first attended His discourses in the Patkar Hall, before coming for darshan."

"No," I replied, "I have read His books and feel ready to see

Him right away. There is no need for me to wait for some days."

"No," she retorted, "you can't see Him right away."

I was determined that I should see Him then and there, so I just sat there and waited. I was thinking, who is this secretary who prevents me from seeing Him! I thought, when He comes out of His room I will catch Him.

I waited until 4 o'clock. The afternoon meeting was over. Then suddenly I had an idea.

"Please give me some paper," I said to Laxmi, "I will write Him a note to read."

Laxmi gave me a note-pad and I wrote this to Him in Hindi:

"Osho I have come from so far away and there was no problem. Now I am sitting here and you are sitting there a few yards away. What are these walls between us? What is this distance? I cannot express why I have come. I have come. This is my expression."

Laxmi took the message in without reading it, and very quickly returned saying, "He is calling you. Just go into that room."

I took a few steps to the room where the master was sitting; Laxmi had not accompanied me. Very softly I opened the door. I had my darshan with Osho. Later, when I came out, Ma Laxmi welcomed me with a cup of chai. I had been accepted.

The young Ma Madhuri, a long-time devotee of Osho, recalls her impressions as a twenty-one-year-old American girl accompanying her mother to visit him in Woodlands in December 1973. She remembers Laxmi as utterly stern. She says that under Laxmi's gaze she felt neither welcomed nor appreciated, rather, guilty and ashamed. Laxmi's advice was that she and her mother attend the daily discourses and 'people then go chew and digest,' as though this would not be a pleasant practice. She added, 'For me, Laxmi was an intense and glowing presence, always a mix of huge power touched with the darkness of old convents.'

Was Laxmi a very stern 'buffer'? She often had to be. Osho was as a rock in the riverbed, a tree in the wind, a white cloud in the sky. He never said no or interfered with whatever existence brought to him.

Ma Dharm Jyoti explained once, 'Laxmi wasn't strict. She was intuitive. If she felt something was not right, or if a person was not ready, she would delay their meeting with Osho in order to protect him. I remember one time she had to be away somewhere on family business. She asked me to take over as receptionist at Woodlands. She gave me a list of appointments and told me all the practical assignments. All went well until some person failed to turn up for his appointment. As it happened another person had come and begged to see Osho. I put my head into Osho's room to ask if he would see this man. Of course, he said yes. As the man passed me I thought he looked funny. Sort of sleepy. And he smelled not good. He had his time with Osho and when he left I went in to ask Osho if he wanted refreshment. He merely asked, "When is Laxmi coming back?"'

To a demanding, sceptical tourist who came knocking on Osho's door Laxmi said, 'If you think that life is three dimensions only, if you think it is defined by what you see and smell and taste and hear and touch, then you'll miss the half of it. You'll miss the silent drumbeat, the infinite realm within. You'll miss what He can offer you. Good day.'

* * *

Neo-*Sannyas* was taking root. Thousands came to hear Osho when he gave talks in halls and public spaces around the country. He usually spoke in Hindi and often there would be a *kirtan* with singing and dancing. Celebration, after all, is central to Osho's perception of the fully-lived life.

By now, the first Westerners had come to stay permanently with Osho. He conducted ten-day camps, every three months at Mount Abu in Rajasthan, which were a major attraction for them. Here he spoke regularly in English, discoursing on the sacred *Upanishads* and other scriptures.

'But why does anyone need a master?' asked one middle-aged German seated beside her clearly enchanted husband.

The right master can be of tremendous help in your transformation. A master responds to what is already present in you. A master responds more to your silence than to your words, your quest rather than your questions. A master will look into the disciple's being and respond to the inner need—expressed or unexpressed. Maybe left alone the disciple will take months or even years, or even lives to find their needs met. [...]The master–disciple relationship is a spiritual relationship. It works on a far deeper level than any other love, on a far higher plane than any other intimacy. You will need great courage.

"Are you starting a new religion, Acharyaji?"

Real religion is a revolution—a revolution from mind to no-mind, from darkness to light, from death to immortality. Religion is the radical change of your inner gestalt.

You can go to the church, you can go to the temple, but you remain the same person. Just by changing from the church to the temple, do you think there will be any transformation of your consciousness? It's not so cheap. It needs tremendous inner work, it needs great awareness.

The basic question is how to become unidentified with the body, with the mind, how to know that you are just a watcher, a watcher on the hills, unidentified with any cloud, totally beyond, beyond the beyond.

My sannyasins don't belong to any religion although all religions belong to them. They are vast enough: they can absorb whatsoever is beautiful in Jesus and they can absorb whatsoever is beautiful in Krishna. Why change Jesus with Krishna?— Because Jesus has something beautiful which Krishna has not got, and Krishna has something else which is beautiful which is missing in Jesus. And you will be far more complete if Jesus, Krishna, Mohammed, Buddha, Moses, Zarathustra, Lao Tzu, Ko Hsuan, Kabir, Bahauddin, all become part of your inner being.

There is no need to be miserly. Your consciousness is so vast it can contain the whole universe; it can contain the whole sky. Even the sky is not the limit! That's my whole effort here: to make you more and more available to all aspects of religiousness. Why choose? Why be this or that? Why not love all that is beautiful? You can love the roses, you can love the lotuses, you can love all kinds of flowers. These are all flowerings of God.

[Osho, *Tao: The Golden Gate*, Vol. 2, Ch. 8, Q. 2]

* * *

Laxmi began to stay in Mumbai when Osho was conducting camps. She would deal with paperwork, have the flat cleaned and perhaps repainted, take care of purchases and administrative matters. In addition, she took the time to organise and order the thousands of books in his library for, during this period, Osho was reading up to a hundred books a month. Laxmi, who was not an ardent reader herself, felt

awed by the ability Osho had to quote key facts and phrases
from any of the books.

She came to understand during these months that a day
in Osho's life was, on the surface, no different from anyone
else's: he valued time and worked to a schedule, needed
breaks and enjoyed company. However, the difference
was that he lived each moment in its totality as a fresh
experience. He was never on auto-pilot. So Laxmi too had
to manage her time meticulously. Osho was up at 6:30 a.m.
each morning. Invariably there were several people waiting
for his *darshan*. Often, to their delight, he would call them
to his room for a spontaneous talk. Laxmi could often sit
in on such meetings. Osho on one occasion explained to
a small group of new initiates the significance of *sannyas*.

To be initiated into sannyas is to be initiated into meditation.
Meditation is the flavour of sannyas. The orange clothes, the
mala, they are outer symbols; the inner thing is meditation.
So remember it, and occasion more and more centring, getting
to the centre beyond all anguish. It is possible. It is within our
reach, it is our birthright, and if we don't claim it then there is
nobody responsible except ourselves. Life has great treasures to
give us but we don't ask. Ask and it shall be given. Seek and ye
shall find. And the seeking has not to be done anywhere else.
The seeking simply means creating the occasion physically,
vitally, psychologically, creating the occasion where you slowly
start moving to the centre. And suddenly when you are at the
centre, you are no more part of the world, you are in God. That
experience is enlightenment, that experience is transformation.

[Osho, *The Sacred Yes*, Ch. 27]

* * *

Laxmi still went home from time to time. One day as the servant cleared away their lunch, her sister Shobana said, 'La, tell us more about the meditations that you do. Why don't you go to his camps anymore?'

'These years of active meditations have put Laxmi in the driving seat. Now the mind purrs quietly along according to traffic conditions. When she sits silently, she feels the boundaries between her and the world slip away. She feels a part of the whole. Sometimes. Not all of the time.'

'Is it that easy?'

'It is easy and not easy. And it's not esoteric. It's very practical. Meditation is nothing but peeling the onion, layer by layer. When nothing is left, one has arrived. There have been tears but now there is clarity.

'Think about it. We read the papers, watch the news; see the madness in this world around us. There's enough going on to scare the living daylights out of anyone. We pile up stress. Fear and tension are an underlying seam throughout our lives. And that's before we drive to work in heavy traffic, have a set-to with a colleague or wait in line for twenty minutes just to get a meal ticket. This mix of stress is why meditation is so necessary. To free the mind. Everything improves with practice. Meditation is the practice.'

* * *

Strange things sometimes happened at Woodlands. Laxmi was learning devotion and surrender the hard way. The more famous Osho became, the more the traditionalists became worried. And they fermented disturbances. One day a young man charged into the apartment shouting abuse. He picked up a paperweight from Laxmi's desk and hurled it at her. The missile just missed her head and smashed into a cabinet with a loud explosion. Shards of glass flew across the room. The man then ran towards Osho's door. Little Laxmi leapt at him, giving the cook and the apartment guard time to rush up and restrain him. He raged incoherently for some time. When, finally, his words became intelligible, Laxmi handed him a glass of water. Now he explained that he was upset because his wife had been initiated into *sannyas* the previous day. People had told him that Osho hypnotised people and ruined homes; that now she would renounce the family. He feared that she would, despite her assurances.

Laxmi started laughing. 'You've got it back to front!' she explained. 'Osho is taking religion out of the temples and bringing it into everyday life. He wants people to make their home a sacred place, not a ruin. Perhaps you should read what Osho says before you rush to judgement.' They released him with a warning. He glanced again at the well-built attendant and left immediately.

On another occasion, a certain Rampal, who helped edit Osho's *Yukrant Magazine*, asked for a copy of the latest edition. Laxmi handed him one. 'That will be two rupees, please.'

'What? But I am an editor!'

'Yes, I know. And it still costs two rupees.'

'This is preposterous. What are you playing at? I have been editing this thing for years now. How can you have the nerve to charge me? Who the hell do you think you are?'

'I'm the one who sells the magazine.'

'Well I think you are a...' The man turned on his heel shouting foul words and disappeared out of the flat, never to be seen again.

* * *

It is not easy to live close to an enlightened being. We are like icebergs with nine-tenths of our awareness submerged in the unconscious. Close to the furnace of a master, the iceberg starts to melt, or, to use another metaphor, we sleepwalk through our lives and only rarely are awake, often only at a time of crisis. Being close to a master demands enormous self-awareness. It was clearly absent in some of those who were Osho's assistants later on, but Laxmi's complete and utter devotion to Osho allowed her, for the most part, to flow with the eddies and cross-currents of that intense life. Without any show of ego, she combined the job of being Osho's secretary with that of driver, cleaner, administrator, accountant and occasional protector. So far so good.

As the months of these Bombay years passed, she felt her joy and self-awareness grow and stabilise. When Osho's caretaker cousin, Kranti, was more and more away in Jabalpur seeing to her own career as a teacher, Laxmi would also serve his meals and sleep in the same room as him. On one of these occasions, she again experienced herself as the separate witness of her body-mind. The following day she watched herself getting dressed, drinking tea, walking, talking and going about the daily business. She came to understand more deeply that she was not the 'I' she had grown up believing herself to be. She told her sister, 'The "I" could no longer get the upper hand of Laxmi. It was fun to see her so engrossed in actions.'

Osho had once talked about a nineteenth century sage called Swami Rama Tirtha who had always referred to himself in the third person singular. From this time, Laxmi started to refer to herself thus; a device she was to use as a reminder until the very end of her days.

Laxmi's joy was now so infectious that it touched most
of those who met her.

* * *

I visited Laxmi's family home when Osho gave discourses
there. That was before Osho moved to Bombay. When
we attended meditation camps, Laxmi was always seen
meditating. She was a devoted *sannyasin* who followed her
master's wishes without bringing her mind in between.

She was very friendly to me and always helped me in many
ways. In those days she used to call me often for meetings
and for Osho's discourses. She would lovingly tell me
to be on time for his talks. She used to be joyous seeing
people taking *sannyas*. Her sense of humour was great. For
example, she would say about the ever-increasing number of
people taking *sannyas* that day, as if reading from a cricket
scorecard, 'four wickets down today and one no-ball'.

[Ma Dharm Jyoti]

* * *

Osho had had an *o.b.e.* before his enlightenment. Meditating
in a tree, he suddenly saw his own body lying on the ground
below him. He was aware of a glittering silver cord joining
him to it. The event is described in *The Long, the Short and
the All*.

*That day for the first time, I saw my own body from the outside,
and since that day the mere physical existence of my body
finished forever. And from that day death also ceased to exist,
because that day I experienced that the body and spirit are two
different things; quite separate from each other.*

[Osho, *The Long, the Short and the All*, Ch. 5]

He continued that he had worried as to how he could return to his body. It happened that, towards dawn, two women carrying milk cans from a nearby village saw the body and went over to it. The disembodied Osho watched them from above. The moment the women's hands touched his forehead, he was back in his body.

Osho later pondered over this and came to understand that complementary charges of electricity from a woman to a man or a man to a woman can anchor the spirit to the body. From the age of twenty-one, his personal needs were seen to by women.

Enlightened beings are aware of the body and are yet
disconnected from it. They use and move their physical form and
yet they must maintain a delicate balance between being in it
and yet at the same time out of it. To an ordinary eye it appears
that the enlightened being lives in the visible physical body like
others. This is not the case.

[Osho, *The Long, the Short and the All*, Ch. 5]

This is an important point to understand. Enlightened beings are likely to have such a tenuous connection with their body that they must rely on others to care for them. In Osho's case, this phenomenon was pronounced and visible, manifesting as extreme sensitivity to air quality, smells and foods. Thus it was vital for his very survival that those who cared for him did so with both love and a paramount professional skill.

Laxmi understood this intuitively: for now she was to be one of his main carers.

* * *

The Neo-*Sannyas* movement had gathered sufficient momentum for Osho to stop public speaking. Now he gave discourses only for his disciples and devotees, usually about a hundred people filling the living room at Woodlands. Dynamic Meditation was held daily at a friend's house, or before dawn on Chowpatty Beach to the wonderment of passers-by.

Osho spoke more frequently in English. Sales of his Hindi language books soared. An English language bi-monthly magazine of his talks, edited and published by *sannyasins*, became immensely popular. Surprisingly Laxmi was always hard pressed for money, or what she later came to refer to as Vitamin M. However, she always made it plain that with trust and with the master's grace, the necessary work would happen and his vision would manifest.

* * *

The new commune will be on a big scale: ten thousand
sannyasins living together as one body, one being. Everybody
is going to live as comfortably, as richly, as we can manage.
But nobody will possess anything. Not only will things not be
possessed, but persons also will not be possessed. In the new
commune everybody will be tremendously interested in the
outside world, and in love with the inner search. The day you
have both together you have become the new man, and the new
man is going to be the saviour of humanity. If the new man is
not born, there is no hope for humanity.

[Osho, *The Golden Future*, Ch. 22, Q. 1]

* * *

A new commune? A new man? A new humanity? Laxmi is going to face ever-greater challenges and ever-greater demands on her devotion to Osho. By late 1973 the need for more space was increasingly clear. Osho told Laxmi that he wanted a place where *sannyasins* could meditate together, work productively together and live together. Laxmi was also aware that the increasingly polluted air of Bombay was having a pernicious effect on Osho's health; his asthma attacks were on the rise.

6. THE POONA ONE PHENOMENON:
CREATION

It is a rare event in history. A sage whose life embodies the eternal values comes to be a lode-star for whoever seeks a better world or deeper meaning to their life. Such people voyage from far and wide; their only link a thirst for the unknown. The Poona One phenomenon (that period of Osho's residency in Pune between 1974 and 1981) was not just a rare event. It was unique. It contained perhaps the largest multitude of seekers, as opposed to pilgrims, ever to assemble on the earth and it had the quality of meditation along with a thriving market place. The spiritual and the material, two sides of the same coin, were embedded as never before. From the very beginning Laxmi was the reeve who kept both sides in service; the coin in circulation.

The start of one of humanity's greatest experiments and a neoteric step of human evolution began with the fall of a ripened nut.

* * *

All day Laxmi had been searching fruitlessly for land and now she stood in the garden of a property that was not even for sale. She was tired and edgy and in need of a shower. The previous afternoon she had set out for the hills; not the

Himalayas this time, but the Western Ghats to the east of Bombay. She had stopped half way up at the old hill station of Lonavla that has magnificent views of forests and hills and the vast plain bordering the Arabian Sea. She had felt strangely quiet and confident as she sipped her *chai* and awaited a real-estate agent. Then a thought struck her. The average monsoon rainfall in Lonavla is one of the highest in India. Asthma and high humidity are not good companions. She apologised to the agent and drove on up to Poona, the former home of more than one enlightened being and an old summer station for the British Army. Poona is set some fifty kilometres back from the Ghats on the high Deccan Plain.

Laxmi found herself drawn to the exclusive suburb of Koregaon Park. She drove back and forth looking at the fine houses and summer palaces of the royals and the wealthy of India. She called a likely estate agent and arranged an appointment for the following morning, then booked herself into a modest hotel.

The month of February is a fine time to be in that beautiful part of India. The air is hot but not too hot, as it will be in June before the monsoon. Spring has painted blossoms on the avenues that frame the elegant streets of Koregaon Park. There are lines of brilliant scarlet Gulmohar trees and pale mauve Jacaranda trees. Hibiscuses are flowering everywhere and on the verges and waste ground there is a riot of pale pink Columbine creepers.

Next morning with the estate agent Laxmi visited a number of cramped and decaying properties. However something drew her to an empty building, named Himalaya that they had passed several times. It was not for sale. A solitary caretaker sat at its gate, eager to talk, happy to break his lonely year-long vigil. His employer was a Maharaja from a distant state whose only visit was for two weeks during the Poona horse-racing season. That would be in July with the coming of the rains and it was only February now. He stood beside the woman in orange, keeping his eyes to the ground. Behind him, the frustrated estate agent kicked his heels and shuffled his feet, wondering how to get his cut from this diversion.

Laxmi was staring up at a tree, a spreading, lustrous, temple of a tree. She was imbibing it, she was showering in its cool shade, she was treasuring its viridian sculptedness. Laxmi felt her body relax and her mind slow down. She was smiling. A cuckoo called its haunting invitation, a grace note rising from the murmuration of the distant traffic. Her smile grew wide. Then the nut dropped. She heard the sound of it brushing a leaf, clattering through a frond or two and landing on the bare earth with a hollow thunk. It rolled towards her and came to rest at her feet. For a while Laxmi stood staring at it. It was the size of an egg, plump and purple, but Laxmi was not seeing that. She was reading the message it bore.

* * *

She handed the nut to Osho in Bombay that evening. 'You always wanted to live in the Himalaya and an omen has told me you shall.' Osho laughed. It transpired that the mansion's owner was an admirer and had meditated in one of his Mount Abu camps. A transfer of ownership was comfortably arranged.

* * *

The move to Poona in 1974 was a festival, a gala, a celebration. It took place on the day of the Spring Equinox, the day that Osho had become enlightened twenty-two years before: the 21st of March.

All day in Bombay, hundreds of well-wishers came to take *prasad*, bring gifts, say goodbye. So that all might have *darshan* with Osho, a long line snaked out of the apartment, down the steps and onto the driveway. In the late afternoon a hundred friends piled onto the train or into a convoy of fifteen cars to make the three-hour journey up to Poona. Laxmi was proud to drive the car containing Osho, Vivek and another pure devotee, Greek Mukta, who had funded the building's purchase.

In the twilight, a small party of glowing orange planets surrounded the ethereal white-robed Osho as he walked around the new property. The house abounded with bedrooms and balconies, sitting rooms and ante-rooms. Behind the house was a line of rooms for servants. Osho chose as his bedroom a large room on the ground floor that happened to be almost opposite the tree of Laxmi's omen, thereafter called the Almond Tree, although its nuts were not almonds. He gave another *darshan* to the accompanying friends who continued to celebrate until midnight.

When the time came to retire, Laxmi took a shower before realising she had nowhere to sleep. From her bag, she pulled out a blanket and finding most rooms already occupied, spread it on the floor of an open balcony. She lay down exhausted yet with a deep feeling of fulfilment. She felt the beating of her heart, heard the muffled sounds of urban life around her, let her eyes trace the crowded constellations of the sky and the dark mystery of the garden.

Then she saw the Tree, black, imperturbable, generous. It called her. Laxmi arose and went to it. She found a hollow that cradled her back between two roots. She closed her eyes. She disappeared.

No body. No mind. No Laxmi. No tree. No time. Only a vast, living, pulsing silence. It may have been hours or seconds before she returned to herself. She felt effervescent, relaxed and refreshed as if she had slept twelve hours. When she walked back to her blanket, her feet barely touched the ground. She lay down and slept.

In the morning, the same silence prevailed as she went about her work. She felt filled more than ever with love, with trust and with gratitude.

Now she was living even closer to Osho; day in and day out in the same house. She had entered her forty-second year: a seven-year cycle was starting again.

* * *

Before long the mansion, now renamed Lao Tzu House, was showing signs of being too small. During the monsoon months, it was not possible for Osho's talks to be given on the lawn and the covered carport by the front door became overcrowded. Osho suggested to Laxmi that a large open-sided auditorium be added to the back of the house. 'The trees and the sky must be part of it.'

Laxmi leapt into the work of finding a designer and builder for what was to become the Chuang Tzu auditorium, later Osho's *Samadhi*. During its construction, a tragedy was narrowly averted and an important teaching was imparted.

One afternoon, when the project was perhaps two-thirds complete, the workers were shuttering and rendering cement, laying bricks and concrete blocks, while chains of women brought the concrete mix in *gomellas* on their heads. Small children played in the sand heaps and by the water butts. Suddenly a tearing, rumbling sound stopped everyone. Amidst the screams, a warning shout rang out. A section of the roof was about to collapse. A great frond of concrete hung suspended for the briefest moment, then steel bars twisted and snapped and the frond crashed to the floor in clouds of dust. There were fifty people on the site. No one was killed, no one was even hurt. The hall was completed on schedule within three months.

And the teaching? The more people go deep into meditation the more powerful their thoughts become. Negative thoughts have negative consequences. Osho was commenting at the time on the writings of the great mystic sage, Patanjali. Osho said that as many as twenty of his *sannyasins* were harbouring negative thoughts about the building, its structure, its cost, the implication of less intimate contact with himself—and those negative thoughts had translated into the disaster. For many Westerners this was foreign territory, for Laxmi it was self-evident. She had always known that thoughts are forceful things, they influence phenomena.

* * *

Some of the trustees of Osho's *Jivan Jagruti Kendra* Trust were business people who had contributed to his living expenses in Bombay. Now that he was living in Poona they felt distanced, even abandoned. They called Laxmi and told her that they were withdrawing their support. Laxmi consulted Osho. The Trust was closed down and a new body established called The Rajneesh Foundation with Laxmi as the managing trustee. All Osho's business was to now happen from Poona. The apartment in Woodlands was sold and the money was immediately used to purchase the next-door property to Lao Tzu House. It was renamed Krishna House.

***

'Money! We need money! We need a Juggernaut load of it!' Laxmi sat at her desk; not the big glass one with the high-back chair that thousands would later remember her by. No, this was a modest green steel desk with a tubular metal and raffia chair. She sat, one hand supporting her chin. 'Money is needed for so many things. For building and rebuilding, extending and refurbishing. We need new halls for the meditations. A proper office. A kitchen with a dining area. New showers and toilets. We need money for spreading the master's words. Ahh!'

Laxmi's train of thought paused. 'His work is his words, he has told me. So how does one scatter the seeds of his words?' She drew a deep breath. 'Books!' She drew another breath. 'More books and magazines and tape-recordings.'

She reached under the desk and pulled out a copy of *The Yellow Pages*.

'Mmmm. Quite a few printers here in Poona. Ahh, here's a likely firm—Sangham Press. We are a *sangham*, an assembly, a community of seekers after truth.' Laxmi reached for the telephone and thus embarked on another new undertaking—publishing.

Within two months, after a lot of bargaining and leaps of faith, the first volume was published. Osho's commentary on the *Vigyan Bhairav Tantra* was called *The Book of Secret*s. Within the next six weeks there were substantial sales both in India and abroad.

Laxmi later said that the publication and sale of Osho's words provided the seam of gold she had hoped for, even though Osho stipulated that his books be sold at the lowest possible prices.

* * *

As Osho's words began to spread around the world, more and more people arrived to see him, to hear him, to meet him in person. Many of them stayed. And many of them helped out with the gardening or the catering or construction work. The houses and the grounds of the Ashram became gradually more beautiful.

Osho now spoke alternate months in Hindi and in English. Laxmi was pleased to see that most of the Westerners sat in for the Hindi discourses whether they understood the language or not. 'They are learning,' she remarked, 'that it's the silent gaps between his words that hold the message.'

The new arrivals brought not only more hands and more money but also some of the skills and technology scarce at that time in India; for example, visual and sound recording equipment.

As time passed, Laxmi decided that the Ashram bedrooms had to be divided into two and then subdivided into four spaces to accommodate more residents. She understood that *sannyasins* wanted to live close to their *guru* and her light manner and loving smile made it easy for older residents to acquiesce to ever-smaller living spaces. 'Laxmi is amazed by so much harmony here,' she said, 'even though so many people do not share a common language.'

* * *

People have commentated on Laxmi's bird-like appetite and her given reason of being too busy and dedicated to the work of Osho to have time for either food or relationship. Perhaps the picture is more subtle than that. For food she seems to have subsisted on a breakfast of hot milk and a banana, then, throughout the day only a few cups of tea and biscuits and a plate of rice and *da*l. In relationships too she seems to have subsisted on nothing but the emptiness of the master. She had clearly understood from her very first meetings with Osho that enforced celibacy is not celibacy—it is perversion. In deep meditation Laxmi examined her primal drives. The low sexual drive that she had could easily be transformed to higher levels of love, clarity and meditation. What for Laxmi had started as both a natural inclination and a Jain-Gandhian abstention from sex and food, gradually became a selfless and flowing energy of devotion towards the master. His work was her work.

* * *

And work she did. In the early era of Poona One, Laxmi was not only president of the Rajneesh Foundation but also responsible for the day-to-day running of the Ashram and its intricate linkages. She was the chief fund-raiser and negotiator with banks and politicians, she was in overall charge of the publication and dissemination of Osho's words, she oversaw the network of Osho centres throughout India as well as worldwide; she drove Osho daily to the

Buddha Hall for the morning discourse; she sat beside him in *darshan* every night, consult him afterwards for major decisions; and she welcomed every new arrival to the commune. A master attracts all manner of people, not just seekers after truth. And Laxmi had to meet them, engage with them and screen them.

Her devotion and her genetic endowment enabled her to lovingly address misfits, nomads, the naturally rebellious, the round pegs in square holes, the lost souls, aspiring saints, the ones who question rules, the martyrs, the religious maniacs, the lunatic fringe and those who wear a different kind of spectacles. Laxmi had to fit them in or screen them out, encourage or discourage them. This she did with visible skill, acuity and compassion.

* * *

Osho lived spontaneously, an already dangerous behaviour in the calculating world we live in. He spoke daily from eternity on the sacred texts of the past. He spoke from the heart of here and now with humour and compassion. The global community of seekers gathered and began their transformation into a commune. Osho spoke of the end of social hierarchy.

Remember here in the commune there is no leader and no led,
no ruler and no ruled. Even the people who are Presidents of the
Foundation or the Commune or the Investment Corporation are
not different from you. They are not rulers; they are servants of
the commune.

[Osho, *From Bondage to Freedom*, Ch. 5, Q. 10]

Laxmi took these words to her heart. She was there to serve her master and there to serve the spiritual intentions of the people that surrounded him; the burgeoning commune. There were old and young here now and Laxmi had to see that they were taken care of. She told a couple who had just arrived with their two children, 'Each child in this commune has a mother and a father and scores of aunts and uncles. The word "family" is included in the larger word, "commune". If that suits you—good. If not, that is also good.'

* * *

Osho would always outgrow his space. There was always a need to expand, always the need for Vitamin M. Laxmi managed to raise the money to buy two more adjacent buildings. They were named after the mystics Jesus and Meister Eckhart. Ashram workers rapidly refitted them to keep up with the commune's mushrooming requirements.

Now Laxmi no longer needed to employ Indian staff but her own work-load was always increasing: more buildings needed to be built, more accommodation rented in the area, more people to see, more concerns to consider. With so many people living at close quarters, health and hygiene become an issue and Laxmi had to enlist some of the qualified medical practitioners to set up a medical centre. So too was nutrition an important consideration. The makeshift cafeteria called Vrindavan was expanded until it comfortably fed 500 people.

* * *

The front gate of the Ashram, known as the Gateless Gate, was majestic. Some years after Osho's death it was torn down and replaced by a functional airport-style gate. Laxmi once told the story of its origins to a group of friends gathered in her office one evening.

'We started work on the Gateless Gate before the plans were ready and before there was money to pay for it. Osho gave the guidelines to an Indian architect who loved him. The architect told Laxmi, "It is Osho's work. We will put our total energy into it and it will surely happen." We trusted.

'Within just two months the Gateless Gate was finished. You, friends, see it every day. Marble and granite, the best Burma teak wood, bronze and brass and glass. Osho himself designed the emblem set in the arch above. You know what that emblem symbolises?'

There were blank faces all around.

'The dot in the middle of the triangle is oneness within the all. The triangle stands for the trinity of the Creator, the Preserver and the Destroyer. They are set within a nine-sided figure which symbolises the planets and our solar system. All is held together by the outer circle. This emblem describes our inner process towards universality. Everything about us is to enhance our inner journey. That's what Laxmi has found.'

All the time new problems demanded new, innovative solutions. Laxmi had to think quickly on her feet.

'We need a proper place for a workshop,' said Asheesh, the engineer in charge of carpentry, once. 'If you want us to make new *malas,* that is.'

Laxmi put her fingers together a moment and closed her eyes. 'Laxmi will move Osho's car from his garage and keep it now in the old car port. Then you have that space. And while you're about it, he needs a new set of glass fronted shelves. And please bring Laxmi a set of designs for the *mala* tomorrow.'

A few minutes later Ma Niranjana, a tall, broad-shouldered Ashram resident from Germany, presented herself. She worked in the gardens. She was angry and upset. She would speak to Laxmi only, not to either Arup or Sheela, satellites seated either side of her.

'How can Laxmi be of help?'

'I'm sharing with Ma Khoji. I can't live with her. *Sheisse*! She is noisy and untidy, she's a smoker and she smells, she wakes me up in the night to tell me I'm snoring, she always...' One of Laxmi's eyebrows arched in a particular way, like a tilde or an S laid on its side. Her small raised hand arrested the flow of words. When silence was established, a smile broke right across her face. 'Laxmi remembers you are a gardener. Right? When you plant a garden, are all the flowers one colour, all the shrubs the same?'

'No. Variety makes everything more...'

'Just so! In HIS garden there are many flowers: brightly coloured ones, pungent smelling ones, small pale ones underfoot, roses with sharp thorns. Gardening is a beautiful work. Laxmi feels you try tending this flower in your room, give it what it needs and watch it grow. Okay? And you come back and see Laxmi in two weeks.'

For a long time after, there was silence. Niranjana stood to leave. Now she was smiling as she bowed her head to Laxmi; an apology of sorts. 'Thank you, Laxmi.' There were tears in her voice.

* * *

Now a word about the word 'surrender', a word r
on the path of self-enquiry. In the East it has ;
meaning to what is understood in the West. Surrender, as
used by a master, signifies yielding as the bamboo and the
willow tree yield to the wind, a graceful acceptance of what
is. 'Surrender' on the way to transformation is never a giving
up, never the abject capitulation that Westerners construe
of it. Here is how Osho used this word:

> *The master is awakened and he sees you are asleep. He says, 'I*
> *am not here to erase your individuality, I am here to erase your*
> *ego, the unreal you, the false you.' He does not teach and yet you*
> *learn from him. You surrender to him yet you stay completely*
> *independent. The surrender must be total; no ifs and buts. It*
> *cannot be conditional. When you surrender to the master you do*
> *not surrender to the master. The master is the catalytic agent. It*
> *is your surrender that transforms you. He does nothing yet you*
> *are transformed.*

[Osho, *The Invitation*, Ch. 19, Q. 1]

Ma Mukti, who worked with her sister Ma Divya in Osho's
kitchen, had mixed feelings towards Laxmi. She said, 'I
admired her devotion. Her path was the Path of Surrender.
In Poona One there were no rules but there was a lot of
harmony. We learned from her to immerse ourselves in the
work, whatever it was.

'Divya, Pragya and I were in the kitchen and also a bit in
the office. Laxmi for some reason wanted someone else to
do the cooking. She piled us up with more and more work
in the office. We accepted it in the spirit of surrender. Until
it got too much. Then I spoke to Laxmi about it. She said,
"Very good. You go do *Kirtan Mandali*, touring Maharashtra
with a group of singers."

"But Laxmi, all that singing and chanting stuff is not my thing. I don't do *kirtan*."

"Then Laxmi suggests you go back to your home."

'I was stunned. After some thought I said, "We will go back to our home. Before we go we would like to take leaving-*darshan* with Osho."

'At *darshan* the next night, I told Osho I was having problems with Laxmi and that I would be going home. He just said okay. So we left Poona to stay a few days with Narendra in Mumbai before the long journey home. While we were there, we got a call from Laxmi. "He does not like the food of the new cook. You come back immediately."

'We came that evening. A few days later Vivek said, "Don't be worried about Laxmi. Osho likes the food cooked by you, so you stay."'

* * *

Osho himself declared to one *sannyasin* that it was very easy to love him and it was difficult to love Laxmi.

Yet unless you love Laxmi nothing is going to happen.
Whatsoever work is given to you, do it as lovingly as possible.
The point is not whether the work is very important or not. If
you do it lovingly, it becomes important, whatsoever it is even if it
is cleaning. The question is not what work—the question is that
you surrender to the Ashram all your energies; and whatsoever
is available, or whatsoever Laxmi thinks is right, you do. Simply
surrender to Laxmi. That is going to help very much. Just listen
to her, and whatsoever she says, do. This is a meditation for
you—surrendering to Laxmi.

[Osho, *The Passion for the Impossible*, Ch. 5]

* * *

Laxmi was attacked on a night in September 1975. The city power grid had gone down at eleven o'clock. Tired and dirty, Poona lay slumped in darkness. Laxmi, as she walked from her office to her bedroom in Lao Tzu House, heard the night sounds of the crickets and the far-off shunting trains, the mosquitoes and the night guards banging on the ground their bamboo canes. She did not hear the stealthy breathing of a man concealed behind Hibiscus bushes on her path. Laxmi had no cause to walk with circumspection; she was in the confines of the Ashram, guarded day and night by volunteer *sannyasins* at each gate, back and front. She was making the journey she made every night after *darshan*, after consulting with Osho and after finishing off her office work. She was enjoying the air's coolness following the sweltering heat of the day. In one hand she held a folder of papers, in the other a beaker of hot water. She was relaxed. Yet something niggled in a back part of her mind. She told herself to trust that Osho, in the morning, would illuminate her.

She brushed against some foliage that leaned across her path. Suddenly a hand gripped tightly round her throat and another grasped her neck. A puff of fear escaped from her. She threw the beaker over her shoulder and the folder slipped from her arm. Now anger surged in her as she felt the pain and saw the papers scatter dimly in the darkness. She kicked and struggled. She felt herself being choked, a weight bearing down upon her, bearing down and down and down. There was no way to scream; she could not even draw in breath to fill her lungs. She felt herself falling into a tangle of branches and Canna lilies, disappearing, dying under a wall of despair and bewilderment.

Laxmi's body and mind were struggling but struggling fruitlessly. Her assailant was strong and grim. Occasional grunts told her of a violent will. He was standing over her, one leg by her ear, the other in her groin. His hands were a steel collar locked round her neck. She felt the flailing of her hands grow weak, the silhouette of Krishna House against the sky grow dim. She saw that niggle of misgiving should have been attended to. Now the end was imminent. She could resist or relax. A soundless cry arose through the pervading panic. '*Bhagwan! Bhagwan!*'

Useless!

She reviewed her options. Basically there were none. Life was all but drained from her. But stop! Who is this who can see it all so clearly? Awareness has arisen. Of course, this body is not me. The remembrance of Nargol occurred.

Now, suddenly, an extraordinary joy rose up in her, an intense and over-arching joy that took in her whole life span. It contained, in an endless, timeless moment, both love and gratitude to her family and the people of her childhood, the women she had worked with and the hundreds who had come to her as spokesperson for Osho, for all who had helped her live this bright and brilliant life. Rising above these feelings was an ecstasy, orgasmic in intensity, that her life had been blessed with Osho.

Even as the joy flooded through her, a hand was shifted from her throat. Her lungs gulped in the air and a great yell arose from her to pierce the humming silence of that atrocious night. '*BHAGWAN!*' The hand was instantly clamped across her mouth and the hot foul breath of the man was on her face. She felt his teeth clamp onto her nose. She felt them puncture the flesh and blood spurt from the wound. She felt no pain. She felt no fear; only a deep and willing surrender to death. 'I am free. Freedom is already here!'

As the body-mind that was Laxmi faded from life there was heard the sound of running feet, there was seen the flash of a torch. Male voices filled the air and Laxmi was aware of being lifted up by tender hands.

'Don't hurt the man,' she heard her own voice say. 'Don't hurt him.'

Laxmi was carried to a quiet room. Then a doctor was tending to her nose, cleaning, disinfecting, inserting a small stitch where loose flesh was hung. Then large pads of dressing were applied.

'Don't hurt the man!'

'We have detained him. Someone has called the police.'

'No police! Don't hurt him.'

'But Laxmi...'

'Laxmi has been gifted. The man has given Laxmi an experience of bliss. Laxmi's body is injured, Laxmi is unhurt. Laxmi is free.'

The door opened and closed. A new voice joined the conversation. 'The man has just told us his target was Osho. It's Osho he wanted to kill, but he wasn't accessible. You kept refusing him access so he decided to kill you, Laxmi. He wanted to strangle you. Then he thought you would become a martyr. So he decided to disfigure you instead. To bite your nose off.'

The doctor's voice intervened. 'You will have scars for a month or two but you will not be disfigured.'

'He said he's angry because his wife has become a *sannyasin*. He is frightened she will leave him. Quite frankly, who would blame her?'

'Osho's grace is matchless. Laxmi is unharmed. The man is known to Laxmi now. Laxmi feels the man is just unconscious. He is behaving out of thousands of years of male supremacy. And when he feels that male power is slipping away, violence happens. See? He wanted to disfigure Laxmi. To leave his mark on her...so primitive. Perhaps he will learn something from this. Please release him before the police arrive.'

The door opened again and Vivek said, 'Osho has heard. He would like to see you.'

'Thank you. Laxmi is fine. She is sorry that his sleep has been disturbed. Please convey to him that she will see him in the morning.'

Osho commented on this incident a few days later in his discourse. He took the opportunity to explain to his people in the commune that there is an individual responsibility and a collective responsibility for the thoughts we entertain. This lesson was to be repeated for *sannyasins* a few years later by events in Rajneeshpuram, the commune ranch in Oregon.

Just two, three days ago it happened that a sannyasin attacked Laxmi. You may not be aware that you all are responsible for it, because many of you have been feeling antagonism towards Laxmi. That sannyasin is just a victim, just the weakest link among you. He has expressed your antagonism, that's all, and he was the weakest; he became the victim, and now you will feel that he is responsible. That's not true. You all participated. Subtle is the law!

How did you participate? Deep down, whenever somebody is managing—and Laxmi is managing things around here—there are many situations in which you will feel antagonistic, in which

she will have to say no to you, in which you will feel
cannot be avoided—in which you feel that enough
is not being paid to you, in which you feel that you ar
treated as if you are nobody. Your ego feels hurt and
you feel antagonism.

If many people feel antagonism towards a person, then the
weakest amongst them will become the victim; he will do
something. He was the craziest amongst you, that's right. But he
alone is not responsible. If you have ever felt antagonism towards
Laxmi, that is part (and you have earned a karma, and, unless
you become so subtly aware, you cannot become enlightened.
Things are very complicated.)

[Osho, *The Alpha and the Omega*, Vol. 2, Ch. 9,
9 January 1975]

* * *

In those days the Ashram lived financially on the edge.
Osho was so controversial that the traditional benefactors
would not come anywhere near him. So I know that Laxmi
struggled all the time. Osho never made it easy for her. If a
penniless person showed up, whether Indian or Westerner,
and he wanted that person to stay, he would tell Laxmi to
look after him or her. I often wondered what went through
her mind at hearing those commands. In Poona One I was
awed by how she faced all these new challenges head on,
simply waving her little hand and saying, 'It is HIS work!'

She came from a fairly wealthy family but nothing could
have prepared her for the deluge of Western people—and
all the challenges they and their egos brought with them...
Sitting in her office in Krishna House she greeted all these
people with love and openness and I don't think I ever saw

her fazed by this bizarre new world appearing in front of her with such speed and such force.

[Ma Prem Veena]

* * *

The extraordinary magnetic attraction that Osho was exerting across the affluent world began to force big changes in Laxmi's connections to her master that would provide her with more opportunities for her growth. Now, so busy was her schedule in the new, elegant front office built onto Krishna House, she would see Osho privately only for an hour in the morning and an hour late in the evening after *darshan*. 'I learnt so much from her. I learnt dedication to the master. Nothing else mattered to Laxmi but work for Osho. I learnt surrender from her,' said Ma Pragya.

* * *

The demands of her job gradually impelled Laxmi to find assistants for her work, some to travel with her, some to stay behind and administer the realm. Ma Anand Sheela from Baroda became her Indian affairs secretary and Ma Prem Arup from Holland became her Western affairs secretary, Swami Krishna Prem her press advisor, Swami Veetmoha her driver, Ma Prashna made robes for her, Ma Anasha kept them ready for use. Somebody, nameless but nimble, kept her topped up with her special brew of *chai*.

* * *

Swami Om Prakash Saraswati had first met Laxmi at one of Osho's meditation camps on Mount Abu. Devotion to Osho came as naturally and as compellingly to him as it did to her. He became a resident in the commune and worked half time in the accounts department. On one occasion, Laxmi, as usual short of Vitamin M, asked him to pay some bills with post-dated cheques. He refused.

'What? Laxmi is asking you to write cheques and you refuse? Swami, this is Ashram business and it needs to happen. Please do it.'

'Laxmi ma, with respect, I cannot do it.'

'This is not the way of surrender, Swami.'

'With respect, it is the way of my surrender. I can only do what feels right to me.'

Next morning Laxmi came to Prakash's desk. She said, 'Laxmi has consulted Osho. He said "Don't force him." So Laxmi is happy you stood your ground.'

* * *

The designer Veena worked in the publication department with Swami Yatri, at the time a well-known British artist and designer. 'It was a massively demanding project. We had our Western ideas and Laxmi her Indian ideas. There were some major clashes of opinion. But we always worked things out in the end...she was always so sweet and encouraging, we had to do our best.'

* * *

Swami Yatri wrote the following account of his relationship with Laxmi: 'Whatever can be said of this beautiful, infuriating, warm, loyal and totally dedicated being will always fall short of the truth. It will sound like some nostalgic, overcooked eulogy.

'For one trying to recapture what she was really like—the

stories coil back around the teller. She was in every facet of our lives from Bombay through to the end of Poona One. Many remember this as, on the one hand a golden age of pushing at inner boundaries, and on the other hand a cash-strapped commune trusting that Existence would somehow provide. The motivator of action was Laxmi.

'Anything that I can say of her is seen from a very small and outwardly inconsequential window and in most ways is set facing a distorting mirror. There is no way you could be objective about this woman. What is most remembered was that she was my friend—and a lot of fun too.

'In the first meeting with Laxmi, this diminutive Gujarati woman called me *child*. She was four years older than me and I am a big man. That odd kinship somehow took root. I worked directly with her creating and publishing books on a 24/7 shift. It took quite a while before we stopped fighting. This was partly because Osho would tell me to do one thing in the morning via his caretaker Vivek; Laxmi would counter it completely by the afternoon and while meeting him in the evening he would directly give me a third, entirely different direction.

'On asking Osho what to do in such a case he smiled: "Always follow Laxmi." And after I had insisted it was not easy to be caught between the two of them he added, "Remember, people think of me as the good guy who says yes, while Laxmi is the bad guy who always says no. But really it's not true at all, so follow her."

'On hearing this I went to Laxmi and kneeling before her in mock surrender asked her how *she* managed Osho's constantly changing landscapes—let alone his even more downright and impossible assignments.'

'"Oh, I just always say *Haan Ji*...yes Lord. He knows I don't fully mean it but never says so, and then I do what I think is the needful. And he knows that too."

'Laxmi insisted that Osho was the mastermind behind her actions. But in order to "do the needful", carrying out his vision in a practical way for the everyday world, some very deft footwork was required. You couldn't pay too much attention to the original script. That was her first valuable lesson to me.

'Looking back however, it is unfortunate for all of us that Sheela, her successor, also learnt a few such strategies at Laxmi's knee; but while, as far as I know, Laxmi never used them for her own personal advantage, her protégé proved over the next five years to be not quite so selfless and a lot more dangerous.

'On one occasion, I had the idiocy to hint to Vivek, Osho's great gossip gatherer, that the "Gateless Gate," though made of the best marble and Burmese teak wood, was a tasteless piece of Indian wedding cake. Later it transpired that while Osho had had a hand in its design, it was Laxmi who had actually outlined the whole vision of it to the architect.

'Osho called me in later and said that he had just heard that I didn't think much of the gate. He pointed out that before building it Laxmi had been trying to get a bank loan. No bank would lend to her. However, she managed to build the gate simply on trust and with no money advanced. They then sat back and waited. The original bankers, who had denied any chance of loans, saw the building work completed; saw a famous architect's name, the expensive marble and the superbly crafted details so they assumed the Ashram must be absurdly rich to be able to afford such luxuries. As rupees tend to attract *crores* of rupees, the bankers queued up outside Laxmi's door offering substantial loan deals. She promptly tripled the sums which they accepted without a murmur. "That is your wedding cake, Yatri!" concluded Osho.

'Yes, Laxmi had overseen its creation. This demolished my preconceptions that a mystic would be a holy innocent of the ways of Mammon. It also gave me a rare insight into just how smart Laxmi had to be in order to maintain the commune and gamble with virtually nothing in the piggy bank.

'Often I would visit a printer to ensure they were doing a good job, yet spend most of the time hearing their complaints about the massive debts the Ashram had built up. In my pocket might be a sweetener cheque of doubtful durability for a tiny fraction of what the printer required. But any mention that Laxmi would deal with it all when next she visited set the machines rolling again.

'Laxmi quickly gained a reputation in Bombay as a successful big-time entrepreneur while in truth it was just a gamble with an outward air of being in command. She often sent us with nothing in hand to furious creditors just to see what would happen. We seldom managed to get them to work to schedule but if she went, it was an entirely different story, with special teas and candies, even though she often didn't pay them either.

'Early in 1975 she visited the general ward of the local Poona hospital where I was undergoing what ended up as an emergency operation for a classic meditator's ailment acquired by sitting on cold floors—a fissure and haemorrhoids. The man in the next bed—unbeknown to his relatives camping around both our beds, cooking *chapatis* and *dal* on a stove—had quietly died. Laxmi appeared to gain six feet in all directions when confronting the dominatrix matron over the wondrously unhygienic state of the ward. I was promptly moved into a private room (on tick) with bowing apologies from anyone who met the fire in her eyes.

'What is not known, except to very few, is that Laxmi also suffered dreadfully from the self-same complaint but, point-blank, refused an operation. Osho once confided to me that he felt that her famed fasts were simply to avoid the after-effects of food passing through her. I was shocked at this revelation but, if anything, it bonded us together as fellow sufferers. It explained the care she took over my recovery. She even had a rubber lifebuoy seat resembling a duck that she lent me for the lectures. It also revealed that there were probably a few other illnesses she had that were unknown to most of us.

'Knowing of these ailments, what always amazed me was the sheer energy and power of Laxmi, completely in inverse proportion to her actual size. She seemed to project the *Kshatriya* effect, a force of some huge warrior of the Hindu caste. On one occasion, a Western *sannyasin* woman was attacked by an unknown Indian who attempted to rape her. Laxmi commandeered a camper-van full of our security guards, jumped onto the vehicle and hung out of the open side doors, brandishing a stick and screaming vengeance, directing these hulking martial arts guards like some Mogul warrior on a war elephant all along the roads around the Ashram, hunting down the would-be rapist. Lucky for him he was not immediately caught but the local paper published an article on it at the time that seemed to have a cautionary effect on any other would-be assailant.

'Laxmi was loyal to those she trusted. This could sometimes be seen as naïve or ill-judged. Early on in 1974 and 1975, she hired a group of cooks connected to her family in Bombay to feed those *sannyasins* working in the Ashram. The cooks pocketed about 75 per cent of the budget and fed us on thinned *dal, chapatis* and *jaggery* (solid cane sugar). Other than being very hungry, many of us came out in boils from the diet of flour and sugar. At first Laxmi would not hear a word against the cooks, partly perhaps because she was so disinterested in food and partly because somewhere she thought *sannyasins* should not indulge in such luxury. It is to her credit that she began questioning her own Indian-Jain-monk fasting programme when big, blond Haridas, whom she loved, sat in the office exclaiming with a small boy's voice, "Laxmi, I'm hungry! There's no food and I'm hungry!" She began to realise big Westerners who were three times the size of many Indian sadhus needed more calories and protein. She then went to check. She discovered the cooks' shortfall and fired the lot but took no further action against them. This ushered in the beginning of *sannyasin* catering.

'The interesting revelation was that she had conflicting loyalties to resolve and this often recurred throughout her reign as secretary. If you passed the test at some time, she stuck by you through thick and thin. You just knew she would try all she could to resolve difficult and contradictory situations—the cooks on the one hand and the *sannyasins* on the other.

'Now I come to a very personal and almost certainly contentious observation about the three women who dominated the Poona commune in the seven years before the exodus to the USA. It is not a cosmetically and politically correct view but it was the reality to this eyewitness. It also highlights the unique differences in the character of each woman.

'There was Laxmi—the first disciple and carer of Osho. There was Vivek—his new and intimate companion and carer of a few years. And there was Sheela—the secretary in waiting. This was a clash of giants and often quite uncomfortable to be around.

'In the case of Vivek and Laxmi there was a real mutual respect even though I witnessed some fiery clashes between them. In the years between 1973 and 1976 they shared a certain—almost virginal—nun-like appearance, both in the choice of clothes they wore and in their outward air of chaste calmness. In 1976, Vivek entered the first of her relationships with men and the difference between them started to become more and more apparent. Gradually, Vivek became the women's role model while Laxmi remained aloof as the virgin queen. The original orange colour chosen by Osho changed as Vivek—also with Osho's blessings—experimented with alternative tones and shades of sunrise colours. These were both created and imitated by her little coterie of tailors and seamstresses in Lao Tzu House. Soon her shades and fashions spread throughout the Ashram, eclipsing the original Laxmi colour.

'Laxmi's work increasingly took her away from Osho. He had warned us during earlier *darshans* that he would not be able to devote as much time to each individual as he had done so far, because thousands would be coming. This change was especially true for Laxmi. The one time and place she could really relax was sitting by his side at *darshan* each night. There she could just enjoy his presence.

'But how did she feel, one wonders, when on one occasion she was locked out of the passage which led to Osho's room. She managed to persuade Prasad, Vivek's lover at the time, to unlock the passage door and let her knock on Osho's door. The ensuing fallout was radioactive. I was an uncomfortable and quickly escaping observer to Vivek's merciless mauling of Prasad for allowing Laxmi in. Vivek was the only woman in the commune I had really feared to antagonise. In that moment I discovered that my intuition was well-grounded.

'Laxmi and Vivek remained opposed in many superficial situations but there was a deep harmony in their overall strategy of caring for their master and for the vision that he was manifesting.'

* * *

Thus finishes Yatri's first contribution. We will read more of his memories shortly.

* * *

It is surprising to consider that the people who invented Tantra and who built the erotically abundant temples of Khajuraho were later to create one of the most sexually repressed cultures of all time. This repression evolved, of course, with the help of both their Mogul occupiers and their British colonisers. However, whilst the Western world was opening up its sexual floodgates in the twentieth century, India was making ever-harsher judgements; 'body bad, spirit good'.

Both Laxmi and Osho were products of that society and responded in their own distinctive ways. Osho became the herald of a new man and a new humanity that honoured both meditation and human love; the inner world of spirit and the outer physical world that included and celebrated sex. Laxmi, who did not meet Osho until she was in her mid-thirties, was reared in a culture where sex was rarely referred to and never described. Growing up she was influenced by her Jain-Gandhian background that demanded sexual energy be sublimated into religious and socially responsible pursuits. She never explored her own sexuality.

* * *

Around the time of the events that Yatri recounts Laxmi had another kind of near-death experience. The story has been told in many, often contradictory, versions. This is Laxmi's account in her own words.

In 1976 Laxmi was driving back alone from Bombay to Poona in the Ashram Mercedes. She had driven alone many times on this road, and would always listen to a tape of Osho's discourses while on the road. When Laxmi was only half an hour away from Poona the car suddenly skidded. There was a loud tearing noise, and the vehicle behind sped away ahead. Laxmi glimpsed at its occupants laughing like maniacs. Next moment her car was rolling down a steep hill. This happened so fast that there was no time to think. Laxmi cradled her head in her arms on the steering wheel and shut her eyes. Her body was relaxed and calm.

When the car stopped, all was still and silent except for soft ticking noises from the engine. Laxmi opened her eyes to see that the car was a wreck except for her seat and the door on her side. The windshield on her side was the only glass still intact. Lifting her head, Laxmi took out a tin of biscuits and opened the door. Sitting on a nearby rock she thanked the sturdy body of the Mercedes that had saved her. While rolling down Laxmi had trusted the master would take care of her.

Suitcase in hand, Laxmi climbed back uphill and looked down at the wrecked car. A vision rose before her. Instead of the wreckage, there were elephants, horses, chariots and soldiers in ancient battle costumes. A king with a crown watched the battling soldiers. Arrows and spears were strewn around. Shields and swords clattered. Krishna, the blue Hindu god, Arjuna and the Pandava family who fought their cousins for the kingdom, all appeared on the scene. This was the Mahabharata, the great Indian epic war. Laxmi was not there; she was witnessing it all.

Then a car passed by, stopped and reversed. Someone came out and asked, 'Ma Laxmi, what are you doing here?' With this sound Laxmi returned to the scene of the accident. Pointing to the wrecked car she asked the friend if he saw anything. But the vision was gone. Seeing the wreckage, the friend asked Laxmi if she was all right and offered to drive her to the nearest police station to report the incident. He took her bag and led her to his car. They drove to the police station where she lodged a report of deliberate hit-and-run. At the Ashram later, she narrated the details of the accident and the vision of the Mahabharata to Osho. He said that if the head is hit in a certain way, people can see glimpses of their previous lives, and she may have travelled into her past. He added, 'Life is a mystery,' as if telling Laxmi not to dwell on the experience.

* * *

Osho was able to use Laxmi's love of cars as a device for raising both awareness and funds.

In August 1978, Osho said:

Indians have become very materialistic: that is true, but with so many buddhas the release of their energy still pulsates in spite of the Indian materialism. Indians have become really materialistic, far more materialistic than any country in the world. And great hypocrisy exists, because they go on claiming to be religious, and they are no more. My own observation is that now the Indian mind is more and more materialistic, more gross than any other mind. Their whole interest is in money, in power-politics, in material things.

Just a few days ago I told Laxmi to purchase the most costly car possible in the country. One thing good about Laxmi: she never asks why. She purchased it. It worked—it was a device. Laxmi was knocking on the doors of the banks to get money for the new commune. We need much money; near-about five crore rupees will be needed. Who is going to lend that much money to me? The day she purchased the car, seeing that we have the money, banks started coming to her office, offering—'Take as much money as you want.' Now she is puzzled from whom to take? Everybody wants to give on better terms, and they are after her.

I have been working in India for twenty years continuously. Thousands of people have been transformed, millions have listened to me and many more have been reading what I am saying, but the Times of India, the most conventional newspaper of India, still the most British, has not published a single article about me or my work. But the day Laxmi purchased the car there was a big article—on the car, not on me!

Now they are all interested. Many people come to the office not to see me or to see you my people. They inquire, 'Can we see the car?' Laxmi says to them, 'You can come to the early morning

*discourse, and you can see the car too.' And poor fellows—they
have to come and listen to me for ninety minutes just to see the
car. What a torture! And these are rich people, educated people.
Can you think of a more materialistic country?*

*Now Laxmi knows that the car has helped her tremendously.
Once its work is finished it can be gone. Never take anything
on its face value here, things have hidden meanings; they are
devices.*

[Osho, *Yoga: The Alpha and the Omega*, Vol. 2, Ch. 9 and
The Secret of Secrets, Vol. 2, Ch. 4, Q. 3]

* * *

Here is another story of Laxmi and cars, this one told by
Swami Veetmoha:

'Osho loved cars and driving. Laxmi loved cars. I loved
driving. So I could drive Laxmi. It was a match made in
heaven. But I didn't yet know that at 3:30 on the afternoon
of December 11th 1975. I was approaching the huge teak
gates of the Shree Rajneesh Ashram in Poona, at the wheel
of an expedition-outfitted Land Rover.

'Ten days earlier, at Bhandar-i-Shapur, an unlikely Gulf
port in Iran with huge parking lots of military hardware
scattered through the surrounding desert, I had reset the
Land Rover's odometer to zero. Now I had just driven from
Kuwait to Poona in ten frantic days of sea and sand and
snowstorms, potholes and border crossings, 3135.9 miles—
which is 5055.5 kilometres—my idea of heaven.

'Once I arrived in Poona I had no trouble finding the
Ashram at 17 Koregaon Park. The closer I got the more
orange robes I saw, and the more fair-haired people were
walking the streets. I just kept driving in the same direction.

Now at the front gate there's a crowd, bustling in and out. The huge gates are open, but a large, burly Sikh in an orange robe is standing, arms folded, between the gateposts eyeing people as they enter. He looks even more effective than the gate. I am about to switch off the engine and get out when he sees me. Instantly he is a flurry of waving orange arms; clearing the entrance, shouting at the crowd to stand aside and let me through, beckoning me forward. He turns and shouts something in Hindi towards the main house, repeatedly.

'It looks as if they are expecting me.

'I drive slowly through the gate and under a huge tent-like structure that I assume has been erected for Osho's birthday celebrations. It covers the whole area in front of the main house. The low winter sun is shining through a purple bougainvillea beside the drive. I note the light and colours of the orange-robed people crowded around and the sudden excitement and activity that greets my arrival. It is overwhelming. I am surprised to feel tears burning my eyes.

'I slow the Land Rover until I'm barely moving. Hurrying towards me is a small group of people. At their front is Laxmi, seeming so tiny from my high seat and surrounded by taller men and women, but moving as fast as her long tight *lungi* will allow her. She is busy tying her headscarf as she approaches, and urges a man jogging along beside her with a trail of yellow flowers in his arms to hurry ahead. Someone else suddenly appears from nowhere with a basket of white petals and, even before I have come to a stop in the middle of the driveway, flowers are showering onto the front of the Land Rover, and smiling faces are appearing at the windows. "Welcome, Swamiji. How was your trip?"

'Now the man with the yellow flowers is climbing onto the hood, trailing the garland around the roof rack and down the sides around the windshield.

'Laxmi appears at my window. "So you are here! How are you, Swamiji?" Her voice sings. It seems both totally personal and for the crowd too, somehow—a public utterance, clearly articulated, rolling her r's, enjoying the scene and the sound of her words.

'"Absolutely fine, thanks."

'"Can you get down?"

'"Yes, sure."

'"We wondered when you would be here. Osho asked me just this morning: 'Where is the Land Rover?'

'"Really?" I am so happy to have brought this gift of a well-wisher and to have made it in time for the celebration. I open the door and slide out of my seat onto the solid concrete of the Shree Rajneesh Ashram. The seat sighs. I'm looking down into two sparkling black eyes. "It's wonderful to be here."

'"Good timing, Swamiji! You are just in time for ice cream."

'Ah, Laxmi, able to both beautifully command the administration of the whole and yet still have space for the sweet small essentials of life!

'Now behind her I see Anuradha approaching. It is her Land Rover that I have been privileged to deliver to the Ashram from Kuwait. She is wearing the modest smile that I remember from our first meeting in London. She is not the kind to squeal with joy and rush up to the front to greet me. It's been more than a year since I saw her.

'Laxmi sees her coming. "Your parcel has arrived, Ma,"

she says. "And here is the postman." She nods her head at me. Anuradha keeps coming, and gives me a big hug.

"'How has it been for you?" she asks.

"'Wonderful." I pat the hood of the Land Rover. "And she's been very well-behaved." I almost said wonderful again but too many wonderfuls would make everybody laugh. They are laughing anyway.

"'If she is well-behaved, then Laxmi is going to drive," says Laxmi, who then puts her tiny slippered foot on the fold-down step, takes hold of the steering wheel and climbs in. The crowd comes forward laughing and cheering. I hear, "Go for it Laxmi," and "It's too big for you, Laxmi," and "Ma, you need longer legs."

'It's true; her legs don't reach the pedals.

'Now she addresses me more intimately. "After tomorrow we will go to Bombay. Now you must be tired. Do you need to rest, Swamiji? Yes? Anu, take him and show him the showers. Make sure he has everything he needs. Then, when you have rested, come and have some ice cream. You'll love it! It's guava ice cream. It is delicious." Anuradha agrees. "Yes, Laxmi, it was absolutely delysseus."

"'Swami, for now, leave the Land Rover outside the office." She points to the drive outside the house a short distance away. "Tomorrow early morning put it by the gate of Lao Tzu House, so Osho will see it when he comes out for discourse. Okay?"

'I nod my head vigorously. Of course, all this is very, very okay.'

* * *

There are many stories of Laxmi's love of cars and driving. Ma Mamta, who was once scared out of her wits as a passenger in a car driven by Laxmi, told her she was driving too fast on an American highway. 'I take after my master,' she shrugged.

Later Laxmi was to find there was a price to pay for the time her Mercedes had been forced off the Bombay–Poona road. Ma Anand Savita, writer and diarist, noted three years later:

'Just before *darshan*, Laxmi in her room was speaking of the problems with her eyesight. Despite the Edwardian lorgnettes and half-moon specs imported from the West, she always comes back to the giant magnifying glass that trebles the little typed characters so she can read.

'"No no no, it is not ordinary short seeing! This is unbalanced you see, it comes from the accident"—talking as if about someone else's car as she outlines the affected parts of her body. "No, it's the accident. Now the vision is unbalanced and the glasses make it hurt more so there is headache. First there was the headache now the seeing is changed, and the arm," she reaches out her right hand, "Goes numb! These tiny little bones, all because there is no room for the new nerves, you see." A big smile, as she explains this decay of her nervous system, eyes bright as ever, "Just those tiny little bones causing all the trouble!"'

7. THE POONA ONE PHENOMENON:
PRESERVATION

Swami Deva told me, 'I arrived in Poona in 1977, midway through the commune's life; Osho's "experiment to provoke God". I was aged forty. Nothing in life could have trained my heart and my eyes for what met them as I walked through the Gateless Gate that morning in December. All I could see was beauty. All I could feel was joy. I was walking out of a monochrome world into a multi-coloured universe.

'We had travelled, my wife and I and three children, from a remote, self-sufficient organic farm on the edge of the Black Mountains of Wales, by car and bus, train and plane, taxi and rickshaw for twenty-four hours.

'All my adult life I had been a traveller. I had lived in desolate suburbs and in vibrant city centres; on remote islands and in intimate farming communities. For my keep, I had lived as an artist-painter, farmer, lecturer, art therapist and carpenter. I had been married twice. Nothing, nothing had prepared me for what met my eyes as I entered the Ashram that sparkling first day. There was abundant glossy nature and there was a brightly coloured throng; both in teeming harmony.

'Tall trees stooped over Hibiscus-lined marble pathways on which a multitude of people moved about their business.

Men, women and children all wore robes of different hues of orange; all had long hair and the men were bearded too. The way they moved, whether carrying a great baulk of wood on their shoulder or a clipboard under their arm, or a baby, or a tray of *chai*, or pulling a trolley or pushing a wheelbarrow or walking arm in arm with someone, they seemed to move with ease and elegance. Little groups of people were sitting on a low wall quietly talking or loudly laughing while others were cleaning out a pond or painting a brick wall or watering a herbaceous flowerbed or poring over an architect's blueprint; they all seemed so relaxed, so happy. So beautiful.

'Someone led us to the office. There sat Laxmi flanked by her two assistants—Arup and Sheela. Laxmi's smile was as dazzling as the day. I remember noticing her little headscarf tied over a glistening abundance of long black hair. "Welcome!" she said. "You wrote and asked about the further shore. The answer is that you will find it hidden on this shore." Her arm swept out in a semicircle that encompassed the office and all that was happening outside the plate glass windows.

'"Is all this your responsibility?" I asked.

'She laughed at the absurdity of the question. "It's Him. He sits in His chair and does nothing. Laxmi just opens the windows and doors and existence floods in with the needful."'

* * *

In 1977 there were perhaps 500 residents in the Ashram. Within the next three-and-a-half years, that figure would explode to well over 5,000. Short-term visitor numbers were in the tens of thousands. If Osho is the still point of the turning wheel, Laxmi is the hub through which all spokes connect. She has a lot of power: she does not take it personally.

This is a crucial time for Poona One; this singular experiment to provoke god is halfway through its life. From Europe and the Americas comes an inflow of distinguished therapists. Their profession is of healing; their problem is the culture that they work in is diseased. Their clients are the victims of all sorts of social malaise. What is the point of healing them to then return them to the same conditions that caused their sickness?

These days such inconsistencies are dealt with chemically; half the developed world's population is on medication when they could be whole and healed with meditation. Here in Poona One, the therapists discovered a saner society, one that valued the sacred and the profane, the inner and the outer. In the commune there were over seventy different kinds of group and individual therapies on offer. These were like the pre-wash cycle in the great brain-washing process. They could clean out and regenerate the polluted and wounded psyches of our age, relieve them of their old conditioning.

More and more of the new arrivals stayed. Most wanted to help in the life of the commune, to reap the reward of sitting with Osho in discourse each day; to learn to fly without wings. Instead of six cooks now there were sixty, instead of eight gardeners there were eighty, instead of nine cleaners there were ninety, instead of ten builders—100. New departments were needed and they materialised. Doctors and nurses, pharmacists and lab-technicians put together a peerless medical centre. Photographers and filmmakers came together and created an imaginative photographic studio. Sound technicians amassed their own technology to record and sell Osho's discourses. Gardeners restored the depleted soils to make bountiful gardens. Architects and engineers designed new buildings. Jewellers, potters, weavers, graphic designers, printers and the makers of scent-free natural cosmetics set up workshops for themselves. Shorthand secretaries and surveyors, tailors and teachers, lawyers and accountants, bankers and brick-layers, philosophers and postmen all found their niches. These diverse enterprises happened under Laxmi's perspicacious eye. At any moment though, someone might be allocated to a new department to learn new skills or a new perspective or just to face their inner processes. Work became the work of transcendence. After all, all were here to learn the art of being in—but not attached to—the world.

From an early age Laxmi had taken care of the education and well-being of the children in her family. In this commune Laxmi always had the welfare of children very much in her heart. A playgroup for the under-sevens and a school for older children were created. A big round house was built for the children's dormitory and their parents slept nearby.

Perhaps one of the most aspirational projects that Laxmi had to oversee was the creation of a university. Osho asked over 100 educationalists and therapists to create a balanced system of learning that prepared people for a new world. In education something is added, in the practice of meditation something is dropped. Only now, some forty years later, are the more cutting-edge governments and corporations beginning to implement the policy of integrating work with meditation, the outer with the inner.

* * *

In this growing commune there were all types of personalities; the master's commune was a giant adventure playground for all to act out their unlived fantasies. If you identified yourself with any of the roles, then a mighty Zen stick would, as likely as not, fall upon your head. At that you might bow in gratitude or you might bow out of the field of play.

'Mistakes and meditation are the main devices Osho offers us,' Laxmi told a baffled young man who came to her desk with a problem. 'Both are vital for our growth and understanding. Then we get to understand the things that are beyond our understanding. So make many mistakes! But don't repeat the same ones. Okay, Swami?'

To another *sannyasin* asking how meditation would help her in her life, she said, 'It isn't just a technique for which you get a diploma. Meditation is central to your very being. Meditation grows out of you as understanding, as lightness of being, as inclusiveness. There is only one revolution. That is meditation.'

Laxmi was to remember these, her own words, when the master's Zen stick fell on her.

* * *

Sometime in early 1979 Laxmi called Deva to her office. 'Swami! Laxmi has heard you know how to make real cheese.'

'That's true, we used to make them on my farm.'

'The Western friends in this commune need more protein. We cannot find good vegetarian Indian cheese. Laxmi requests you make cheese for the Ashram.'

The only response to those bright eyes, indeed the only response to anything in those exciting times, was a resounding 'YES'. However, he did ask for a special dispensation.

At the time he was working in the garden department, growing organic vegetables for Osho. And he loved working for Greek Mukta, the department's overall head. 'You do both jobs,' responded the smiling Laxmi with her head in oscillating motion. 'Deeksha will give you whatever you need.'

Indeed she did. Deeksha, the head of the catering department, gave him more than he needed—a headache and a hard time.

Cheeses, once poured into their forms, need to set under pressure and in peace for a few weeks. Deeksha's minions in the huge kitchen known as Vrindavan were forever cleaning. Twice a day, tidal waves of water pushed around by squeegees flooded the floor on which the forms were standing under pressure. Then the minions wanted the forms moved from one site to another. They cleaned behind them, under them and even the forms themselves. Deva asked Deeksha for an undisturbed space. He begged her, he pleaded, he demanded, he insisted. What he did not then understand was that the independent cheese factory's very existence was a trespass on her empire of food.

He went to talk to Laxmi. She listened, nodded and then dismissed me. A day later he was summoned to Laxmi's presence, this time with Deeksha sitting beside her in all her fulminating glory.

'Deeksha says you make much trouble. You are negative. She says her people do not interfere with you. She says your problem is ego. You need to give yourself totally to the work.'

'The cheeses need to settle undisturbed. I wouldn't bother you if that was happening. Ego is my problem but I think not in this case.' After a few more questions, Laxmi turned to Deeksha.

'Deva will have a new space on the roof of Jesus House. And later, when available, a space in Number 70. Laxmi believes his word. Deeksha, this Buddhafield is here for all of us to become more aware. It is a rare opportunity to see without judgement how we are possessive or hungry for power. Deeksha, don't miss! And please don't lie to Laxmi.'

Laxmi's kindness to him did not end there. He had often felt her sharp antennae took continuous remote readings of everyone's moods and states of mind. Their material lives were stripped down to essentials; most people owning just two or three robes, a shawl, two pairs of sandals, a tape-player, a toothbrush and some bedding. But their non-material lives were profuse with wealth and opportunity: everyone could and would explore all kinds of occupational skills and all sorts of emotional states and all manners of relating. Some nine months after starting the cheese factory, he became very ill and spent ten days in a ward of the medical centre. Later Laxmi saw him with an eye patch because the left side of his face was temporarily paralysed. 'Swami Deva,' she said, 'please go to the office and ask for money for a holiday. Take the bus to Mahabaleshwar in the mountains. Laxmi has heard your marriage is in difficulty.

You go and be with yourself a while.' Laxmi's intervention was fitting; those ten days out of time were metamorphic for him.

* * *

Laxmi gave with ease and took with ease. Swami Dayananda related this story from that time:

'I was living outside the Ashram during Poona One doing some handyman work for the Maharaja of Baroda, the owner of a big house in Poona. I had the plan to rent it from him. It was Number 70 Koregaon Park. But he didn't want to let go of it because it had belonged to his father who had died in a car crash. He even had his father's English Jaguar car walled up into a room in the garage.

'For more than a year I tried to rent it. Finally he agreed. I had already planned how to divide the rooms and how I would profit from renting out sections to *sannyasins* as living accommodation. Shortly before the deal was finalised, Laxmi called me into her office. "We heard you are negotiating for number seventy," she said. She was very brief. "The Ashram needs number seventy." There was not much to say. It was clear. They want it, they should have it. Nothing to argue about. There went my dream of making some extra money!

'However, when I decided to become a worker at the Ashram, she sent me to number seventy to be the coordinator of the handymen there.'

* * *

'Sw Atul speaks of Laxmi as a hollow bamboo, a flute playing only the melody that came from Osho. "She received her energy from him. She was always jubilant despite long hours and an intense work-load. We took inspiration from her. Her work was her meditation. For many of us she exemplified Osho's teaching—'Be in the world but not of it.'"

* * *

Laxmi found that meditation was very difficult for some new arrivals. After all, the West has no tradition of sitting silently with intentional passivity. Watching thoughts pass by without becoming enmeshed in them is an alien concept: the best it can do is explore the personality by means of psychology, a relatively superficial process. Only in recent years, and largely thanks to Osho's work, has meditation emerged from the monasteries and caves of the Himalayas. Now it is to be found in the corporate offices and boardrooms worldwide as well as in suburban village halls.

Laxmi understood that silence and presence are inherent in everyone, so in her heart she bowed to the divine essence within them—a silent *namaste*. Thus it was that amongst the tens of thousands of *sannyasins* moving in the commune there were few who resented or rejected Laxmi in her role.

Like her master, she would emphasise the value of meditation but she also recognised that Westerners would often have to use other routes to arrive at it. To one worker she would insist repeatedly, 'Swami, just be in the here and now.' To another, 'Ma, be total in whatsoever you are doing.' To another, 'Who is looking out of your eyes? Who sees you cleaning and painting the walls.' To another, 'Be creative. How can you make your typing a play? Make it a piece of art?' To someone else, 'Be open to love.' To one complaining, disabled worker she listened then said, 'Friend, be grateful for whatever comes your way; be it sun or rain, joy or sadness, pleasure or pain. All are messengers of existence offering you a gift.' To an overzealous therapist she said, 'Meditation is not therapy. It is therapeutic.' Often she told workers and visitors, 'Life is a play, a *leela*. It has no goal. I have heard Him say we already are what we seek. So trying to attain enlightenment is just following another desire. Celebration is the climate where ego falls away.'

And celebration was the climate Laxmi fostered in this Buddhafield of Osho. For herself, in her devotion, she always knew that meditation is the fast track. She had heard Osho say that with the silent mind problems are no longer problems. What the mind cannot solve, the no-mind dissolves.

I teach a religion less religiousness—and that is the need of today and of all the tomorrows that are going to follow. The old kind of religion is outdated, its time is finished, in fact it has been living a posthumous kind of existence for centuries. It is dead already, we are only carrying a corpse and it is stinking.

Meditation is the only way to experience God, to experience religion. You cannot get it from the Bible, from the Gita, from the Koran, from the Talmud—no words, no scriptures can give it to you. Only silence is able to receive God, is able to become pregnant with God, to carry God in your belly, in your very heartbeat, in your breathing, to feel him everywhere, in everybody.

[Osho]

* * *

Laxmi had no immediate concern with politics. Since relinquishing her connection with all things Gandhian, she no longer had any ambition to 'make her mark' or change the course of history. Likewise, she had no immediate concern with the poisoning of the earth or the decay and corruption of religions or the overpopulation of this planet. She was, of course, aware of these issues but Laxmi's focus was always the vision of her master, which included, parenthetically, all these things and her own self-realisation. To change the world we must change ourselves. In the day-to-day running of this growing commune, her concerns were particular and immediate. She strove to create a world that was beautiful, economically viable and spiritually enriching

She was rarely duped: her lack of guile enabled her to see to the heart of any matter. In the course of her days this now ex-'spinsterish good-doer' had to confront the whole range of human conditions, from every kind of relationship crisis to serious illness, from devious plotting to spiritually drunken disorderliness, from economic insolvency to personal hysteria, from political bullying to subtle aesthetics. With her master behind her, she used laughter, irony and a gentle teasing to obtain desired results amongst *sannyasins*. And if that failed she was an adamantine blade, sharp and swift and deadly. All this she did with quiet authority, without rush, without an intrusive personal agenda.

'But Laxmi,' said a visiting business executive to her. 'I am a neighbour and I have experience of fund-raising. Where is your development plan? How will it be financed?'

Laxmi sat behind her desk, elbows on the clear glass surface, fingertips together, unmoving for a moment. 'Development plan is sleeping right now. Laxmi brings him *chai* at five past five when he wakes up.'

The executive had the look of one talking to a child. 'Yes,

but you must have some idea of where you want to be five years from now. The steps you'll take to get from A to B to C. Else how will you provide the necessary funds?'

'Laxmi has no idea where she wants to be even tomorrow. Look! Laxmi's hands are empty. All is in the hands of existence.' With that she throws both hands in the air as if greeting a long-lost friend. 'Does an amoeba have a development plan? No. It divides and divides and divides until it's the size that's needed.'

Now the corporate man was looking for support. Around him in the office were only smiling faces. He turned back to the motionless Laxmi almost pleading with her. 'But the money? How can you live with such a short-term view? I am here to offer you my skills. Communication is one of them. I can help you.'

'Communication is of the head. Here the word is communion, which is of the heart.' Laxmi settled back in her capacious chair, 'Chief fund-raiser will awake at five past seven. Laxmi will apprise him of your offer. But be aware; it's not the money he will take from you, it's your business mind.'

'Then where does the money come from?'

'It comes from love.'

The smartly suited executive began to think he has come to the wrong place. 'Love?'

'Yes, love.'

He reaches for his bag. 'Love?'

'Love drives this economy. The more people give, the more they have. Sometimes the purse is empty, sometimes overflowing. Here love is our climate.' Again Laxmi's arms are raised as if feeling for rain. 'Money comes as needed.'

'A miracle,' says the gentleman standing up.

'Yes,' says Laxmi. 'Everything is miracle.'

* * *

Sometimes the teaser was teased herself. Vivek and Savita and a few friends were setting Laxmi up for a hypothetical date. The names of a some alpha males were called out. When Teertha's name was mentioned (he being the senior group leader and reader of sutras in discourse) declared with her impish grin, while at the same time pulling a face: 'Too much used!'

No other prospective consorts where whisked away so quickly.

* * *

In a five-star hotel in New Delhi, Laxmi sat behind a green baize table on which were neatly ordered piles of Osho books and a cluster of microphones. Before her in a smoky haze were the massed press of India, Europe and North America. Behind her was a large photograph of Osho, to her left was Swami Krishna Prem and to her right Ma Madhura and Swami Nishant. The time was late 1979.

Hitherto Laxmi has had an ambivalent relationship with the press and publicity. In 1978, in the face of opposition from her press advisors, she had given a German yellow-press magazine permission to have a reporter and photographer attend one of the Ashram's powerful and infamous No-Limits-Encounter therapy groups. Within days, photographs of naked men and women hugging and wrestling were on every bourgeois German coffee table with captions that invited puckered lips and knowing sneers.

Laxmi was learning. She sat immaculate and motionless in her crimson robe and headscarf, her eyes shining with anticipation.

Krishna Prem tapped the microphone and a noisy silence fell upon the room. 'Welcome to you all,' he began. 'We have invited you here in order to introduce ourselves and to let you in on some of the things that are happening in the Ashram of Osho in Poona. It is also an opportunity to clarify a few of the misunderstandings that have cropped up over the years. At present, the Ashram hosts visitors from over fifty countries; there are about a thousand residents and, on average, five thousand visitors every month.

'Osho has published over one hundred and fifty books to date and two new ones are brought out each month. One title has sold a million copies here in India alone. I don't need to remind you that that one is entitled *From Sex to Super-Consciousness*.

'The Ashram has over thirty separate, autonomous departments that include the various book departments that transcribe, edit, lay-out, print, bind, and sell Osho's words. There are cleaning and catering departments of course, maintenance and transport, gardening, photography, carpentry and construction, schools and educational facilities for adults and children, a boutique, cosmetic manufacture, cabinet-making and cheese factories, departments for different creative arts and crafts such as weaving, pottery, sculpture, jewellery; there are all sorts of physical and psychological therapies, martial arts and yoga and last, but most importantly, meditation.

'Osho's message is for each one of us to re-discover our true selves. He gives us the tools. And the Ashram is a blueprint for how we all might live; in celebration, in harmony with ourselves, each other and with Nature.

'I now introduce Ma Yoga Laxmi. She is Osho's personal secretary and administrator. We invite you to ask her questions.'

A hand shot up from an aisle seat near the back of the hall.

'Good morning, Laxmi. Sandip Battliwallah from the *Hindustan Gazette*. Would you confirm or deny that free sex is allowed in Ashram?'

'So far as Laxmi knows, no one is charging.' [Laughter ensued]

'Please answer question. What is Rajneesh's position on sex?'

'Osho has been speaking for twenty years on every conceivable subject known to man. One subject only interests the Indian press. Sex. Religions and states have turned us into slaves. You ask how? Everyone has sexual feelings. Priests and politicians instil a sense of fear and guilt about the feelings. Through fear and guilt anyone can be exploited and controlled. Sex is the basic, fundamental energy of all life. Repress it and then men and women can be ruled their whole lives. So the answer to our friend's question is yes, sex between loving and consenting couples is not condemned and freedom in all its forms is encouraged. That way the energy is not stuck and is free to move to higher things.' [Small applause]

'Hi. Praful Roy of the *Indian Daily Star*; *gurus* are available, two for a penny in India. They are part of the exploitation you just referred to. Why should we listen to them? Why's Rajneesh any different?'

'Praful, have you read His books? Here, please accept this one. His latest. You will see a real master comes into this world for the raising of human consciousness, the transformation of humanity. His or her work is always to return paradise to its proper place here on earth. Yes, you heard Laxmi correctly. Paradise belongs right here, not the hereafter.

'No real master wants to start a religion or to make people good or create belief systems. Nor does he or she want to endorse some kind of a god. So read the books of Osho, listen to His words on tape and you will understand. He freely offers His own understanding, His own vision, His experience. No god, no commandments, no beliefs; instead freedom, celebration and awareness. That is His non-serious *leela*, His play. Laxmi has heard Him say that when we live with awareness we are in union with all that is.'

'Are you saying that he's trying to change human nature? That's pretty ambitious.'

'Osho is faced with an awesome task. It is not to change human nature but to reunite humans with their true nature. We are less than what we can be, ignorant of who we are. We live in a region of slumber. We are beggars sitting on a gold mine. So we live in fear and desire and that's what suits the people of power. If we offer ourselves to a real master such as Osho, He will use every device and every opportunity to wake us up, open our eyes and stand us on our own two feet. Osho is very skilled. He's a well-read philosopher, an artist and trail-blazer. He is also a mother, a warrior, a prankster, and psychologist and a playful child. As a master, He lives in an infinite now—available whether embodied or not. Praful, please read Him. Then authentic sharing with your readers will happen. Perhaps?'

A regal Laxmi, circa 1958

At the feet of her master, circa 1971

Every night in *darshan*, silent and alert

A secretary always jubilant, 1977

With Swami Krishna Prem and a friend in front of the 'Leela Restaurant on Wheels', operated by Laxmi

A playful Laxmi with friends, circa 1982

L to R: Mamta, Preeti, Chetna and Yog Prabhat with whom she lived in Woodstock, USA and Swami Om Prakash Saraswati

Laxmi was popular with the Western Osho *sannyasin*s, seen here with some of the friends who loved her

Being in the here and now and happy with it

Laxmi with friends from India

Dinner time with a former gardener from Poona I

Laxmi with Gary, a dentist friend and supporter in Woodstock, circa 1983

Back from the USA, Osho arrives at Span Resort with Laxmi and Vivek,
his caretaker

Laxmi with a warm smile, her
usual demeanor

At Rajyoga Meditation Centre, New Delhi, with Ma Dassano, her caretaker kneeling (left) and Swami Om Prakash Saraswati, founder of Rajyoga Meditation Centre, Oshoworld and Oshodham

With Ma Sohan and her husband, Manik Babu (Bafnaji)

'Err...err...thank you Ma. They will be most enlightened I'm sure.' [More laughter]

'Best you transform yourself first to show them how. [More laughter] Another question?'

'With respect, Ma Laxmi, I'm John Spencer of the U.A. Press. What about the colour orange? Some would say the wearing of it is a travesty of traditional Hinduism, the final stage of worldly renunciation.'

'They would and they do. But what do *you* say?'

'I say it's very cheeky. Would you explain?'

'Orange has no meaning as such. You can take it as a reminder of your purpose on this earth, to find out who you are. You can take it as a play, as a symbol of the rising sun, as a send up of expired traditionalism, as a fashion statement. Laxmi agrees it's very cheeky.'

'Hernandez da Silva, *Mirror Magazine*. Does *Bhagwan* have anything to say about the ever-present nuclear threat? Or the dawning environmental crisis?'

'He lives in the here and now. Laxmi has heard Him say humans have always lived with one threat or another hanging over them. Some events turn into tragedies, some turn into blessings, some into nothing at all. You never know! So best you live a full life now. Find out who you really are. This knowing brings with it song and celebration. Don't postpone. Then death will bring you no regrets. And consider this: do people who celebrate life make wars? Do they destroy forests? Do they try to dominate others? Understand this. We are moving from an old world order to the age of the New Man and Woman; away from control and fear and terror and aggression. The New Humanity lives in love and celebration, creativity and joy. Only the light of self-awareness will help us through the dark and gathering storms that loom before us. Laxmi believes that ignorance, and ignorance of our ignorance, will only be dispelled by the light of self-enquiry. What Laxmi calls meditation. So Mr da Silva, be happy, celebrate life here and now. Then transformation can begin. Who knows what tomorrow will bring.'

'It sounds like some sort of revolution.'

'Yes. There is only one real revolution—the inner one. It's never been tried before on such a scale.'

* * *

Back in the hotel or friend's house after such a meeting, Laxmi would see to the welfare of her helpers and then, once in her room with the door closed, she would shower, bring order to her small wardrobe and then sit silently. An hour or two later, a soft knock on the door and a cup of *chai* would remind her of her role to make decisions for the next few steps and the next few days.

* * *

The following account by Ma Prem Anando, an actor from Italy, describes Laxmi's compelling and inspiring presence:

'I first met Laxmi in her office when I went to inquire about *sannyas* in September 1978. She was the one who asked the first questions, she "checked me out" with those very wide-open eyes of hers... I vividly remember that during this brief meeting I couldn't take my eyes off her. I couldn't stop thinking how she reminded me of myself as a little girl; she laughed and joked as if she still was a child herself. But it wasn't only that. Laxmi for me was like a magnet of some sort, her energy seemed part of everything around us and everything around seemed to be part of her... She made me aware of my own self, including parts I didn't yet know; it was astounding.

'Later in time, after months of living at the Ashram, just to see her little shape glide by, would give me bouts of happiness and huge enthusiasm...

'I went to ask her if I could become an *Ashramite*, and have a food pass. I was trembling inside, knowing my chances were small, but I had no money to pay for my place, and I categorically wouldn't go back to Italy. She looked at me very carefully, in silence, and after what seemed to be a century and a half, she said: "Yes."

'When she began her travels, when her chair became empty, the middle one of the three behind the vast glass desk in the big marble office, I really felt some part of me was missing: the family was not complete. Other power-house Mas and Swamis with important responsibilities never affected me as much as the few times I was face to face with little Laxmi. She had a way of looking deep into you; it was scary, but at the same time totally reassuring—there were no judgments labels or assumptions; just depth.

'She was a small colossus of a woman who meant a lot to me and many others.'

* * *

Savita reports:

'I complained, or rather my *ego* complained, because it thought it should and might regret it later if it didn't. So I swept into her office saying, "You said I could have the first-floor room number 6 and now you're giving me a ground-floor room number 4 which I don't want just because it's noisier and..." She was looking into me with her massive well-deep eyes as my voice tailed off. She shook her head as if blessing me. "No. You have room 4." And that was that.'

* * *

Once, in her office at the day's end, Laxmi talked to a few friends about the difference between the enlightened and the unenlightened life.

'Laxmi knows only one enlightened person. He lives an ordinary life. He's gone to bed already, like other sensible people. He wakes up early though, at half past six. Vivek brings him a cup of tea, always the same kind of tea, always in the same cup. At seven, he goes to shower and bathes for half an hour. At seven thirty, he has yet another cup of tea with an apple. On the dot at eight he will be in Buddha Hall. As you know, he speaks for ninety minutes, finishing at exactly half past nine. Then he reads till lunch at half past eleven. His lunch is vegetables, a lentil *dal,* green salad, rice and *roti.* His cooks may become bored of cooking the same old meals but Osho never tires of them. Each time he eats, it is afresh. There is no past involved. It is a new dish and a new taste each time. He eats with complete awareness. He uses mind only when required. For the rest of the time he is in a state of no-mind, of meditation.

'Often when Laxmi visits him, he is sitting in his chair, his eyes closed in a state of total relaxation. He told Laxmi recently, "For me to talk is arduous. The sooner you are able to understand me in my silence, the better it will be."'

* * *

In December 1977, Osho spelled out Laxmi's importance to his work. A female American *sannyasin* asked him why the guards at the Gateless Gate had refused entry to an Indian *sannyasin*. She said that when she had asked Laxmi, she had been 'more or less told to mind my own business.'

Osho replied:

Laxmi is right. And always remember that Laxmi never does anything on her own. She is a perfect vehicle. That's why she has been chosen for the work. She does not have her own idea of what is right and what is wrong. She simply listens and does. Whatsoever is said, she does. [...] This is not going to be a democracy. This should be remembered from the very beginning.

People are prevented from entering but nobody is prevented from leaving. If you want to be here, you have to be totally here. This place is to change you; it is not to be according to you. This place is going to be a transformation for you.

[Osho, *The Diamond Sutra*, Ch. 8, Q. 5]

* * *

Despite the ever-increasing pressure of people to feed and accommodate, no one ever saw Laxmi stressed or tense. There were always the bright eyes, the joke and the logical explanation, 'It's HIM.' But there was also the hard Zen stick. Here's the story of how Osho used Laxmi to hit the proud and cerebral Krishna Prem, journalist, writer and first head of the Ashram press office.

During the monsoon of 1979, Krishna Prem had developed pneumonia. After a long convalescence, he had energy *darshan (shaktipat)* with Osho. The following morning, he dropped by Laxmi's office. This story is shortened and lifted from his book, *Osho, India and Me.*

'Good news, the body is better,' she says. 'It was beautiful last night the way He held Krishna Prem's hands. And this morning too He spoke of Krishna Prem.'

'Really?' I was moved and flattered.

'Yes,' she continues, looking me straight in the eye. 'One word *gets* Krishna Prem and that word is Laxmi. Now he is vulnerable. *Get him.*'

The floor disappears from under my feet.

She returns to her papers. 'Just so you know.'

For the next months, Laxmi was on his case. She criticised him relentlessly, finding fault with his work, his behaviour and with his deep-seated, overflowing negativity. After some weeks he protested,

'But Laxmi! I don't feel negativity! I don't know what you're on about!'

'See?' she shouted back, 'exactly what Laxmi means!'

I wrote to Osho asking why I was being continually berated by Laxmi. The answer came back: 'See Laxmi.'

With a sinking feeling Krishna Prem, a mature, intelligent and forceful man, entered the tiger's lair.

'Laxmi looks up from her papers. 'He says it has nothing to do with Laxmi. He says to start smoking again.' As I rise to leave, Laxmi's hand thrusts a book into the air, her eyes still fixed on the piles of paper spread across the desk. 'This is for you.'

It is one of Osho's books signed by Osho with a loving message and the date of my birthday.

Over the coming weeks, Laxmi makes greater and greater demands on me. Nothing I do is ever right. One day, in exasperation, I too yell back at her, 'Why do you have to shout and scream at me?'

'This is Laxmi's way. If you deserve it, take it; if you don't, just laugh.'

It took Krishna Prem a while but finally he got it. He heard Osho's words of counsel, to live from the heart and from intuition, not from the head and from logic. He went to thank Laxmi. 'Thank Laxmi? For what? No need for thank-you,' she smiles. 'Laxmi enjoyed.'

Laxmi had become a master of the well-delivered Zen strike.

* * *

Swami Keerti, editing in the Hindi book and newsletter department, also recalled her countless hits to him. 'She told me, "Hurry up. This is needed as of yesterday!" And she was right. I was a lazy man. You see we all had this great respect for her. Osho gave her a function—his secretary—not power. Because she stayed with that, being just a medium, people had respect for her, totally trusted her.'

* * *

Two seven-year-old children were caught stealing money from purses in the Ashram's bag-and-shoe check; they told this story forty-four years later. They came before Laxmi in her office. 'You, Deepti, if it happens again, you will be expelled from the commune. Then how will your parents manage without you? And you, Puja, your punishment is to be happy from now on. Can you manage that?'

* * *

As the commune evolved Laxmi was required to spend longer and longer periods away from Osho. 'This does not affect Laxmi,' she declared to friends one evening in her office. 'Laxmi trusts. Laxmi has understood that Osho does not want to make anyone dependent on him. He represents freedom. He lives for freedom. He *is* freedom. If you cling to any kind of crutch, including a *guru*, you lose your freedom. Laxmi sees that independence makes one grow and helps one to be centred.'

'But don't you miss him when you have to go away?' asked one of her assistants.

'The Master is both physical and non-physical. A presence and an absence. Form and formlessness. Laxmi is aware of Osho's presence even in his absence. This formlessness is not in time. With trust and love Laxmi feels his energy and guidance in any place at any time.'

'What if he sent you away permanently?'

Laxmi smiled her mischievous smile, 'He makes suggestions. Only suggestions. Whether to implement them stays with the individual.'

When events took an unsettling turn, would Laxmi come to regret such settled self-assurance?

* * *

During a morning discourse in May 1980, a Hindu fundamentalist threw a dagger at Osho. It whizzed over the heads of *sannyasins* and landed on the ground a few metres from him.

The Ashram security *sannyasins* caught the man and handed him over to the police. He was tried by the local judiciary and acquitted.

Laxmi protested to the Press, 'The judgement is clearly prejudiced. That bigoted judge sitting in judgement couldn't believe that all those present would sit undisturbed in meditation. He would not even listen to the tape recording of the event. What Laxmi finds most shocking is that, as an Indian, he failed to appreciate the beauty, grace and forbearance of the three thousand meditators present, just because of his bias against Osho. It is strange too, that this land which has been the birthplace of so many great mystics seems to have made no impression on the judge.'

Laxmi enlisted extra security guards from amongst the black-belt martial artists in the commune.

* * *

Osho is a paradigm or exemplar for the contemporary, globalised world where, between leaps of technological brilliance, we stumble around leaving a wake of destruction behind us. He used every means at his disposal to illuminate our way. At that time he was reading books, magazines and newspapers from around the world. Thus he gathered the materials for his insightful discourses.

Swami Satyananda was a best-selling author and journalist, well-respected for capturing the zeitgeist of that epoch. He described for a magazine in 1999 how Laxmi conspired with the master for his growth in an article titled 'The Ballpoint Pen', excerpted below:

'Here are 4,000 Swiss francs,' said Ma Hari, giving me a bundle of bank notes. 'With this money you are supposed to buy two gold ballpoint pens for *Bhagwan*—eighteen carat and studded with diamonds.'

She sorted through her handbag and pulled out a scruffy page torn from a magazine. 'This is what they look like,' Ma Hari said. '*Bhagwan* found them in a *Playboy* magazine.'

'*Playboy* magazine?'

'Ballpoint pens with diamonds?'

I looked at the advertisement. The pens were being offered by a company in Geneva and my mind moved into gear. Why on earth should my master want to possess this kind of vulgar toy? Diamond-studded ballpoint pens! Have you ever heard of an enlightened master sporting diamond-studded pens? Was not 'relaxing into ordinariness' his message? These kinds of pens one saw lurking out of the shirt pockets of Mafiosi types and oil sheiks. Status symbols of the *nouveau riche*. And why on earth was he reading *Playboy*? Was this a suitable publication for the man whom I considered to be the spiritual master for the 21st century?

Suddenly I was angry. I didn't want anything to do with this.

It was in the fall of 1979 and I had been a *sannyasin* for only a year. Ma Hari, who had taken *sannyas* four years earlier, was a little more experienced in the ways of the master and so she simply said:

'How about just buying them?'

'I've more important things to do. You better buy them.'

Ma Hari quietly took the 4,000 francs back. 'You don't say "no" to the master,' she said.

Ma Hari and I—'Ashramites' in Poona One—were touring the West. My book *Ganz Entspannt im Hier und Jetzt* (recently translated as *The Cosmic Madhouse*), was to be launched at the Frankfurt Book Fair and I was in Germany to promote it. Ma Hari had come along because Laxmi had the funny idea that she should. Osho had called Laxmi 'My perfect tool'—whatever Laxmi said was supposed to come straight from the master. No need to argue with her.

One day Laxmi had called me into her office. 'Ma Hari has nice energy,' she revealed to me. 'You buy her plane ticket, OK? She will be good for you.'

'We'll be flying first class, of course,' was Ma Hari's first constructive idea. 'This we owe to *Bhagwan*'s reputation.' I tried hard to understand the logic, but missed. So I booked economy as usual and took off a few days before Ma Hari. We reunited in Hamburg. She managed to locate the manufacturer in Geneva and ordered two ballpoint pens. The pens sold like hot cookies; there was a three months waiting list. We proceeded to the Frankfurt Book Fair— dressed in orange and maroon of course and wearing the *mala*.

When we arrived in Frankfurt at the *Bhagwan* book booth, a crowd of *sannyasins* were waiting for us. 'There's a telegram for you, Satyananda,' they shouted.

It must have been the longest and strangest telegram I'd ever received. In a roundabout way, it reiterated what I already knew and then added that it was of extreme, if not fundamental importance, that *exactly* the pens that were pictured in the magazine are bought. I was asked to give this task absolute priority and my full attention and energy—any other plans I might have were of secondary importance.

What a button pusher! These ridiculous pens were supposed to be more important than my book which was about to become the publishing sensation of this year's Book Fair? I left in confusion, to put it mildly, to see my publisher at his booth. There, an excited PR agent yelled at me:

'Mr Elten, there's an important telegram...we've been looking for you all over the place.'

I ripped open the envelope—the telegram was identical to

the one I had read just five minutes before at the *Bhagwan* booth.

'Bad news?' the agent asked, looking at my face.

'No,' I replied, 'just something crazy.'

When I arrived back in Hamburg there was yet another urgent telegram waiting for me, nearly as long as the two previous ones. This time Laxmi was asking me to telegraph her a full report of the progress I was making in procuring these pens.

I wrote back: 'Ma Hari making great efforts getting the pens STOP Good progress STOP No need to worry STOP His blessings. STOP Satyananda.'

Back came the reply: 'Urgent! *You* are responsible. Give it the utmost priority...' and so on and so forth.

After the Book Fair I would have liked to get back to Poona right away but here I was stuck in the Hamburg winter waiting for these goddamned diamond-studded, gold ballpoint pens; and the price of gold was rising day by day...

When we had finally, after the three months, reached the top of the waiting list, the price of the two pens had risen from 3,800 Swiss francs to 5,800.

'What now?' I asked Ma Hari. 'One pen will also do, don't you think so?'

She didn't think so at all. She thought that the wish of an Enlightened One is law to his disciples. It would be utterly inappropriate to decide on our own to cut this order in half.

To avoid any further complications and to get over with this mad game I could have, of course, simply paid the difference—2,000 Swiss francs out of my own pocket. After all I had been living for free in his Ashram for a whole year, writing a book about my experiences in his presence. The book was on its way to become a bestseller, and nobody had asked me to surrender the royalties to the Ashram.

If I had been in my heart, I would have paid. But after only one year with the master, I was still in my mind. And my mind was very busy thinking up all kinds of arguments which would allow me to hang on to 2,800 francs with a good conscience. I still believed that a master would fulfil my expectations.

So I suggested to Ma Hari that we send a telegram to the rich Austrian Ma who took the part of the donor in this game. We asked her if she was prepared to push another 2,000 francs over or if she felt that one ballpoint pen would be fine. Her answer came next day: 'One pen OK.'

No sooner had Ma Hari reduced our order to one pen another telegram arrived from Poona: 'Where are the pens?' Pens in the plural, not one pen! Was Laxmi still assuming that we were bringing two? Where should the second one come from if the donor wasn't ready to cough up more money? Again the ball was in my court. What should I do after all...? My 'Higher Self' began to assert itself. Only a little consciousness was needed to defeat the mind. But this consciousness was, in reality, painfully lacking. My mind refused to support what it thought was bad taste. The truth of the matter was, of course, that I was simply too stingy to buy a little luxurious present for my master. A year later I donated all the money I still possessed unconditionally. Obviously I had by then arrived on a higher spiritual plain.

A few days later we collected the pen from a jeweller. Now off to Poona asap! But all flights were fully booked. And there was another urgent telegram: 'Where are the pens???'

It so happened that Ma Astha was leaving in a couple of days, and thank God she was prepared to take the precious gift to Poona. 'Maybe it will help with my enlightenment,' she grinned.

Ma Hari and I departed a week later and when we met Astha in the Ashram she greeted us with a 'You'll never guess what happened!'

She told us how she had gone to Laxmi's office and handed over the package with the pen. Laxmi took the pen from its box, held it under her nose, looked at it sideways and upside down before exclaiming: 'This is supposed to be for *Bhagwan*? I don't know anything about it.' Astha quietly left the office.

The next morning, she was in the medical centre with a fever. Suddenly the Swiss Doctor Sw Hassid burst into the waiting room, shouting, 'My God, listen [to] what happened...*Bhagwan* gave me this thing!' Hassid stretched his hand out and there was our diamond-studded ballpoint pen!

'You're joking,' I exclaimed, a hot flush passing over me.

For years I felt ashamed of myself. Even after I had donated my life insurance and put almost all of my cash into the Ranch in Oregon, a bad conscience plagued me. And there were moments when my mind (which cherished this situation!) whispered into my ear: 'You see all these wonderful diamond-studded watches and bracelets which the master gives away to almost everybody? And what did you get? A Chinese straw hat two sizes too small!'

By now I know that a master is never disappointed nor is he grateful. He has no illusions and simply helps people to grow. His game with the ballpoint pen was simply a masterstroke and I feel almost honoured that I received the hit. And grateful to Laxmi too.

* * *

A few *sannyasins* came to see Laxmi in the office. They told her that, in the evenings after *darshans*, they had been improvising with scenes from the Shakespeare play, *A Midsummer Night's Dream*. Laxmi jumped at the idea of putting the commune on the map of cultural Bombay. She called in an Ashram resident who was a professional theatre director, to get the ball rolling.

Within weeks a cast had been gathered together and rehearsed, while theatre and costume designers, sound and lighting technicians worked frantically to create the necessary scenery and props. The performance in Bombay drew rave reviews. Laxmi then had an international children's theatre group formed, and they staged *Peter Pan* in Mumbai. The audience greeted their presentation with continuous cheers. Later there were shows in Delhi too. Laxmi relished the wide publicity that they brought to Osho and his work.

She then thought to expand and embellish the theatre performances with an exhibition of *sannyasins* working at their particular crafts: weavers wove, jewellers made jewellery, potters crafted ceramics, sculptors sculpted, designers showed their work with fabrics, carpenters their work of elegant ebony and rosewood cabinets. All the while musicians played live music. And sometimes a professional ventriloquist with his dummy had the crowds in stitches.

Indira Gandhi, the then prime minister of India, was invited to a performance. Unfortunately, she had to cancel at the last moment for reasons of state but she invited the whole caste to her residence for tea and cakes afterwards. Laxmi told her that the displays were an example to the world of the love and trust, meditation, creativity and gratitude that Osho evoked in his people.

* * *

Indira Gandhi was India's fourth prime minister and, like her father, interested in the spiritual life. From an early age she had been touched by the words and the being of Osho. She was however, first and foremost, an ambitious politician, so she never actually came to his Ashram even when she was in Poona because Osho was already a controversial figure by then. Until 1977 when she was temporarily deposed from power, Laxmi was given a 'green pass', an entitlement to visit Indira in her home or office at any time. Indira received thankfully every new book of Osho as it was published and during the Fourth World Book Fair in Delhi she made a special point of visiting the Ashram stand.

In 1980 when Indira was again prime minister, her son and heir Sanjay died in an airplane crash. Indira, when Laxmi next visited, took Laxmi's hand and entreated her to go and talk with Rajiv, her younger son. She wanted Laxmi's help to persuade Rajiv to give up being a professional pilot and enter politics. Laxmi went to his room and spoke with him for a long time concerning the contribution he might make to the country's progress in the 20th century. Rajiv had married a Roman Catholic girl. He was reluctant but he did subsequently enter politics and become prime minister following his mother's assassination in 1984. However, he was to become more and more influenced by his political advisors than by his own heart,

* * *

Chuang Tzu, as we hear Osho tell the story, was sitting by a tranquil lake when two envoys of King Wei of Chu appeared. 'His Majesty requires your presence at his court to take up the esteemed office of chief minister. We bring gifts and a thousand ounces of silver.'

Chuang Tzu remained silent for a while, gazing at the small waves lapping the water's edge. Then he turned to the messengers with a laugh. 'That's a lot of silver. And to be chief minister is an honoured position. But hey! Think for a moment of the great ox that is sacrificed each year. You feed it rich foods and give it a blanket with golden embroidery. It is continually groomed and stroked. But when the time of the sacrifice comes, don't you think he would rather change places with that obscure little turtle playing over there in the mud?'

'Indeed he would,' replied the envoys.

'Then please be gone. I am happy playing in the mud.'

Osho went on to say that Laxmi is his Chuang Tzu; she is in the world and not of it. She dealt with tricky politicians, angry neighbours, hard-nosed businessmen, effusive visitors and adoring spaced-out *sannyasins*, yet she still preserved her meditation.

* * *

When Laxmi was in Mumbai and had politicians to meet, she would stay overnight, at the Oberoi Hotel. Veetmoha, as her then driver, said he has so many memories of Laxmi sitting on the bed, on the phone, arranging meetings— sometimes with a small team of people around her, ironing, preparing food, showing samples of paper or bookbinding cloth, discussing construction blueprints or what to serve at the next festive celebration. Then it was, 'Let's go, Swamiji!' and rides in elevators, car doors held open by huge Sikhs for the diminutive Laxmi, climbing in with her red slippers, always excited and upbeat about the next event.

He wrote too of her kindness, her deep maternal generosity:

Laxmi often stopped by her family home, Vatcha Villas, during Bombay visits. If Laxmi's nieces and nephews were home it was a zoo; very similar I imagine to what the household sounded like when Laxmi was a child. Feeding the driver was always on Laxmi's mind, and I would sit on a stool in the kitchen while chapattis were made and food prepared for me. Laxmi knew of my fondness for Indian sweets, and introduced me to some rare and special ones. 'You will love it!' she would say, offering me a plate. She never forgot the sensation caused by Gulab Pak, when I first tried it in Kutch. It is a boiled milk sweet made with rose petals. Ineffable!

* * *

Around Osho, change was always in the air. With the success of Laxmi's work in publishing and Osho's words flowing to all corners of the globe, the trickle of seekers to Poona had become a flood. Osho asked Laxmi to find a new place where his commune could thrive and expand. After only three years in Poona, by 1977, Laxmi was searching in Gujarat.

Veetmoha, her driver, writes:

The meeting with the Maharaja of Kutch was the most formal and impressive of the many meetings I attended with

Laxmi on her travels. The reception room in the palace in
Bhuj was magnificent. Laxmi and I and one or two of the
Maharaja's staff were seated round the edge of the huge
room. We stood as the Maharaja descended the stairs for the
audience. He was a tall good-looking man and I was struck
by his regal bearing; how the chair he approached became a
throne when he sat in it. He was gracious.

Laxmi, conveying a message to princes and politicians, was
a remarkable sight! First, there is a long tradition in India
of powerful women, and also simple women, making a big
difference through their work and example. And secondly
there is a long tradition of women in spiritual garb revered
as saints. The ongoing surprise was that tiny Laxmi seemed
to command both these traditions, and accept them as the
most natural thing in the world...

Sometimes, if things had been difficult, Laxmi would
vent, addressing me in her own delightful rendition of my
sannyas name, Veetmoha: 'Veetamoh! These people! Really!
It is such a thing!' This was not exasperation so much as
puzzlement and disbelief. Then she would immediately
turn to what was needed to be done next, to which politician
might hold the key, to whose influence might be sought to
move things along, to making the necessary phone calls as
soon as we were back in the hotel room. When things were
going badly she would sometimes just give a big sigh: 'Oh,
Bhagwan!'

* * *

Ma Prem Madhura, who had once worked for the UK's
prestigious *Sunday Times* newspaper and helped in the
Ashram's press office, remembers travelling to Mumbai with
Laxmi. 'Veetmoha was at the wheel. Laxmi was speaking of
the changes ahead of us. She told us that we had, as yet, no

idea what the meditative life was all about. One day we would become silent within. At that time, Saswad, a semi-desert site, some twenty-five kilometres from the Poona Ashram, was about to be designated as the stop-gap, overflow commune. Laxmi said that perhaps when we moved there and had withdrawn from the market place, then only would we know this profound inner silence.'

Madhura felt that Laxmi herself was a prime example of a meditator in the market place. She had seen her in the home of India's Prime Minister Indira Gandhi, 'She was no different from usual. They were relating almost as soul sisters.'

On one occasion, Laxmi told Madhura to visit the editor of an influential Bombay daily newspaper that was now presenting Osho in a negative light. 'Tell them they are riding their bandwagon back to front. Times have changed again. Now Osho is an internationally recognised figure. Tell them that they owe it to their readers to present him again.'

'I followed Laxmi's guidance to the letter T. Next week the paper carried a full centre-page spread on Osho.'

Laxmi never hesitated or felt fazed with the high-ups: the chief-ministers, collectors, state officials, know-it-all intellectuals of the press or academic life. Teasing was her favoured prod for overriding someone's resistance.

Sw Atul brought a very important, indeed very self-important, New Delhi lawyer to see her. The lawyer, by his manner, indicated he was rather too good for Laxmi and her business. The casework was discussed in a hotel room. When business was completed, Laxmi said innocently, 'Would you like to hear a tape of Osho speaking?' It was an offer the gentleman could hardly refuse.

The tape deck whirred into crackling rotation and then settled down to the clear voice of Osho, saying:

One of the most interesting words in the English language today is the word 'fuck'. It is one magical word. Just by its sound it can describe pain, pleasure, hate and love. In language it falls into many grammatical categories. It can be used as a verb, both transitive (John fucked Mary) and intransitive (Mary was fucked by John), and as a noun (Mary is a fine fuck). It can be used as an adjective (Mary is fucking beautiful). As you can see there are not many words with the versatility of 'fuck'. Besides the sexual meaning, there are also the following uses:

Fraud: I got fucked at the used-car lot.
Ignorance: Fucked if I know.
Trouble: I guess I am fucked now!
Aggression: Fuck you!
Displeasure: What the fuck is going on here?
Difficulty: I can't understand this fucking job.
Incompetence: He is a fuck-off.
Suspicion: What the fuck are you doing?
Enjoyment: I had a fucking good time.
Request: Get the fuck out of here!
Hostility: I am going to knock your fucking head off!
Greeting: How the fuck are you?
Apathy: Who gives a fuck?
Innovation: Get a bigger fucking hammer.
Surprise: Fuck! You scared the shit out of me!
Anxiety: Today is really fucked.

And it is very healthy too. If every morning you do it as a Transcendental Meditation—just when you get up, the first thing, repeat the mantra 'Fuck you!' five times—it clears the throat. That's how I keep my throat clear!

Laxmi's laughter failed to infect either the lawyer or the deeply embarrassed Atul.

On another occasion another self-important guest was thirty minutes late. When finally announced by the hotel reception, Laxmi told them to send him up. She then vacated her room, watched him from down the passage and kept him waiting fifteen minutes.

Laxmi liked to cheer up serious politicians with a gift-wrapped box. When it was opened, out popped a jack-in-the-box.

* * *

Swami Lokesh had first met Laxmi in 1974. He wrote this:

We talked on several occasions. Laxmi was a sweet and intelligent woman. She was a joker and utterly devoted to her master.

I only ever wrote a single letter to Osho. One afternoon, I was in a flippant mood and what I fired off was flippant. I took the letter to Laxmi and she gave me a funny look as I handed it over.

I left the Ashram and bicycled down to the late enlightened Meher Baba's wee house down on Bund Garden Road. The caretaker there would let me come and go as I pleased.

I chose a book from the small library and hunkered down in a corner. I read a few lines about the master being playful like Lord Krishna, but never to forget that the master is an embodiment of the Supreme, the All-That-Is. I flashed back on the flippant letter that I handed to Laxmi half an hour before. I realised I had fucked up big time.

I hurried out to my antique bike, squeaked my way back to the Ashram at hyper-speed and rushed in to the office. Laxmi was waiting for me, with my unopened letter in her hand. She chuckled and handed the letter back. 'Swami Lokesh,' she said, 'I thought you might return for this.' Her dark eyes sparkled. 'Thanks, Laxmi,' I said with obvious relief. I *namasted* and left.

I adored that woman.

* * *

Ma Deva Fatima, writer and actor, wrote this anecdote of Laxmi's presence in her life:

In Poona One I entered the office that was nearly empty save for my own heavy self-consciousness. Seated in a chair too big for her, Laxmi appeared frail, almost a non-presence. Her eyes had luminosity with a look intensely close and hazily distant. I started to recite the message from a friend that I had come to deliver. She held me in her eyes; I had the feeling she was listening to the words below the words. In the middle of a sentence she said, 'Why don't you take sannyas!'

I could not find an answer. Her look softened and she repeated, 'Why don't you take sannyas?'

Noting my dumb incomprehension, she pointed to the waste-paper basket. 'Your mind should go in here. The mind keeps us tied to the mundane. It limits us, prevents us reaching higher levels of consciousness and .connectedness. Each lifetime is an opportunity. We keep side-stepping our best chances, life after life. Sannyas is the short cut to *nirvana*, to ultimate truth.'

The office door opened and an assistant reminded her of other waiting visitors. As I walked out I felt her eyes following me. I turned and looked at her.

'Take sannyas,' she said with a faint smile.

I did.

8. THE POONA ONE PHENOMENON: DESTRUCTION

Yatri has described the beginning of the end of the Poona One phenomenon:

'I was aware of the deep harmony that existed between Laxmi and Vivek in the caring for their master. That harmony was disrupted however, as early as 1979, when it became apparent that there was a direct challenge to both Laxmi and Vivek from a third party. While both of them were only interested in caring for Osho, his health and his vision of awakening as many of his disciples as quickly and comprehensively as possible, it was evident that, for Sheela, the major thirst was to be his Number One disciple.

'About that time Laxmi was away for long periods; searching for land, meeting government officials and pursuing other Ashram business including bookings for the theatre group performances. Her greatest effort was in trying to persuade the Indian government to allow a commune to be built in surroundings more suitable than the polluted industrial city that Poona was becoming. Vivek was suffering from what could have been some hormonal disorders that limited her ability to look after Osho the way she had done before. Other carers were drafted in when she was ill each month.

'So while his two true carers were indisposed Sheela stepped in, taking over the general running of the commune and carrying out his direct instructions. It is difficult for most of us to understand why Osho gave her such freedom, especially in the light of what was to happen later. The ways of the mystics are, however, mysterious. Nevertheless, knowing Sheela from 1975, it was easy to see that she was a natural leader with all the attendant strengths and weaknesses.

'What Sheela seemed to long for was to be both Osho's secretary and top disciple. However, she did not fully realise the job came with small print attached; the same small print that Laxmi had discovered. Apart from a daily commune business meeting, she would spend less time with the master than any new Westerner might have with him in *darshan*.

'Sheela had the power and guile of Laxmi yet lacked the integrity that such power required. This made for a volatile and dangerous mix. She became a very powerful leader, almost a Moses leading her tribes into the new land. And we followed. When Laxmi finally returned, empty handed from trying to find a location for the next paradise in India, the caravanserai and her beloved master had already moved on and with it the passing of both her era and all she had fought for.

'For me her grace and acceptance was heroic. She was not a saint in any way nor would she ever have aspired to that dubious stratum. She was perhaps even a flawed mystic with a little too much interest in esoterica, but she was the very core of Osho's early vision of a Neo-*Sannyas* universe. And that is her lasting legacy. Her devotion and loyalty to her Beloved remained unshakeable. Her loyalty to the new secretary was another matter.'

* * *

In those days Laxmi appeared to be in an elevated state, both outwardly and inwardly. But, and it is a big but, being with a master is an extreme affair. Joseph Campbell, the great writer on comparative religion, has called our journey through life 'The One Great Story': 'In the beginning, we are one with the source but we become separated from it and now we must find a way to return.' The way is perilous. It costs us nothing less than everything. A master burns the dross to purify the gold. Many of those close to Osho could not take the heat.

Events were piling up, herding Laxmi to another death, a not-so-little death. We approach the final phase of her primacy in Osho's communes. Osho was one of a long line of masters who used shock and provocation to destabilise the habitual barriers that we erect against reality. All he was really doing was providing situations for people to become aware of who and what they really were. He was ruthless with the ones who loved him totally.

* * *

Difficulties for Laxmi were piling up both at home and away. The commune had outgrown its topography. This once desolate eight-acre compound was now a seething oasis in a polluted city. Within its walls were tall trees and silence, a complex of lush gardens, marble pathways and a pulsing plurality of folk moving about their business. Visitors professed themselves stunned by the order and serenity of such an over-crowded place. There was always so much construction work happening that Osho joked during discourse one morning, 'In this Ashram, the shortest distance between two points is a building site.'

It was time to move on again.

* * *

Laxmi's prime target area throughout most of 1979 and 1980 was, of course, the Himalayas; for countless centuries the home of mystics and sages, seekers and *sannyasins*. She scented, at one time, the sweet possibility of success when talking with the state government of Himachal. She thought they might sell her a hotel with extensive land in Chail. However, the financial arrangements were never clear and Sheela, when standing in for Laxmi on one occasion and for her own ends, sabotaged the negotiations by inimical behaviour.

Laxmi focused her attention on more familiar ground, Gujarat, the state of her family's origins. She was trying to buy a palace with a farm of about 20,000 acres that had several lakes and fine old trees.

Indian bureaucracy is a legendary Sloth. Things moved slowly at first then froze into immobility. To make progress, Laxmi had to gather together in one place the landowner, the local community and the state government for negotiations. The federal government of Moraji Desai lurked implacably behind the scenes.

Years later, it transpired there were two undeclared concerns never ever alluded to in the meetings. They were the possibility of secret nuclear tests in the area and the usual fear that foreign agents would gain entry into the country from nearby Pakistan in the guise of *sannyasins*. Laxmi discovered these caveats some five years after her protracted negotiations had stalled. Then it became clear that the real and major barrier had been Moraji Desai, the prime minister who succeeded Indira Gandhi.

Moraji Desai was one of India's most ambitious and plietesial politicians, the kind that flower but once in a lifetime. In 1977, at the age of eighty-three, he finally made it to the top. Back in 1960, he had his first tussle with Osho when he was the finance minister and Osho a hardly-known *Acharya*. They both happened to be guest speakers at a big religious conference organised by the Shankaracharya Tulsi before an audience of over .

At a get-together prior to the main event, Moraji Desai demanded to know why Tulsi should have a raised dais upon which to sit while he and the other nineteen speakers had to sit on a carpet on the floor. Desai rejected all Tulsi's justifications. Osho asked if he might intervene and Desai, expecting support, assented.

'Look,' he said. 'There are nineteen people here, most of them illustrious and eminent people from all walks of life and not one of them has made a complaint.' He then asked the group if they had felt hurt or offended. 'If it has not occurred to you, please raise your hands.' All hands were held up.

Turning again to Desai he said, 'Not one of them is feeling hurt. Only you. You must be suffering from an inferiority complex. And may I further ask, if you had been offered the high seat with the Shankaracharya, would you have invited the other honoured guests to be on the same level as you?'

Some eight or ten years later, Prime Minister Indira Ghandi, in a private conversation with Osho, mentioned that Moraji Desai was causing many problems in her cabinet. Osho responded, 'If your deputy is so against you, why not throw him out?' And she did dismiss him. Osho's remark was reported back to Desai by one of his spies and it further fuelled his resentment. Many years later, having become prime minister, he declared that he had only one further ambition and that was to know God.

'Ambition and God?' queried Osho publicly. 'They are mutually exclusive. A contradiction in terms. Ambition is external and comes from a covetous ego. And anyway God does not exist: godliness can be known as an inner experience. And what would Mr Desai say if he did meet God? Would he talk about politics? Moraji Desai is a hypocrite who calls himself religious as a political strategy.'

It was this same Moraji Desai who was making sure that hidden obstacles were put in the way of Laxmi's search for land. So the days and months and seasons passed. Laxmi, despite frequent absences from her master and despite the stone-walls of bureaucracy, remained ever trusting, ever expectant of positive results.

This fierce positivity, noticed and referred to by many people, may prove to be a quality that transmutes into a dis-quality, a feature of worth that becomes a curse.

The positive results never materialised.

* * *

At the last hour, Laxmi again turned her attention to the Himalayas. She visited several palaces in poor repair because the maharajas who owned them could no longer afford to maintain them. Some were just a mound of rubble yet the price shot up as soon as the owner learned that Laxmi represented the Rajneesh Foundation.

Laxmi now had to add to her many administrative skills the knowledge of climate, of culture, of local food and water and of the diseases common to the areas she visited.

She had long-since become expert at living with a shortage of funds. 'Currency must move; not stagnate,' she told her assistants. 'The Foundation has a perpetual funding crisis, though it never stops us working. Money comes in and we spend it immediately. One knows it appears that the Foundation is fabulously rich; few people see the narrow financial path that Laxmi treads. This never holds us back because money is just a means.'

This attitude was later to prompt a Rajneeshpuram bumper sticker: *Moses Earns—Jesus Saves—Bhagwan Spends.*

* * *

Back in the Ashram, in late 1980 and early 1981, a palace coup was under way. Like so many of Sheela's undertakings, this happened below the surface of the Ashram's flourishing life, unseen and unknown to all but a few of her associates. While Laxmi was away, Sheela was visiting Osho daily to deal with Ashram business. But it was her own business that Sheela was furthering.

She informed Osho, during one such secretarial meeting, that people were unhappy with the way Laxmi was running the Ashram. She told him that many people wanted her to be in charge because of her more contemporary outlook. Osho asked her to verify her claim. Sheela then had a few primed heads of department sign letters of support for her.

Osho never told people what to do or what not to do. Unless, of course, they asked him. In this case, Osho went with the prevailing energy as it was presented to him. Thus it came about that, almost invisibly, Laxmi was superseded.

It wasn't that she hadn't been warned. In February of 1981 Laxmi, while on some mission in Mumbai, had visited Vatcha Villas with Sheela, her assistant. At the table after lunch there was talk of various sites for the new commune—Gujarat, the Himalayas, America. Laxmi was urging members of the family to commit themselves. 'We need meditators,' she said. 'We need His lovers.'

'No!' Sheela interrupted. 'We need workers.'

After the meal, Laxmi's sister Shobana told her loudly so that all could hear, '*Leki ben!* Your seat of power is slipping!'

Was Laxmi too complacent, or too naïve, or too trusting, or too fixed on her purpose to heed the warning?

* * *

This clandestine supersession happened in early 1981, when Osho's health was causing alarm for his carers, his doctors and for all his *sannyasins*. Twenty years of constant travelling the length and breadth of India was taking its toll on his body. In addition to severe back pain, his allergies were aggravated by the growing pollution of the city of Poona. His diabetes, however, was now under control.

A few days after Osho's Enlightenment Day celebration, both his morning discourse and evening *darshan* were cancelled because of an outbreak of chicken pox within the commune. It was announced the next morning, when *sannyasins* assembled for the eight o'clock meditation that Osho was entering into a period of silence and seclusion.

He was satisfied that he had found his people. 'What can be said in words I have said; what cannot be said I continue to transmit.'

With the deterioration of Osho's health, it was decided by Sheela and her current American-born husband, together with Osho's British doctor, that America, the land of the free and of opportunity, would be the place for him to have treatment and, if possible, become a home for the new commune. Thus Sheela would consolidate her power and distance Osho from Laxmi.

Osho himself was initially averse to such plans. However, such was Sheela's insistence and the seriousness of his physical health that he agreed to a short stay in New Jersey.

Laxmi, in the Himalayas or in Delhi or Gujarat or Bombay, following hopeful leads and waiting on empty promises, knew little of these stratagems. The few hints and clues that came her way she seemed to ignore. Sheela had quietly whittled away her position and her supports. Veetmoha was no longer her driver; Sheela's own stooge had replaced him. He reported back faithfully to her—as long as she held the power.

* * *

Laxmi was not a politician; she spoke and moved from intuition, thus she was a perfect channel for Osho's work both in the world of politics and in the commune itself. As he told his people one day 'Even if Laxmi is wrong and tells you to do something, do it as if it comes from me. Right or wrong—do it! To a master surrender is easy; to Laxmi it will require a bigger let-go, a bigger dispensation from you. So ceding yourself to Laxmi is an important step in the life of the commune and in your own development.'

Yatri remembered asking Osho if he should therapeutic group to deepen his self-awareness. 'No need,' was the answer. 'You have Laxmi.'

This concept and the possibility of Laxmi being right or wrong was a theme he referred to himself as well.

Enlightened ones are fallible, he told his people. I have said again and again, I am a fallible, ordinary man. And to be a disciple of a fallible, ordinary man is disturbing. But that simply shows your ego and its longing. You would like to make me a God, because then you become also God's disciple. Then there is a direct communication line between God and you.

Forgive me, I am not God, and there is no one who is; no one who has ever been. It is your psychology that has created the prophets, the messiahs and the avataras. They have fulfilled your desire. And naturally, it was good business: they became messiahs, and you became the special apostles of the messiah. Unless man drops this stupid psychology, it is very difficult to get rid of messiahs, prophets, great masters, because you are so insistent on being a great disciple. How can you be a great disciple if the master is fallible?

I am trying in every way to destroy your psychology, which has dominated humanity for centuries. It has made you almost unintelligent, but the balloon of your ego goes on becoming bigger and bigger. You, your individuality, your consciousness, go on diminishing in the same proportion.

What do you want? Should I say things which satisfy you? Or should I say things as they are, whether they satisfy you or hurt you? It is your responsibility, it is not my concern.

[Osho, *From the False to the Truth*, Ch. 15, Q. 1]

* * *

This period of the search for property, with Laxmi's long absences from Poona in Bombay, Gujarat and Delhi, had lasted for a year and a half.

Laxmi noted down:

The government of Himachal Pradesh had been keen to allot land to the Trust for an Ashram, as it would be a major foreign exchange earner for the state. A lobby of senior bureaucrats and politicians had shown special interest in the project. But, during this period, Osho's health took a turn for the worse, and it was decided that if the state government did not meet a certain deadline he would leave for the United States. The deadline passed and it became clear that a commune in the Himalayas was not going to be possible.

We see with hindsight that events had taken a somewhat more complex and sinister turn than Laxmi's writing suggests.

On 1 June 1981 Osho left for America.

* * *

Osho drove with his friends and helpers in convoy to the Bombay Airport. Laxmi in Delhi was forewarned by a friend and flew immediately to Bombay. According to her assistant Arup, and quoted by Max Brecher in *A Passage to America,* Osho, about to board the plane in the heat and roar of the airport, asked Laxmi to stay behind in India and continue negotiating for land near Shimla. 'As soon as he left, Laxmi got into some sort of panic. She was either concerned for *Bhagwan*'s health or afraid that Sheela was going to keep him in America. I don't know exactly what happened, but she dropped everything. She stopped dealing with the government, stopped negotiating on the land and followed him to America. Laxmi actually went against the request that *Bhagwan* had made of her.'

There are those who question this version of events. It seems probable that Laxmi was not at the airport but met Osho in the home of Manu and Hansa during the day prior to his evening flight. However the consensus is that Osho himself made it clear he was unwilling to stay in America. He wanted the new commune to flower in India. And finding the land was to be Laxmi's ongoing task.

* * *

The glory days of Poona One were over. Laxmi sat cross-legged on a mattress in a darkened room in Juhu near the Bombay airport. Around her were the sounds of trunks being slid across the floors, *sannyasin* migrants coming and going. To Laxmi's ears the sounds of disintegration.

In her head arose the harsh and brittle voices of self-doubt. She could sense and almost hear the spring of self-worth heart dry up, her every gene began to shrivel. It was like an infection. The alien germs of rejection, fear and anger invaded her mind. The turning world had juddered to a halt. All hopes and dreams, all strivings had been emptied out into a void. The Ashram soon would be abandoned, the Almond Tree a decomposing splinter in the memory. Laxmi was assailed by shame and ignominy. She felt crushed. A decade of devotion lay shattered on the cold marble floor at her feet.

What must she do? The future had faded away; the present moment had no foundation. Laxmi sat silently. For a long time, there was nothing; nothing but a strong ache in her belly. Her mind appeared as a carousel of sadness, anger, jealousy and fear, of what might have been and what was hoped for. 'This cannot be! This is some mistake. He has been deceived. He has been kidnapped. Laxmi needs to be available. Laxmi needs to pull herself together and take action.'

The door of her bedroom opened, a cleaner with bucket and mop came in, stood still and withdrew.

Laxmi slept. When she awoke the disparaging voices were softer. 'Laxmi has heard Osho say that it's easy to be spiritual when in power. The ego inflates with authority, it grows big on other's admiration. Laxmi thought she had advanced well down the spiritual way: how much of that was due to her status? Her being the mouthpiece of Osho? The test of someone free of ego comes when the spotlight falls elsewhere. Laxmi has to wait.'

For forty-eight hours, Laxmi stayed in her room. Sometimes she mined the memory of her father's early death, sometimes she saw the teenage Laxmi bullied by her schoolmates, sometimes she saw the brutal streets of Bombay brimming with the destitute. Pain consumed her being.

She slept, she sat and meditated. The fog of shock began to clear. With the first thin shaft of light at dawn one day, Laxmi found a clear decision had been made, 'See to Osho's safety and well-being. He told Laxmi to remain and find a property. That will have to wait. This pain is of a wounded ego. It is the work of the master to destroy the ego. Laxmi's work is his well-being.'

* * *

Osho lived to help humanity step back from ego; to clear away the mists of unconsciousness. Laxmi trusted this work. That is why she was with him. She had offered her Self to Osho. What was happening was painful, terrible. But it was necessary.

Over the following hours of meditation, between bouts of busyness, Laxmi reached deep into the midnight silence within until acceptance started to rise like the slowly waxing moon. 'Ha! *Ye sab unki leela hai*. This is the Master's play.'

Yet clearly this acceptance was not fully digested; it was not thorough-going. Laxmi would have to pass through more dark nights of the soul.

9. A NEW LAND—A NEW TRIAL

Within eleven days of Osho's departure, Laxmi was in New Jersey at the Castle, a Victorian folly rented by Sheela as an interim step to finding medical help for Osho and a site for the new commune.

Osho had asked Laxmi to continue with the Shimla negotiations, to prepare a base for his work in India. Why was Laxmi in New Jersey? Was not surrender to her master central to her life?

Laxmi was in painful disarray. The conflict in her being was this: her heart was saying treatment in America is what the master's body needs, Laxmi is released from many chores; the other half of her, her head, was saying; this is a betrayal; Osho has been hijacked, Laxmi has been swindled.

With the mismatch of these voices, she felt unbalanced, unsure of the ground beneath her feet. However, in some recess of a hidden cave there was trust. It would take time and meditation for that trust to reassert itself. In the world's most sacred traditions, surrender is a tried and tested path to self-realisation, to freedom. It is a beautiful word despite its modern overlay of giving up and abject defeat. Surrender is the ancient path of the *bhakti*, one who is ruled by the heart; in love with an enlightened one or an esoteric tradition. It is a method for disciples to merge with the master; to become a master themselves.

Laxmi repeated silently to herself, 'This is the Master's work, this is His gift for Laxmi's growth.'

* * *

Swami Jayapal, a native of New York wrote about this time for the online *Osho News*:

Laxmi got into her head that she could ingratiate herself with Osho by buying him yet another very expensive watch. Mind you Sheela was 'in' and Laxmi was 'out' by the time we arrived at the Castle. The competition was on!

Somehow Laxmi had squeezed financial commitments out of a few wealthy sannyasins to pay for this bauble. Off we go to Madison Avenue. Laxmi had on her wrist a very expensive Patek Philippe watch to demonstrate to jewellers that we were affluent and meant business. Being in New York with a twenty-thousand-dollar watch on her wrist was a magnet for some clever low-life so we made sure her sleeves covered the watch until we were in a shop.

We found a jeweller who had just what Laxmi wanted. All kinds of Rolex time pieces—some gold, some platinum, some with diamonds and sapphires surrounding the face, all for $30,000 or more. So Laxmi says to the store owner we would like to take a few of these watches back to New Jersey to show to the client. The obvious response was that if the client wished to see the watches he must come into the city. After heated negotiation, the owner allowed us to take the watches, along with an armed guard from the store, back to the Castle.

So, driving through Friday rush hour traffic with a very uncomfortable guy riding shotgun, off we go to New Jersey; and to make things even more bizarre, Laxmi insists we play the famous Osho 'fuck tape' for our unsuspecting pistol-packing friend. When we got to the Castle, Laxmi grabbed the watches and ran upstairs while the armed guard looked on—mouth open—having totally lost control.

The bottom line, as Laxmi told it: Osho asked which was the most expensive and ended up with platinum surrounded by diamonds. $35,000. And then we were off to New York to complete the transaction.

* * *

Some six years after the big switch, the writer Max Brecher interviewed Laxmi about the American exodus and her attitude towards Sheela. Were her feelings hurt? 'Look at the beauty and the grace that is showered on Laxmi. Jealousy has withered away. ['I don't believe this,' notes Max Brecher in the transcript.] Laxmi understands that we are living in a market place. When the mind is uppermost, all temptations are bound to happen. However if HIS work is happening beautifully...well that is the only life that Laxmi has now— Osho and His work. When friends ask Laxmi, aren't you hurt—don't you miss your high-back chair? Laxmi replies, 'The chair was a chair-less chair, a toy, a joke. When the play is over, Laxmi is still enjoying. This is what He wants of us; not to cling to power, not to be greedy, to accept life as it is and to enjoy.

'This is what He wants.' Laxmi has not said these things are happening of her volition, they are happening because Osho wants them and she is willing to pay the price. Enlightenment does not come cheap.

Osho was not happy to see Laxmi in America. Behind closed doors, Osho repeatedly asked her to return to search for a base for him in India. *Sannyasins* working in rooms nearby told of hearing her raised voice of refusal. Osho had no plans to stay long in America. He had even said in a discourse just a few months previously, that if he were to speak of his vision of the New Man and the New Woman in America they would kill him. As we shall see, Laxmi's refusal to return to the search drove Osho both deeper into the clutches of Sheela and into the fateful fulfilment of his prognosis.

* * *

From New Jersey, Laxmi was expelled to Oregon, to the newly purchased Big Muddy Ranch, ahead of Osho. Why the word expelled? Earlier she had entered, uninvited, the Castle press office where the new PR team were conversing with a few top American journalists. She had laughingly interrupted the *sannyasin*'s pitch of Osho's spiritual message for America, picked up a bundle of 100 ten-dollar notes, stripped off the wrapping and placed a bunch of notes in everyone's hands. The cameras flashed and clicked. No one else was laughing, least of all when the photos came out across the States. That incident had given Sheela the excuse to banish her from Osho's presence.

Laxmi arrived at the Ranch one blazing afternoon; 64,000 acres (26,000 hectares) of dry grass and Juniper trees, eroded and shrivelled creeks, a couple of clapped-out houses and one or two barns; a furnace in summer, freezing cold in winter. This semi-desert habitat was, for six months of the year a habitat of dust, for the other six months, mud.

During the early days that first summer on the Ranch, before Osho had arrived, Sheela would visit for short periods. She would convene and address regular meetings of the

growing number of working *sannyasins* there. In one such
meeting, she warned everyone against leaving the key in
their vehicle as Laxmi might take advantage and make off
with it. This instruction, designed to publicly humiliate
Laxmi, followed an incident to which many had been a
witness.

Meals were eaten, at that time, in and around the old
Ranch House. At lunchtime on this particular day, someone
had parked his massive D8 bulldozer, the size of a small
house, very close to the makeshift cafeteria. They had seen
the diminutive Laxmi climb up into the driver's seat and
attempt to start it up, laughing and calling out to bystanders.
A few people laughed but most were disturbed by this
behaviour. The driver and a few friends went to entice Laxmi
down because it seemed to most people she was behaving
with a manic recklessness. *Sannyasins* were accustomed to
her high energy and high spirits that had always seemed
appropriate in the days of her administrative supremacy.
Now, however, it seemed out of place; forced and dangerous.
At all events, someone must have passed the story on to
Sheela who used it to further subdue and isolate her.

* * *

The insight Laxmi had had at Nargol was crucial for her
emotional survival in the weeks that followed Osho's move
to America. It was not enlightenment but it did illuminate
her path. Repeatedly, in the ensuing months she told herself,
'Laxmi is not the body-mind. Laxmi is not separate from the
whole. There are no separate objects called Laxmi and Osho:
there is only subjectivity. This is part of the play.'

And indeed a new Laxmi was being born. This one had

short hair and wore jeans. She worked in the commune laundry or helped lay turf for instant lawns. This Laxmi explored new states of mind and new feelings. She was in turn downcast and cheerful, unsure and certain. 'Do not cling to anything. When one door closes another ten open,' she chanted to herself.

* * *

Osho, when at last he arrived at the Ranch, sent Ma Pragya to Laxmi's trailer with a message. 'Everything is good. Sheela is taking care, so you relax, meditate and drop all other things.'

Ma Sunshine was working as a guide and receptionist in the early autumn days.

I gave a tour to Laxmi once...[She] was not interested in the facts and figures about the size of the Ranch, the date we purchased it or anything like that. She was more interested in knowing who I was and whether I felt I was in integrity working as a 'Twinkie', tour guide and receptionist. I told her that I would rather have worked in the greenhouse, but considering the weather was so cold, I was happy to be driving around in a warm van and I enjoyed the company of both Veena and Isabel. Laxmi warned me that I should be wary of Sheela, that she was not honest. I told her that I didn't know Sheela well but that I trusted Isabel. Laxmi suggested that I stay vigilantly aware of my purpose for being on the Ranch so that I do not get involved in the politics. I thought that was good advice and often remembered the conversation whenever I felt that I needed to keep my behaviour in alignment with my values.

When I brought Laxmi back she was escorted to the parking lot even though she had hoped that she would get to see *Bhagwan*.

She was not welcome on the Ranch and she knew it. I found that quite uncomfortable but she seemed to accept it. I didn't really know her but I trusted her for some reason. Of course, after the tour, Sheela asked what she said to me and told me that she's very negative and that I should consider anything she might say as a cunning gesture to get back into power.

* * *

From September 1981 onwards, Laxmi was less visible to those working on the Ranch, overwhelmed as they were with the task of making space for the hundreds and thousands yet to come.

Osho now asked Sheela to give Laxmi special status despite her having over-ridden his earlier requests that she return to India. He told Sheela that there was no need for her to work in a place where people were working all hours of the day, that her meals would be cooked separately, that her laundry would be taken care of, her mobile home cleaned for her and that she would have a car when few cars were available. Osho also sent the message that Ma Anasha, a youngster from Italy, should be allocated to her trailer as home help. This request we construed as a token of his love for Laxmi. It also has the hallmark of a masterly device for the growth of both Sheela and Laxmi. They must co-exist without strife in the emerging new order.

Friends who visited Laxmi reported mixed findings. To Krishna Prem she appeared hurt, angry and negative, not wanting to be a part of this experiment. To Ma Madhuri she appeared as 'diminished, en-sorrowed, bowed and thin as if the loss of power really had showed that there was more work to be done'. Friends saw she wore the brave face of the ever-devoted disciple, yet she could not mask the underlying tenor of her discontent. In truth all these appearances merely reflect the process of hardship and growth through which Laxmi passed in this period. She was in the painful course of laying down an illusory ego. She was dying in order to be reborn.

And not just Laxmi. In those days of 1981 and early 1982 all the Poona One alpha males and females were being rapidly cut down to size by a rampant Sheela. Osho's self-appointed bodyguard was now driver of the 'shit-truck' emptying septic tanks, a work from which he soon found cause to jump ship and run off to write a self-justifying memoir commonly referred to as *The Guard that Failed*. DevaGeet, Osho's dentist, was on a crew shoring up and stabilising the mobile homes towed in for the growing population. Another friend went from running the farming to working in the kitchen washing pots.

'You relax, meditate and drop all other things,' Osho had said. But Laxmi is Laxmi. This simple message from her master was too difficult for her to process at that time. She would have to undergo more hits, more meditation, more transformation.

Sw Nishant was a CEO and member of the Indian Institute of Directors. He had helped Laxmi in Delhi at a press conference. In 1981, on his first visit to the Ranch, they both stayed in the same trailer.

'So Swamiji, welcome. You have come at the right time.'

Nishant bent to touch Laxmi's feet but was fended away.

'Why is this right time, Ma? What is happening?'

'Now is always the right time, Swami. And more than
ever the master's work needs willing hands and hearts.'

'That's true. One can see there is much work to be done
here.'

'Here is not the right place.'

'Oh, you mean...?'

'Laxmi is feeling this Big Muddy Ranch is not a right
place for Him. He has chosen to give America a chance, the
world's most powerful state...yet...His health. His work...'

'What?'

'Perhaps closer to the West Coast would be better than
this far away wasteland, closer to those who want to hear
Him. And the climate would be better for His body.'

'Has he asked you to find somewhere else?'

'His body is not happy here.'

'Are you being too protective, too worried?'

'Laxmi knows very well the condition of the master's
body. It has been her concern for many years. Laxmi wants
to find another place near Ashland.'

'But Laxmi, you are always telling us to listen to the
master, to surrender to his word. And if he is here on the
Ranch why would I go to Ashland?'

'We will buy a property more suitable. His body is not
strong. Laxmi knows. When everything is ready, He will
come.'

'Has he asked you to find land?'

'Swamiji, a master is unfathomable and in worldly ways
the master is not well acquainted.'

'Laxmi ma. With the eyes of my heart I see you are not
on a power trip. I see you want what is best for him and
his work. But...'

'Sometimes a disciple has to follow their gut.'

'We heard he has told you to relax, to enjoy, to meditate...'

'Laxmi must follow her gut and her heart.'

* * *

The following account by Veetmoha, Laxmi's former driver, is significant:

'...[S]ometime in February 1982, when I had been at the Ranch about six months, I got an invitation to visit Laxmi at her trailer home half a mile up the canyon from downtown Rajneeshpuram.

'...I walked up to Laxmi's trailer and knocked on the door. "Come in, Swamiji! Hello, how are things?" Her beaming smile and bird-like gestures welcomed me in. She indicated towards the chair. "Come, sit down." Someone had given her a bottle of Amaretto, and she asked me if I would like some. "This is America!"

'When it came to the sins of the flesh, Laxmi had a familiar response, especially if others were present who might be surprised that a *sannyasin* in the traditional orange colour of renunciation should be drinking: "Osho celebrates everything!" she reminded me. I must say though, I never saw her pay anything but lip service—literally—to alcohol. There had been no alcohol in the Poona Ashram till the final days. Readers will remember, however, that her father would often sit after work with a drink and play with the children.

'Scattered on the bed where Laxmi was sitting were some glossy brochures with photos of cars—and, I could see at a glance, not just cars, but Mercedes.

'Laxmi told me she had recently spent some time with Osho, and he had approved of her idea to travel round the

States visiting all the places where *sannyasins* gathered in meditation centres and communities. It would be a goodwill tour, reassuring Osho's people that all is well, that their centres are recognised, encouraging them to visit Rajneeshpuram and—and this is the crucial point—letting them know that Osho himself would soon be travelling to visit them! Then Laxmi asked if I wanted to be her driver and join her on her grand tour—in a new Mercedes 300D. Heaven multiplied! Of course! "Laxmi thinks this dark green one is very beautiful, no?" "Oh yes, Ma, yes!" Laxmi did love cars.

'So Osho seduced me with a Land Rover; Laxmi seduced me with a Mercedes. I was happy to be offered such bribes, though they must have known that neither was necessary. Why did they do it? Just out of love.

'Of course the critical thing I have not said here is that I thought of Rajneeshpuram as Sheela's creation, a creation whose creator I trusted less and less as time went by. When I first saw photos of the "Big Muddy"...my heart sank. This was the outcome of all those years of searching! A dry creek bed winding through the barren sagebrush with a few dilapidated barns! This was the coup that Sheela had made! And I was to commit myself to it and throw myself into it?

'Now all that would change. Now there would be a network of communities, recognising Rajneeshpuram as the home city—the capital and source of energy if you like—and the place to visit for gatherings and celebrations, but each relatively independent and free to develop its own lifestyle and means of support. The fact that Osho had approved this idea, and had imagined a time in which he would travel to his centres throughout the States and around the world, took the future of *sannyas* in a whole new direction, one which I was totally enthusiastic about. After six months at Rajneeshpuram—the Big Muddy Ranch—I had lost all hope that the city that was rising in the desert of eastern Oregon could become the Shangri-La that I had driven all those hundreds of miles around India to find.

'A few days later I was sitting having dinner in the cafeteria with my rationed glass of draft Henry Weinhard beer, when Sheela appeared. She came up to me. "Veetmoha, do you want to be Laxmi's driver?" That's all she said. "Yes!" is all I replied. Sheela turned and walked away. Of course I thought that I had set in motion a series of events which would end with me driving away up the Big Muddy road in a green Mercedes with Laxmi on the back seat—the waves and goodbyes and bon voyages of well-wishers still echoing around us. How naïve I was.

'A day or two later I was called into the office that handled people's visas—upstairs in the warehouse. There I was told that, as I was no longer supporting what was happening on the Ranch, the Ranch would no longer support my continuing presence. As the first extension of my original six-month tourist visa was due to expire at the end of March, that day therefore would have to be the last date of my stay in the United States.'

* * *

Keerti would often make the trek out to Laxmi's trailer after work, just to spend an hour or two with her. One day she said to him, 'What is this Hitler business? This censoring of everything?'

'What do you mean?'

'Those letters that Laxmi gave you last week to post in Antelope, did you post? Did you inform Sheela?'

'What? Yes. No. I posted them. I didn't say anything to Sheela.'

'So how does Sheela know?' Laxmi suddenly put both hands to her head. After a few moments she lowered them slowly and lowering her voice she said, 'This is not a safe place for the master. Laxmi will find him a place elsewhere. In Ashland perhaps.'

A few days later Laxmi told him, 'Laxmi received another Zen stick from the master. He said, you and Sheela are my two hands. If one hand fights the other, how will the work get done? So Laxmi drops the Ashland scheme. He also said that Laxmi should retire. But Laxmi can never retire.'

Keerti said he thought it was hard for her to adjust to letting others care for Osho after ten years doing that herself.

* * *

One day in March, not long after the conversation with Veetmoha, Laxmi received a message that Sheela wanted to speak with her—immediately. She put on her boots, her commune-issue too big boots, her scarlet down-jacket and pulled a red woolly cap over her now short hair. She trudged the muddy road with her head bent into the icy rain. She was feeling both dread and relief. What is this dread? she asked herself. What is the worst that can happen? That Sheela wants to pick a fight with one? That she'll send one to the Pot Room in the kitchens? That Laxmi will be told to leave this place? The worst that can happen is not bad. The master is running this show. Let's see what new events will unfold for Laxmi.

Laxmi waited barefoot in an ante-room for fifteen

minutes before being called into a spacious office. Here was Sheela reclining on a sofa; around her were six or eight of her aides, all Westerners, seated in chairs or lounging on the carpeted floor with files or clipboards. No one offered her a seat.

'You have to leave the country when the visa expires,' said Sheela. 'Or find a way.'

Laxmi, still standing by the door, was knocked in the shoulder when someone closed it behind her. The bluntness, the coldness felt like blows to the belly. And the dead-eye stares of those who had been her assistants. A silence stretched out. Laxmi considered the words 'or find a way'.

'Marriage is out of the question,' she said, and the sound of her own voice gave her impetus. 'Sheela, is it not possible to address the subject of visas and residency in the States in a more intelligent way? Laxmi suggests we frame proposals for the immigration people that would allow not just Laxmi but the thousands of people who love Osho to come here. That is, if the plan is to remain here permanently.'

Blank silence filled the room.

Laxmi turned to the woman in charge of accounts, with whom she had previously worked long and fruitfully in the Ashram. 'Laxmi has no funds.'

The accountant looked at Sheela a moment then back at Laxmi. 'You have to take care of yourself.' Laxmi was dismissed.

The next morning she hitched a ride in a commune van that was travelling the fifty miles to a small airport in Bend. She kept silent on the long drive as the pale brown landscape streamed past her. The worst that could happen had happened. She was an outcast. Utterly alone. Now she must align herself with a completely new set of realities.

any times had she had heard the master say, 'Do not cling to anything'? Two voices in her head were arguing on that cold bright drive through semi-desert Oregon. One voice told her meditation grows with challenges, the other said, 'this is wrong. Laxmi knows what's right for Osho; she should be in charge.'

She remembered Osho's words:

Meditation is the art of transforming loneliness into aloneness. [...] Great courage is needed for this transformation. [...] This is the work of every sannyasin, to go into your aloneness. There is no need to go into a monastery or the Himalayas. Live in the world and yet work silently to create the space where the world disappears, where one becomes profoundly silent. Out of that silence love arises. [...] Meditation alone is not enough, nor is love; both are two aspects of the same coin and for both, courage is needed. But the basis is meditation. Begin with meditation and end in love. That is the whole journey of sannyas.

After two bumpy hours on traffic-free roads, the van slowed down in a built up zone. With a hesitant voice, Laxmi asked the driver, 'Would you lend Laxmi two dollars for a telephone call?'

'Oh Laxmi! Of course. Lend? I'll give. We never see you very much but this place won't be the same without you.'

Ma Chetna, an old friend from Poona, was living in Ashland. She arranged a ticket over the phone while Laxmi waited at the bleak, windswept airport.

Deep in Laxmi's psyche was a doubt, a regret. By leaving India she had delivered Osho into Sheela's clutches. This sentiment she would have to live with.

10. INTO THE WILDERNESS

For the next three months Laxmi was an illegal immigrant, moving through the giant mall of America, learning its ways and at the same time deepening her meditation so that understanding and love might prevail.

Laxmi knew, had always known, that her journey was not just her own journey but everyone's. No one wants to live in suffering and separation; all aspire to love and peace. We are on a path of restoration whether we know it or not.

Towards the end of the last century, it was becoming increasingly clear that we humans were both inheriting and passing on a frightful liability; dysfunctional institutions, decaying cultures, broken traditions and a ravaged earth. Laxmi, in her distress understood the necessity of humanity's transition from the old-carbon era mentality to the New Man and Woman. Through meditation she was beginning to sense the unity of all things, that we are not separate from this living organism, planet earth, the living Gaia. This is what her master lived and spoke about—this is what she drank from him. The needed revolution is individual. He pointed Laxmi to herself. She was the one she was looking for.

Was she relieved to quit the Ranch, to head out into an America so much at variance to what she held precious?

Were there regrets in Laxmi's mind at leaving a commune to which she had contributed so much? Would the memories of her childhood rejection after smallpox be reshaped? How would the secular life impact her Indian religious conditioning?

Laxmi had courage. Everything was possible.

* * *

Shortly after Laxmi's exodus from the Ranch, Sheela sent out a directive to all Osho Meditation Centres proscribing any contact with Laxmi, saying '...a door closed in her face is precisely what is needed for her growth. No one should therefore interfere with Laxmi's process.'

But Laxmi would be surrounded by *sannyasins*, despite this boycott, for the rest of her life. Leaving the physical presence of the master was a difficulty to which she had been schooled over the previous years and leaving altogether the *sangham*, the community of the master, was not going to be an issue. Laxmi is a 'real' disciple, a heart disciple. Heart disciples listen to the deep, soft murmurs of their heart. They follow the sunken road to that hidden chamber of love. A heart disciple such as Laxmi might even disobey the master if that was what true love demanded.

What is a false or 'professional' disciple? One who follows the rules as they are perceived. Be obedient! Be loyal! Be holy! Be celebrative! They are acting from outside dictates, not from their inner consciousness. In this way they avoid being responsible for themselves; 'we are only following orders.'

Laxmi, when the still small voice within was talking,

had to listen. This was to become a monstrous issue when Osho's health was at stake.

* * *

From the hothouse of the commune, Laxmi launched herself into that lonely league of foreigners who come to struggle with the aspect of American mind's inherent dog-eat-dog philosophy, with racism and xenophobia.

She stayed for four weeks in Oregon, then moved on to Washington DC. After some months there, she travelled to New England. Swami Atul, on his way to Oregon, often visited her till she returned to India. 'She was never the dethroned queen. Every happening was an opportunity for her growth. It seemed to me she saw herself as just a player in Osho's great theatre. Sitting at his side in *darshan* or arguing with a hostile reporter or being excluded from his commune, she was just a player in His play.' Atul said what impressed him was: 'There was no change in her behaviour from when I first met her ten years before as Osho's receptionist in Woodlands. Now in exile in America she was as upbeat and enthusiastic as ever.'

That is not to say she was never sad or worried. 'She foresaw the problems,' Atul continued, 'that would ensue from Sheela's short-term strategies and subterfuges, just as she foresaw the waste of pouring so much energy into a semi-desert expanse of the American West. She told me, "Coming to that place was a big mistake."'

* * *

Laxmi did not worry about her survival. She had no money but she had a large deposit of trust. Earning her living in the concrete jungle, she knew, would be precarious business. She stayed with various friends in New England, moving from place to place.

It was finally in Albany that the Immigration and Naturalization Service (INS) caught up with her. It happened like this. Ma Chetna, in Ashland Oregon, called Laxmi to ask whether she would be coming to the Ranch for the First Annual World Celebration in July. For some time they discussed the impossibility of that because the commune insisted all visitors should have valid US visas. They concluded the talk with pleasantries and messages for friends. Hardly had Laxmi's phone been replaced in its cradle when it rang again (These words below are Laxmi's own words recorded by Max Brecher while researching for his book *A Passage to America*.)

Laxmi: 'A voice said, "May I speak to Ma Yoga Laxmi please?" "Yes. You are speaking to Laxmi." So the voice said, "Oh! This is INS, Mr Casey from Portland. You know we know who you are, and that you are not coming for the festival." Laxmi said, "Well, one cannot come to the festival because one doesn't have a visa." He said, "As a special case, if you want to attend, we can give you a visa." Laxmi said, "Great!" Casey said, "Okay, when you book your ticket, you give us your flight number and we'll be there to meet you. Don't tell anyone about this. We will issue you a visa as a special case."

'Laxmi put the receiver down and immediately called Chetna, "You'll be surprised! But don't ask! Can you book a ticket for Laxmi?" It never occurred to Laxmi at this stage that the phones had been tapped. She never thought that they would be particularly interested in Laxmi.

'Chetna sent a ticket. And then Laxmi phoned the number that Mr Casey had given—and babbled everything to them. Three people were waiting at the airport. One of them asked, "Are you Ma Yoga Laxmi? Please give me your passport. Don't worry about your luggage. It will be taken care of. Please come with us." They took Laxmi out through a side door saying, "We don't want other *sannyasins* to know how you receive your visa."

'They took Laxmi to a Holiday Inn. And they booked the suite in some made-up name. Then Laxmi became worried. "Hey, wait a minute. Laxmi hasn't got money." "You come up. Then you will see." Then Laxmi said, "Look friends, what's going on? Why are you treating me like this?' They said, "We have heard so much about you, and we are your friends. And you just relax. Would you like to have some drink, some food? Whatever you want, you just order."'

[Brecher interrupted her here.]

Brecher: 'From where were they getting information about you? I think, from a woman named Deeksha, who had been in charge of catering in Poona One, right?'

Laxmi: 'No, no. Deeksha was not like that.'

Brecher: 'She gave a lot of information to the US Government. I have read the affidavits.'

Laxmi: 'Perhaps afterwards.'

Brecher: 'Then you tell me. Explain to me.'

Laxmi: 'Deeksha helped Laxmi to survive in America. We were very connected. There was a circular put out by Sheela that Deeksha and Laxmi are trying to create an alternative commune. That circular made Deeksha very angry. And she came to Laxmi and said, "What is this? We are so naïve. Why don't you speak out! Look, nobody supports you, and you are just going on about Him, Him, Him!"

'So Laxmi said, "Deeksha. First thing: are we starting a separate commune?" She said, "No." Then Laxmi said, "Thank you. Then, why are you getting so angry? These circulars are bullshit. Throw them into the bin."'

Brecher: 'What I'm asking, though, if it's not coming from Deeksha, then who is it coming from? Who is giving information from the inside to the US Government already, early in 1981 and 1982? Who's doing it?'

Laxmi: 'As far as Laxmi can tell you, it was a game of Sheela and her party to get rid of Deeksha.'

Brecher: 'To get rid of Deeksha? Explain this to me.'

Laxmi: 'In the Castle Laxmi saw that Deeksha and Sheela were not getting on together. When this Ranch land was being purchased Deeksha was against it. She was saying, "There are no trees. The land is barren. It is muddy. Please, you don't go after it." Sheela's brother Bipin was the one insisting on the Ranch. There was a difference of opinion. So Sheela became very much aware that Deeksha was another person who could be a thorn in the side. In the end, Deeksha got fed up. She told Laxmi in anger, "I hate all this stuff. I don't care if the INS do know everything." It was in 1983 that she talked to the INS I think. That's when *sannyasins* were turning their faces from us. Laxmi used to tell Deeksha, "Don't blame them. See rather that they are helping us to look within. Be aware where this anger is coming from. If ego is there, then anger will come. We should be intelligent enough to use the situation as a challenge to see what is behind the anger." Later on she became much too aggressive. Laxmi had to say, "Deeksha, we will remain as friends. You have taken beautiful care of Laxmi's body. But now it seems that existence is indicating our paths separate."'

Brecher: 'Okay. So let's go back. Back to the Holiday Inn. Mr Casey was saying, "What would you like to drink?" and was very cordial.'

Laxmi: 'Laxmi said, "Look. Get on with it. Do whatever formalities have to be done. Laxmi needs to catch the bus and go to the Ranch. Why don't you get to the business?" Mr Casey said, "Okay. If you want it that way, then as a friend, I want to tell you that I am the INS officer. I have the power to give the visa." So Laxmi said, "Well in that case, can Laxmi ask you a question?" And he said, "Yes, most welcome." So Laxmi said, "What is the status of *Bhagwan* Shree Rajneesh?" He said, "This country is not ready for him. No matter that you people may go to the Supreme Court; America will not allow him to be in this country. And secondly, this is not my decision. This is the decision coming from higher-up. I'm just a servant. I read his books. I respect certain parts. But I can tell you one thing, that he is a very intelligent, genius man."'

Brecher: 'Did he say anything about who those higher-up might be?'

Laxmi: 'Yeah. Laxmi asked, "Is it the President?" And he said, "My lips are sealed." He actually said that to Laxmi.'

Brecher: 'Was he really being authentic?'

Laxmi: 'Laxmi felt so. He was, considering the circumstances, very open with Laxmi. He said, "I can tell you, you are an innocent woman, and that's why I respect you. But I have to do my job. If you cooperate with me, I will see that nothing goes wrong for you. But if you don't cooperate, then...I don't know." So Laxmi said, "But what cooperation do you want?" He said, "There are a few questions. The first question is how much is *Bhagwan*

Shree Rajneesh involved in the activities of the institution?" Laxmi said, "You are asking the wrong question. Laxmi is neither on the Ranch nor in any way connected with the administration. How can one answer this question? But because you have put this question, Laxmi feels to say, don't miss the fragrance of this beautiful flower." He said, "Okay. Forget it. What about the money? Where is the money coming from?" Laxmi just laughed [and then said], "Laxmi, in Poona would have answered that. Again you are asking a wrong question to a wrong person. Unless one is involved in the administrative side, how can you expect one to know from where the money is coming? As far as Poona was concerned, the money was coming from books, from tapes, from videos. And from entry fees at the gate. So much creative work was happening; we were creating cosmetics, pottery, weaving, restaurants, photography, a boutique: all that money was coming in." So he said, "Well, what about the marriages? What you have to say about the marriages?" Laxmi said, "Again you are asking the wrong person. Laxmi's not married." "No, no, no, no," he said. "We are talking about other people marrying for visa." Laxmi said, "If it is the question of a visa, don't you think that Laxmi would have been married already? Why should one come to you?" Casey then smiled. He said, "Well, you are very shrewd." And Laxmi said, "It is not shrewdness. It is the response that is spontaneously happening to you." He said, "But we have heard they are getting married for the visa." "If you have heard that, then you go to the Ranch, and find out from Ma Sheela. Because you are asking the wrong person. Laxmi is no more on the Ranch, no more in the administration." "Well, if you don't cooperate, then we have to be strict."

Laxmi responded, "If that is the case, then Laxmi has the right to call for a lawyer." "Why do you want to waste your money on lawyers? Why don't you cooperate?" "What is there to cooperate about? These questions cannot be answered by Laxmi. And if Laxmi gives answers you expect, they will not be the facts. They will just be lies." "Well, in that case, if you want the lawyer, which lawyer would you like to have?"

'Laxmi had heard the name of a lawyer through a friend who had wanted some legal advice. So Laxmi said, "Mr Robinson." And Mr Casey himself dialled. And he asked for Mr Robinson, and gave the phone to Laxmi. And Laxmi said, "Please, Mr Robinson, if you can spare some time, and come to Holiday Inn, one needs your help." And he said, "Who are you?" Laxmi said, "Ma Yoga Laxmi." So he said, "Okay, I'll be there." And within maybe ten, fifteen, minutes he was there.

[That's an unbelievably quick response time. MB]

'As soon as he entered, all the three people saw him, their faces changed. They were curt. They were strict.'

Brecher: 'With you?'

Laxmi: 'Oh yes. With Laxmi and with the lawyer. Mr Robinson said, "What can I do for you?" And Laxmi said, "Here are the friends. Now they have asked certain questions to which Laxmi does not know the answers. She has said what she knows. But they are still insisting. So please explain to them?" So Mr Robinson turned to Mr Casey...'

Brecher: 'Are you sure it was Mr Robinson that you were talking to? What I mean is, I wonder whether it was somebody working for them who they were passing off as Robinson.'

Laxmi: 'Laxmi had not seen him before.'

Brecher: 'It could have been one of their people.'

Laxmi: 'Perhaps. Who can say now? But this man turned to Mr Casey, and he said, "Well, what do you want to know from my client, and how will she benefit?" [*This is practically a smoking gun for my supposition. MB*] So they said, "If she answers the questions, she will be given immunity. And not only that, she will regain her former power. Because we want Sheela Silverman to be…you know…to be taken." They said, "We want to prove Sheela Silverman has done something wrong in the institution." The lawyer said, "Well, I'm meeting my client for the first time, so I cannot say right now whether she has the answers." Then Casey said, "But we can't afford to keep this suite for much longer. You have to expedite things." Mr Robinson replied, "Perhaps tomorrow by four o'clock." "But suppose she doesn't cooperate?" said Mr Casey and he took out a document from his pocket and showed it to the lawyer. He read it and returned it. "Tomorrow by 4 o'clock we can meet here."

They said, "Okay, fine." And they left.

Then Mr Robinson said to Laxmi, "I can tell from looking at your face that you are not going to cooperate in any way. If you don't cooperate you are in trouble because they will put you to jail. They have the summons and perhaps you may not be able to see the sunshine again. And if you do cooperate, then also there will be trouble for you. My suggestion is that you better escape." [*So they could tail her and see what other criminal activity they could discover? MB*] "Meanwhile, Chetna had come to the airport and was searching all over for Laxmi. And then—this is very surprising—she met Mr Casey. And Mr Casey told her, "Laxmi is in the Holiday Inn." [*How is any of this possible? Chetna would have arrived to meet Laxmi at the airport early. So when was she supposed to meet Casey, who left immediately with Laxmi? MB]*

Brecher: 'She met him by accident?'

Laxmi: 'Yeah. Or what may have happened, Casey knew who Chetna was...'

Brecher: 'He definitely knew who she was if he's tapping her phone.'

Laxmi: 'So that was how he gave her the hotel address. So Chetna came running to the hotel. The lawyer said, "Great that your friend has come. Here's the plan. Let her check in just below your suite. Take your suitcase, remove the tag and replace with her tag. I will walk you out. After two hours, she can come with your luggage and her luggage. The suite key, she just casually drops in the box." [*Who is paying this 'lawyer'? And why is he over-eager to participate in criminal activities for the sake of someone he has just met? MB]*

Laxmi: 'So everything was figured out. We agreed to meet outside the hotel. Then the lawyer told Chetna, "Don't take her to Portland, she will be caught. Look, my hands are tied! But in New York, there are lawyers who will perhaps be very helpful. And your case can go through them. But not through me. I can help you up to this point only. Don't loiter at the airports. You just stay in the toilet, come out, and take the plane."'

The recorded interview ends abruptly here.

* * *

Casey called Laxmi shrewd. Wrong word. Laxmi was right to contradict him. She was truthful, speaking from the heart. She was also somewhat naïve. Casey was professionally devious, attempting to entrap an easy prey. She wanted a visa, a green card, access to her master. But Laxmi's simplicity outwitted him. In retrospect, she admitted to her foolish thoughts of surrender. It was ingenuous of her to be sitting so comfortably with a man whose job required duplicity. Laxmi stayed with her own plain truth. It was a bizarre story with an unaccountable outcome: Laxmi escaped.

During the Poona One days when the Ashram was participating in a crafts fair at the Mumbai *Maidan,* it became clear that certain of the organisers were on some sort of fiddle. Laxmi would have none of it. She pulled out. 'We will not lower ourselves. We will not blemish our integrity, she told her staff.' In that office Laxmi was often heard directing workers that she would never allow the payment of one paisa of *baksheesh,* or bribery—this in a country where bribery is the very lubricant that makes anything happen.

* * *

Veetmoha saw Laxmi in Woodstock, New York, at this time. He wrote:

'I was in London towards the end of that year, 1982, and received a letter from Laxmi suggesting I come to Woodstock and help her write her autobiography. She had a tape recorder and had recorded many hours of memories and stories, which were in the process of being transcribed by a local friend...

'...Laxmi was beginning to adopt some aspects of the American lifestyle, though it would be a few months and the arrival of summer before she launched her curb-side lunch wagon selling home-made samosas on the streets of Woodstock. I remember her reaction to her first few months as a free spirit in the market place that is the United States of America: "It is really something what this country has achieved in such a short time—just two hundred years. And India! Thousands of years, and we still can't make a toilet that flushes!"

'Laxmi had a publisher for her book. One of the Ashram photographers knew the publisher of *Aperture*, the fine art photography magazine whose headquarters was not so far from Woodstock. In addition to the magazine, *Aperture* also published a variety of books in which the quality of the printed image was primary. The publisher had visited the Poona Ashram a few years before and met Laxmi, and seen the quality of the photographs taken in Poona, and was willing to take on a book of her story using them as illustrations. The key would be getting the photos from the Ranch...

'...A few weeks into Laxmi's editing work, I ran out of money and began to feel the need for income. It was then that I had my one and only argument with Laxmi—and indeed saw Laxmi really angry. I have never been good at being straight with money matters, and had jumped at the opportunity to work with Laxmi on her book without promise or even hope of financial reward. But there must have been some expectation that Laxmi would find some way to support me, or find a place for me to live. Just like it had been in India. I knew she had no money herself, but expected that she might have been able to get an advance on the book, and that some of that could be sent my way. That was not the case.

'I got upset with her. Laxmi shouted back at me and swore there was never any arrangement, and that I had come freely to help her, and that I had no right to expect payment, and that I should leave and she will find someone else. That was something totally new and unexpected; the sign of a change, even a maturity in my relationship with her. I would never have challenged her in the Ashram years. There was nothing to complain about.

'As the weeks went by nothing was heard from the Ranch about the photos. It became clear that Sheela was not going to let Laxmi use them. That meant no book—at least no book to be published by *Aperture*.

'I left Woodstock at the end of March and went to live in Massachusetts, and never saw Laxmi again.'

* * *

In the 1980s Osho's *sannyasins* everywhere were embracing his maxim to be *in* the world but not *of* it; to live the worldly and the spiritual life combined. Anyone can attain to silence by sitting in a Himalayan cave or a monk's cell for twenty years, but what happens when they come down to the market place and someone treads on their toe? Where is their silence then?

Osho himself personified this ability to live in both the outer and inner worlds. He named this mode of being Zorba the Buddha. Zorba is one who delights in the material world with all its beauty and its perils, its joys and its disappointments. Buddha, on the other hand, is one who explores and honours the silent universe within, the transcendent, non-dual world of spirit. Zorba the Buddha is the New Man, the New Woman, humanity's hope for the planet's future. Zorba the Buddha is one of Osho's great, life-changing gifts to humanity, along with Dynamic Meditation and the powerful meditative therapy called The Mystic Rose as described in the Appendix. For many, Laxmi running the complexities of the Poona One Ashram, was a shining example of this intent—worldly wise and deeply meditative.

In many cities of the developed world a new phenomenon arose in the form of a restaurant or a discotheque or a hotel or a café called Zorba the Buddha. The milieu was one of simple excellence, be it in food and drink or dance and music. It was usually smoke-free twenty years before that became a norm. It was wholesome, celebratory and an elegant environment. In Germany alone, where there were well over 50,000 *sannyasins*, there were Zorbas in most big cities. They netted for themselves, and to support the Ranch, an estimated eight million dollars a year.

* * *

Wherever Laxmi was, she had no shortage of friends, despite the prohibitions of Sheela. In Albany, 150 miles north of New York City, a group of them put together enough money to help Laxmi's re-entry into the world of Zorba. They purchased and fitted out for her a van to be a mobile kitchen and *chai* shop offering the glories of Indian street food: *pakoras, samosas, chat, dahi bhalla, papri, idli*. And, of course, *chai*. And Earl Grey and herbal teas. Laxmi would be sole proprietor and staff member of Leela Catering.

People who saw her at this time describe her as always happy in her red outfit with its red apron, always cooking as though for her master, as though selling his produce. She was no longer Osho's administrator but her usual upbeat, often wacky, behaviour was unchanged. 'Laxmi can find other ways of doing Osho's work,' she said. 'Isn't celebrating everything in life HIS work? Isn't adding love to every snack and every cup of *chai* HIS work?'

She had by now largely come to terms with her loss of position. Power had never been her goal. When she had it, she had never abused it. Her goal was always Osho's vision; his health and well-being. She had lost the position and now, with the passing of time and the deepening of her daily meditation, reconciliation was arising.

She knew she had to work on herself. That prospect, though daunting, excited her. At weekends she would host lively meetings and meditations. Ma Mamta remembers, 'Her first thing was to make *chai masala*, spiced tea, for everyone. When she served it, it had a different taste. Her aim was to make you feel so welcome and relaxed that you would automatically be open to participate in things. She was wonderful with children; she included them, made them paper toys. After the *satsang*—literally a meeting to experience truth—she would cook. Then the stories and discussions till late into the night. The talk was never about politics or movies or other people, it was always about Osho and our inner journeys. She never spoke against Sheela—at most, she might say that Osho's work would not prosper in the current situation. She pointed out to all that losing her job as Osho's secretary was his gift for her internal growth.'

In Woodstock, an hour's drive from Albany, she told Swami Prabhat she felt some internal block had shifted, that she never felt any sadness and was always in bliss. He said that when Laxmi left the States he asked her if he could have her mattress. Thirty years later, he still sleeps on it.

Laxmi was never the *guru* or even a mini-*guru*, always just a finger pointing to the moon. Laxmi understood that no purpose would be served by claiming priestess sta other than to nourish the very ego that she was with Osho to eliminate. 'Laxmi needs no recognition; she's just a body and a mind who was lucky to meet a rare and beautiful being.'

Osho often forewarned his people of the potential rise of the priest in all of us. The position confers power to the few and keeps the many dependant. In the East especially, priests are honoured above and beyond their, as a rule, worthless worth. Laxmi saw that tendency and steered clear of it. 'Laxmi finds that those who seek truth are much preferable to those who think they've found it,' she commented.

Skilled though Laxmi was in the ways of commerce, New England was not ready, back then in the eighties, for such foreign products as Ma Laxmi; her meals on wheels and her *guru*. The project broke even; no one lost money and in 1984, after a year, Laxmi sold and left the East Coast together with her good friend and long-time supporter Ma Mamta. They headed back to Washington DC.

On one of Atul's visit that year, Laxmi took him to see a couple of properties near Washington that were large enough to house the commune and were available for sale. Did Laxmi really think that such a move was then likely or even possible?

* * *

In the spring of 1984 Laxmi decided to fast in silence for fifteen days. She spent most of the time in her room, seated cross-legged on her bed. Sometimes her mind would be silent and she would occupy the open sky within, free of thoughts, free of the past and future. Then ineffable peace descended on her. At other times her thoughts would flare up like wildfire and she had to leave the house to walk the green grid of suburban streets. 'There's so much of the master's teaching that Laxmi hasn't yet digested. He's sent one out into the world...and yet one has not settled, not met it fair and square. Why are there no people in these streets! Streets wide enough for six cars abreast and only one passes every hour. There aren't even any dogs! And where are all the kids? Why aren't they shouting and climbing in these leafy trees? And why did that Sheela purchase such a treeless desert when Osho so loves trees?' A stab of pain passed through her body. 'Ah, Laxmi's mind is active yet. It longs for HIS silent presence. That crazy radiant master of mine; he baffles many, but so many more he helps on their way.'

Laxmi walked and walked in the torpid hinterlands of Washington suburbia. 'This world! What does Laxmi have to do with it? HE walks beside me, even though we are a thousand miles apart. This all-over-consciousness of which Laxmi has a tiny inkling, is who HE is. Laxmi needs to keep returning to the heart. It does get easier and easier. The pain passes. All is as it should be.'

With the dimming of the day, when the vacant streets were briefly vitalised by workers coming home and settling to their suppers and the oscillating light of Soaps, Laxmi turned her footsteps home. Silently she helped prepare a meal with Mamta then retired to sit in silence and finally to sleep.

After the fast, friends from India stopped by to see her on their way to Rajneeshpuram. Ma Shashin, a new young *sannyasin* at the time, described the lasting impression Laxmi made upon her. 'She was so soft-spoken, light and spontaneous. One time we sat for a couple of hour-long meditations with her, followed by a meal she cooked. Then we all bombarded her with questions about Osho and his vision. She loved these occasions. Osho was the permanent centre of her life. I admired how she gave her full attention to whoever was asking the question and at the same time seemed to be aware of whatever else was going on in the room.

'I remember someone asked her, "How often do you meditate? How often should we meditate?" Laxmi smiled then and sat back in her chair saying, "Laxmi goes deeper with her eyes closed for an hour than ever she does with them open. On top of that Laxmi has come to understand that meditation is not something she has to do once or twice a day, but something that emerges from one. Meditation is now happening in the supermarket and the bus station and walking through the neighbourhood. Laxmi sits to meditate each day but the whole point is that meditation comes to be one's state of being. Meditation becomes one."'

* * *

All was not well with the body of Laxmi, the body she ever reminded herself that she was not. To begin with, she suffered in silence. The problem was somewhere in her belly. Strong pains. She decided to reduce her input of foods and liquids.

Mamta had trained as a nurse. One day she questioned Laxmi closely about the pain. That very evening she took her to a local Catholic hospital and they admitted her straightaway.

* * *

Laxmi sat against the pillows. They were to operate the next day. The nurses had tidied her up and left. Mamta had driven off home. The pain was intense. So this is how Laxmi will die. Cancer! A malignant growth! Laxmi alone, alone in a foreign hospital! *Bhagwan!*

She looked round the room. Her eyes took in the pale gloss walls, the slatted blinds across the window, the dark veneer-wood furniture, the shiny white-tiled floor. And the cuckoo clock. She stared at the cuckoo clock, watched its pendulum swing. Back and forth, back and forth. Tick tock tick tock. The pain was intense and pervasive. Laxmi closed her eyes. Tick tock tick tock.

Who am I? Who is the one who asks? Laxmi is not this body and mind. Who is aware of this pain? Tick tock tick tock. Mind slows down, slows down and gradually stops.

An audible silence is heard. It reverberates inside her and outside in the sterile room. *Who am I?* This is Laxmi's quest; it is a reaching into silence, an expansion into stillness. Tick tock tick tock is just the sound of silence, this body just the shape of stillness. Who Laxmi is, is awareness of this whole phenomenon. There are no instant cures for cancer. There is only the light of awareness. Light. Bright and boundless light.

With a slight start, Laxmi noticed the pain had disappeared. Even as she noticed, the pain was back. Laxmi's got it! Laxmi understands! Silence equals stillness equals awareness. Laxmi launched herself back into silence again, into luminous space. Tick tock tick tock. The weight of sheet and blankets are felt on her legs as skin, the ticking clock as her heartbeat, the something in her belly is the *leela* of existence.

This doesn't make sense. Not to Laxmi's mind. The heart knew exactly what was going on: awareness, no time, no space, no body, no mind, no limits but a singing, ringing awareness of all that is. Awareness too of a fizzing pressure in the forehead just between the eyes. Slowly, slowly Laxmi opens her eyes. Yes. Still the room is there; the slatted blinds precipitating light onto the polished floor; light that leaps to dazzle one, the patient pendulum, two crimson shoes beneath the chair.

Now Laxmi notices a faint vibration in her body: a quivering that starts beneath her navel. This shaking, is it fear? Yes. Fear resides in the body-mind, which she is not.

She is free of care; if an operation happens or it doesn't, if death comes or it doesn't Laxmi is free. Everything is as it should be. No need for anaesthetics. All is Osho's *leela*.

* * *

In a prompt operation, surgeons removed from Laxmi's stomach a malign tumour.

At first Laxmi had been reluctant to go to a doctor or a hospital. Then she was reluctant to undergo an operation and finally she was reluctant to have an anaesthetic. In fact, she told the surgeons, 'Just put this photograph of Osho in front of Laxmi and one will be OK. It will be a test of Laxmi's awareness.' By law, the doctors had to anaesthetize her: they insisted and Laxmi submitted gracefully.

Surprisingly, within a day or two, Laxmi was up and walking gingerly. Mamta even saw her wielding a broom, cleaning the private ward to her exacting satisfaction.

When news of Laxmi's operation spread amongst the *sannyasin* community, people came from everywhere round about to sit with her. Despite a warning phone call from Sheela's lieutenants on the Ranch, the Osho Devadeep Meditation Centre, a community of seventy or so *sannyasins*, arranged amongst themselves to have people always at the hospital with Laxmi. So great were the numbers coming to support her that the hospital authorities put aside a special space in the building and on the lawns for over a hundred *sannyasins* to sit in silence together. Laxmi spoke of this outpouring of love as 'HIS grace'.

She asked of one visitor who was staying in the house she shared with Mamta, 'How are the house plants in Laxmi's room?' He replied, somewhat embarrassed, that he had noticed them wilted and dying. 'Then please go and talk to them, give them water and apologies from Laxmi.'

The hospital staff of doctors, nurses and administrators said they were inspired by Laxmi's bearing and by that of her friends. They waived all her fees and charges and the hospital provided a limousine to take Laxmi home. Mamta said, 'The whole episode was an unusual manifestation of Osho's energy at work.'

* * *

Laxmi returned to her room in the house she shared with Mamta. The stitches were soon removed and again friends old and new, Western and Eastern, came to visit; to sit with her in her convalescence.

One of them was Ma Dassano, a bubbly Afro-American with whom a great and enduring friendship was formed.

One morning she entered Laxmi's bedroom with a flourish. 'How is Her Highness today?'

'Pain is there, my dear slave,' replied Laxmi, 'that is

certain. Sometimes it is only a disturbance happening far below.'

'That's cool. We're all such novices beside you.'

'Laxmi is blessed with Osho's presence in her life for fifteen years. You boarded the train only now. Many friends are joining every station. All will arrive at the final destination. Just you have to pay the correct fare.'

'And who is the ticket collector? You?'

Laxmi laughed and held her painful belly.

'And the cost?'

Laxmi laughed again in spite of herself. She pointed an outspread hand at Dassano. 'This trip costs you your ego. Nothing less than everything you think you are and own.'

Another friend had entered and asked, 'Laxmi why are you banned from being with Osho and the Commune?'

'Who says Laxmi is not with Osho? She is never, ever, not with Osho. The banning? *Ye sab unki leela hai*. This is the Master's play. The Zen stick that brings transformation was lifted when this wooden-headed disciple got too busy. Now who is making *chai* happen? Or is it time for Jack Daniels? Ahh Dassano...'

* * *

Laxmi said to Atul and Mamta, as the dawn showed pale in the kitchen window after a lively night of talking, 'Silence has happened in these last few weeks. Some garbage has been thrown out and the rubbish-collection crew have been round.'

11. THE INQUISITION

The very air was steeped with disinfectant: sweat and cigarettes, fear and boredom formed the lower registers. Laxmi and her friend Nadamo sat amongst the rows and rows of chipped steel chairs in a room that might have been a cattle market built for humans. For an hour they sat and waited. Nadamo was from South America; he too had fallen foul of Sheela's regime and was living in New York. He was here to give Laxmi what support he could. From the ceiling hung a dusty flag whose message, stamped across an emblematic eagle, was 'Welcome to the US Immigration and Naturalization Service'. Around them sat the hundreds, waiting in hope and trepidation.

Above the subdued hum of voices, she at last heard her name. 'Kuruwa!' The voice was uninviting. Laxmi rose and followed a man into one of the stalls or cubicles that stretched down either side of the barn-like room. He closed the door and sat himself behind a green steel desk, chipped and stained like all the chairs. Laxmi sat across from him. He studied some papers. Laxmi knew well about bureaucracy and the creatures that it spawns. She waited without expectation of a human look, a human word.

The voice was surprisingly metallic. 'Your visa request has been denied. You must leave this country forthwith.'

Laxmi winced. She had had hopes. The lawyer had been optimistic. 'One has been called at such short notice. Laxmi would like her lawyer to be present.'

'Just leave! Before we deport you.'

Laxmi gathered her papers and rose. When she reached the door the metallic voice cut in, 'Sit down.'

She sat. Now the man re-shuffled his papers. He didn't look at Laxmi still. He found a plastic folder in a drawer and stuffed them into it. 'Get up! Follow me!'

Laxmi noticed impatience arising in her. She also noticed curiosity. She followed the shiny grey suit in front of her and noticed that someone was following her. Oh, now we visit another cubicle. The smell in there was dreadful. This cabin has a dusty, crooked-hanging photograph of Mr Ronald Reagan on the wall.

'Sit down.'

Are they trained to speak in exhortations? Laxmi faced another man who also would not look at her. The first one and the follower had vanished. This one seemed more senior. He was middle-aged, bald and, like the furnishings, seemed worn and dusty. Two deep furrows ran either side of his nose and his mouth, which itself was a down-turned furrow. When at last he raised his eyes there was a poor attempt at a smile. He said, 'Your visa has been denied. But...If you were to help us with some small matters your status could be changed.'

Although Laxmi was not fooled by the dead smile, nevertheless hope rose impulsively in her heart. She offered him the papers and her passport that she clutched, pushing them across the desk. 'Please change it.'

'The help we need concerns the place called

Rajneeshpuram. How it works and who's involved.' He leaned across the desk and lowered his voice. 'This is for your ears only. They're planning to pick up a few of the top rankers there. Osho himself would not be implicated.'

'Pick up?'

'Arrest, nab, pull in, take into custody. The leaders only; those running the show. You'll have your visa and then you can get your old job back. Things are getting pretty out of hand there. We just need a few names. Then...'

Then it dawned on Laxmi. They were playing hard-cop-soft-cop with her. She said, 'We crucified Jesus two thousand years ago and now, when a flower of such beauty again walks the earth, you want to do it again?'

'Look,' said the man, reaching for Laxmi's passport. 'We are not after him. We want the high-ups who are causing trouble. For us and for your lot. Names. Give us a few names.' He opened Laxmi's passport and studied it.

'Sir, one is not with Osho for power and playing politics. Now, will you please allow Laxmi to call her lawyer?'

'Look,' he repeated himself. 'Do you know who I am? I have flown across America from Portland just to give you your visa and put you back in your place. I'm John Feher, Criminal Investigation.' He edged his right hand across the desk for Laxmi to shake. To no avail. 'You don't seem to know what's good for you.'

'What is your telephone number here? I would like my lawyer to speak with you.'

Mr Dusty Feher opened a wallet and passed a card across. 'I've given you a chance. If you change your mind, give me a call. Collect. You can call collect.'

'But Laxmi would like to call her lawyer now.'

For a long minute Feher studied some pattern in the ink blots on his desk. The fingers of his right hand drummed the plastic covered file. 'Get up! Walk this way!'

Now Feher led her towards the back of the barn. The man who had walked behind her before was behind her again. Laxmi looked for Nadamo among the chairs. The far end of the room was in a blue tobacco haze. Laxmi stopped. 'My friend. I need to tell my friend.'

'Keep walking.' The minder behind gave her a push. Feher reached a pair of armoured doors and pushed one open. Laxmi turned to look for Nadamo again and the minder pushed her hard through the door, clipping her head on the reinforced glass window. She let out a cry. He grabbed her wrist and pulled her towards a lift. When the lift door opened he pushed her in. So unresisting was the body of Laxmi that this time her face caught the wall of the lift. She watched it ascend to the twelfth floor. 'Walk!' He twisted her wrist, already in pain, and now a spasm shot up her back.

'You have no right to treat Laxmi like this. One has no weapon or intention to escape. Laxmi has the right to a lawyer. What you are doing is illegal.'

'Nothing is illegal here.'

Another pair of steel security doors and another barn-like room. This one also had cubicles and men and women clattering on typewriters. Feher led her the length of the room to an empty desk. He kicked a chair towards Laxmi. 'Sit.'

He and the minder disappeared. Laxmi sat facing a wall. The smell was different here, more smoke and scent, less disinfectant. And the voices less muted, more assertive.

Time stretched out. She closed her eyes. Beloved *Bhagwan*!
Help me. She held the locket of her *mala* to her forehead.
Laughter arose from the typing pool. She put the locket to
her ear. More laughter ensued. She kept her eyes closed.
They have no idea. What has Laxmi to learn from all this
hanky-panky? She watched the rising and the falling of her
breath. Pain in the back and the head. Pain in the heart.

She heard the words 'Kuruwa' and 'raise bail' followed by
another voice, 'five thousand'. She looked around. The voices
came from a cubicle nearby. Laxmi looked at her watch.
Two-and-a-half hours had passed. What is going on? Why
do they play with Laxmi so? It's Friday afternoon. Soon the
banks will close. Soon the lawyer will be off for the weekend.
Laxmi rose and walked towards the cubicle. 'Laxmi is here.'
The clatter of the typewriter grew quiet. She knocked on the
cubicle door. 'Laxmi is here. She has a doctor's appointment
this afternoon. Hullo? Who will attend to Laxmi?'

Feher's head appeared round the door. 'Forget any doctor.
You'll be here as long as you need to be here.'

'Laxmi is not a child, nor is she stupid. She is aware that
refusing to allow her to call her lawyer or contact her friend
downstairs is setting her up for a weekend in jail.'

'That's for sure where you'll be if you don't shut up and
sit down.' Feher now left the cubicle and strode off through
the armoured doors.

Laxmi returned to her seat. Breathe and relax. Breathe
and relax. These people are doing their job as they see best;
they have to obey or lose it. Breathe in, relax. This is the
play of existence.

* * *

Time ticked by in heartbeats and Laxmi needed the toilet. She rose and found a man at a desk set apart. 'Would you direct Laxmi to the bathroom please?'

The typing pool had hushed again. The man looked at Laxmi, then at the typing pool, then pointed to the corner where Laxmi had been seated.

'But Laxmi needs the bathroom.'

'Does she really?' This raised a snigger or two. 'Tell her she'll just have to wait.'

'One needs the toilet now.'

A woman in the typing pool called out, 'It has to be arranged. I'll call someone.'

Soon the minder appeared. 'Walk.' He led her through the armoured doors, past the lift and down a concrete staircase. 'In there.'

Laxmi was entering not a toilet but a cell. For a moment she hesitated on the threshold till a great shove sent her flying across the concrete floor to land on her knees against a bench. She stood immediately, turned to hear the cell door slam and a bolt shot home. The man's eye was at the spy hole in the door. Laxmi stared at it until it was withdrawn. Then she tended with toilet paper her grazed knee and wrist. She used the toilet.

When she had finished she banged on the door. Nothing. She banged again. She could not reach her eye to the spyhole, it was too high. She sat on a low steel bed. She listened to her beating heart. The bruise on her cheek was throbbing, her wrist was red and swollen. Who am I? Where is the blessing in this?

* * *

Footsteps. The bolt withdrawn. The door opened. Laxmi looked the minder in the eye and he turned away. 'One is walking,' Laxmi said pre-emptively. She followed him back through the armoured steel doors, this time to another office. He kicked a chair towards her. 'One sits,' said Laxmi sitting. The door was closed. Despair welled up. Tears. No! Laxmi has to stay cool. Act intelligently. You are with me *Bhagwan*.

After a few minutes of gathering herself, Laxmi opened the door and walked towards an office she had noticed earlier. It had glass in the door and windows in its walls.

'Please will you assist? One has waited for hours, one has not been allowed contact with one's lawyer or the friend downstairs and one is cold. Also one is in pain.' Laxmi held up her grazed and swollen wrist.

'Your name?'

'Laxmi Kuruwa.'

'Indian?'

'Yes.'

'Wait.' He lifted his phone and dialled a number. 'I have a Krewer here. Indian.' He listened for some time then replaced the receiver. 'You are now under arrest. You may not leave. Your purse, your wallet. Put them here.'

'Then Laxmi must certainly call her lawyer now. The friend downstairs has his number. Should one go down or should he come up?'

'Neither!' But he pushed the phone towards her. He kept his hand on it. 'Won't you help us with some information? Give us the dope on Sheela and we will see you right.'

Laxmi turned her face away.

'You're a tough one. Look at me woman!' Suddenly he

was standing over her. 'But not as tough as you think. Look at me! Do you know how long you face in prison? And prison isn't nice here in the States. How long would a shrimp like you last in the system? I'm telling you...'—then he gripped her upper arm and squeezed—'...you help us or you rot in prison. Do you understand me? Now tell me everything. Let's start with Sheela.' He shook her arm so her whole body shook. 'Who are her associates? Give me names or you are in the trashcan.' Laxmi looked him in the eye then. Much as she saw that Sheela was the sad, misguided pilot of the ship in which her master and his people sailed she could not bring herself to sabotage that vessel for the sake of her own safety. Least of all to this neo-fascist setup. She turned away her head again.

The man sat down. A long silence ticked by.

'Dial nine to get a line.'

Laxmi slowly, tentatively reached for the phone expecting another assault. She remembered the lawyer's name over on the West Coast. She received his number from directory enquiries and when he answered her, she spoke to him in Hindi. He was immediately pragmatic. He would call a New York lawyer and bail could be arranged: now he must speak to the interrogating officer. She passed over the phone.

Laxmi sat and listened while an argument ensued of which she only heard one side. The man put down the phone and picked it up again. 'Send Chuck with the friend Nadamo.' To Laxmi he said, 'Wait outside.' He went back to his files on the desk.

Nadamo came with an escort. He hugged Laxmi and helped her on with her red felt jacket. His hug caused her back a sharp pain. She started to tell him her story. 'So far

so good,' she reassured him. 'Laxmi is still alive and may
yet see the light of day if bail is on its way.'

The minder interrupted them. 'Both of you. Walk this
way.'

Again the steel doors, again a lift. This time to the
basement. A cell door was opened and they were locked up,
with a dozen other prisoners. Nadamo said, 'Here, Laxmi,
drink this water. Tell me everything.'

Laxmi drank and recounted her tale. When she had
finished she started to laugh. Nadamo too was laughing.
'In this cell we are becoming a monk and a nun after all.'

After an hour the cell door opened. A new man stood
before Laxmi. 'Kuruwa. Walk!' She followed him down the
bare, windowless passage of the grotesque building. The
smell changed to mild disinfectant and vinegar now. In a
small room, she stood before a wall with a plastic board
of numbers hanging from her neck. The man clicked and
cursed with a camera. 'Wait,' he shouted. 'No film.' He
banged around in drawers and cupboards for a while then
grabbed the number-board from Laxmi. 'Your right hand.'
He held Laxmi's delicate thumb and pressed it on an inkpad
and then on a white surface. Then all the fingers, one by
one. 'Now clean them with this wipe.'

She held it under her nose. 'Laxmi has sensitive skin. Do
you have a non-toxic solution to wipe them?'

The man snatched the tissue from Laxmi, held it under a
tap of cold water and handed it back to her. 'Now sign this.'

Laxmi looked at the form. 'Laxmi cannot sign it. It says
one had free access to a lawyer. All day she was denied. Till
late this afternoon.' The man made a gesture with the back
of his hand as if to strike her. He scribbled 'Refused to sign'.

'That also is not true.'

This time he hit her on her shoulder. 'You stupid woman. Playing games!'

He led her back to the cell. Nadamo put his arm round her. They sat in silence for another hour.

At five, the New York lawyer arrived. 'Your officer upstairs has three thousand five hundred dollars.' Laxmi felt relief, and peace and joy erupt. 'His grace, His play! What a lot Laxmi has to learn.' She hugged Nadamo again. They laughed all the way out of the building

* * *

The institutional religions, as Osho often pointed out, create saints and martyrs to validate their own beliefs, their egos and to escape from individual responsibility. Osho offered no belief system and anyway preferred the company of sinners.

'Sinners are nice people. I have never seen a sinner sad and I have never seen a saint joyful. It is strange; it should have been otherwise if religions were true. But religions are not true.'

Laxmi was no saint, nor did she aspire to be one. 'Laxmi is not concerned about enlightenment. Her play is His work.'

Laxmi had her flaws, some recognised, some not. Ma Sangeet, one of the commune's lawyers, told me of an interview she had with Osho three years later in which he referred to Laxmi coming to the States against his wishes.

'Betrayal is my word for her action,' said Sangeet. 'And one I stick to. By not trusting him and doing what he asked, she left him in a very bad situation. He had no one to buy property and he had a choice of exposing Sheela and splitting the community or staying in the US and working behind the scenes, which is what he chose to do. I call this betrayal, and though Osho didn't use that word, I had the sense of [his] deep disappointment and sadness. And remember, this was after the World Tour and into Poona Two when he was talking about it. Within a year or so she was banned.'

Devotion was the chosen path of Laxmi. This does not mean she made no errors or misjudgements. She had her inner work to do and did it till the very end.

Ma Shunyo wrote: 'Osho said to me privately in Rajneeshpuram that if Laxmi had accepted the new situation, her change in role, and done nothing then she would be enlightened by now.'

12. COMING HOME

Illness is the symptom of a body out of balance just as extreme weather is a planet out of balance and economic crises, an economy out of balance. However all phenomena contain the seeds of their renewal, albeit in a multitude of different forms. Out of the imbalances, a cure is being born; a new awareness rises to restore the balance.

If we listen carefully, below the sounding brass of politicians and the press, below the harsh percussion of the multinational corporations, gentle voices can be heard that offer answers to the questions that we hardly dare to ask ourselves. 'Let the dead bury their dead.' The old, separatist, competitive, carbon-era culture must bury itself before it buries all of life on earth.

To whom belong these voices questioning our fundamental attitudes and concepts? They belong to the cutting edge of science, to the sages and the mystics and the artists and the worldwide flowering of millennials. They come too, from the domain of meditation and of love.

Our choice in this age is between love and fear. The new way, the only way now, is the way of the heart, of connection and cooperation. This path does not come with maps and plans and formulas; it comes from not knowing and from trust.

   The new shift of consciousness has already started to
happen on a scale not hitherto seen. We will never know the
full extent of Osho's contribution to this nor the full scale of
his esoteric work. A master is not bounded by the logical or
visible. Recent scientific work in forests has discovered that
each tree communicates, along vast and ancient networks of
mycelia, with neighbours and especially with its offspring
and relatives. These fungal colonies also act as channels
for the transfer of nutrients to other forest trees in need.
Osho has laid down unseen networks that will help this
world renew itself through the hearts of those who tap into
his wisdom.

                              * * *

Four months after the momentous assassination of Indira
Gandhi, at four o'clock on the morning of 14 February 1985,
Laxmi returned to India. She arrived in South Delhi where
there had always been many friends and much support for
her. At the previous Fourth Annual World Celebration on
the Ranch, now named Rajneeshpuram, in a tent among
10,000 tents, two friends of many years, had met and almost
without words, found agreement. One of them, Swami Kul
Bhushan, was an Indian journalist in East Africa, the other,
Swami Atul Anand, ran and still runs, the Rajyoga Osho
Meditation Centre in south Delhi. He was looking for nearby
accommodation for Laxmi. Kul had not quite completed
construction of a house there. He promised part of it for her.
   Now Laxmi settled in the upstairs rooms of the house
known as E2 in an affluent and bustling quarter of south
Delhi. Kul's wife Rashma remembers Laxmi arriving in the
small hours of the morning. 'She had just endured a fifteen-

hour flight. She walked round the rooms tapping a wall here
and there saying, "These are not cardboard houses. Laxmi
is not in America now. India may be dying of poverty but
the West is dying of power."'

Sheela's ban on *sannyasin* contact with Laxmi was, of
course, still in force but luckily for her there were enough
*sannyasin*s everywhere who had the intelligence and the
courage to disregard specious diktats from a centralised
authority. Laxmi was without personal funds. That had been
true for her since first she started as Osho's secretary in
1970. Now, however, she was bankrolled in a modest way
by her Delhi friends.

She was not alone because Ma Dassano from Washington
had accompanied her out of love and the wish to take care
of her. She was not in good health but apparently not in bad
health either; her cancer was in remission. Her digestive
system was impaired: when she ate, she often vomitted. Her
psychological energy was not impaired. Laxmi was always
jubilant, always looking for ways to enhance Osho's work.
And now, since the operation in Washington, something
had changed inside her. Distance from him was no object,
he was her subject.

E2 became a hub of activity. If her physical form was not
strong, her spirit was unquenchable. 'His needs come first.
Vitamin M! We first set up a restaurant; Zorba the Buddha
for Delhi. Then also Laxmi must be looking at properties.
A car is needed.'

Did she know something that other *sannyasin*s don't
know? Did she see some half-written writing on the wall?
It was rumoured in the Osho meditation rooms of Delhi
that the master had said to Laxmi, 'You find a new site for

the commune in India. I want to leave America—leave this place to Sheela.'

* * *

A new green Mercedes was at Laxmi's disposal, a gift from the friends at Rajyoga. 'Laxmi has another toy,' she tells Dassano. Dassano was a true friend. She loved Laxmi and she argued with her, worried about her health and sometimes gave her plain but playful rebukes. 'Eat this lovely food or I quit.' 'If you go running off to Almora without resting for a day or two you might find your toy has a puncture.'

Laxmi told Swami Anuragi, her new driver, 'Laxmi's concern is for His health. A place for Osho to live must have four conditions met; humidity below 70 per cent, good communications to the outside world, a big enough city within reach and roads well maintained. Such a site should be able to accommodate ten thousand people.'

That was a big ask for Himachal Pradesh. Not only was the terrain tending towards the vertical but the state had passed protective laws to safeguard tribal people and peasant farmers, laws that limited how much land anyone could buy. Lastly there were still old mandates from the Moraji Desai-era hindering the purchase of land for anyone connected to Osho.

But Laxmi was moving ahead with her accelerator hard to the floor. Sometimes she set out knowing clearly where she was going, sometimes she was merely sensing out an area, wandering, looking, talking to locals. After one such long, tiring day, Laxmi and her crew, all wearing the orange clothes and Osho *malas*, checked into a small hotel. Laxmi, ever mischievous, said to the startled proprietor, 'Today Laxmi wants to drink a rum and Coke.'

Anuragi tells another story. 'I was at the wheel of the green Mercedes heading to the mountains. After the long drive from Delhi we were reaching the foothills when Laxmi's voice came from the back seat of the car where she sat with Dassano. "Laxmi would like to drive." I pulled over. The car was left hand drive. She stood out in the cold while I piled her up some cushions. When she was comfortable and I was in the passenger seat, she took off like nobody's business. She drove up a steep hill very fast. We came to a small humped bridge, then we were airborne. After a very heavy landing she stopped the car. "Laxmi thinks she will return to her seat."'

On other forays into the mountains, Laxmi liked to share the driving, laughing and singing as she swung the Mercedes round the hairpin bends. Once as their route was tracing the course of a broad rushing river, Laxmi stopped. Everyone piled out of the car for a break and within minutes the figure of Laxmi, jumping from rock to rock was a small red dot in the distance. A car full of strangers parked nearby shouted in alarm to Anuragi and his wife Urvashi, 'This river is dangerous. Call your child to the shore.' They shouted back to the strangers, 'She's not our child, she's our mother.'

* * *

'Laxmi needs to drive to Ahmedabad,' she announced one morning.

'Drive?'

'Yes drive.'

'But it's so far. Laxmi ma, why not fly? Or take the train. You know how far it is? Eighteen hours away.'

'Laxmi knows. She also knows how to find Vitamin M in Gujarat.'

'But why the car? The too-long drive?'

'A new green Mercedes draws money better than an old white Ambassador taxi.'

Those partaking in the conversation rolled their eyes. Someone muttered, 'Laxmi is Laxmi.'

'Yes,' she responded amidst the laughter. 'She is and she isn't.'

Over the months, there were many journeys of reconnaissance, many meetings with state officials, and royal families, many visits to ruined palaces and great houses. Laxmi had no material funds, only promises from friends and supporters and yet she started into deals with a total and convincing confidence. This characteristic, this proclivity to assert something that was not necessarily actual as actual, this trait which we have noted before used with publishers and politicians, is a double-edged sword. In time it could turn to harm her.

* * *

On one occasion when Laxmi was travelling in the Kullu–Manali valley with Dassano, Anuragi and Urvashi, someone told them that the Dalai Lama would be driving through that very afternoon. 'Let us stand by the roadside and welcome him,' said Urvashi.

'Why do you want to welcome a Lama when your master is a living buddha? Laxmi is not interested.' The friends looked at each other sheepishly. That afternoon after lunch, Laxmi took her afternoon nap. Very quietly and with difficulty masking their giggles, the friends locked a sleeping Laxmi in her room and stood beside the road. Soon enough the cavalcade of cars swept up on its way to the Circuit House. It slowed down for the three red-clothed figures, and their *namaste* was returned.

Laxmi never knew.

* * *

Kul's daughter Neela was in her early teens when Laxmi was living in the E2 rooms upstairs. She remembers going for regular, early morning walks with Laxmi in the Lodi Gardens.

They were Zen walks. Slow, silent, watchful. In the day she had so many visitors. From ten until twelve thirty and again from three until seven thirty. She was trying to raise funds. All the grown-ups told her she was unrealistic. She remained persistent, in the flow of something larger than herself. If there was a problem with something she would sit in her chair, close her eyes and she'd be gone. Five minutes or an hour. I learned a lot about a lot, including raising money. At the end of the day she would say, 'What's the score? Three *lakhs* not out.' Of an evening she would often tell us stories of the strange and superfluous wealth in America.

* * *

Shortly after her arrival, Laxmi had decided to buy a building to start a restaurant in Delhi. She encouraged the Osho Centre and other friends to put work and money into the project in order to raise substantial funds for Osho in India. There was an opening night with gala guests. But Laxmi's body was not strong. She could not sustain the momentum. One day Atul visited her. She was in bed, her health flagging. 'Let's give up this Zorba the Buddha project,' he said. Laxmi considered his suggestion for a moment then, in a relaxed, matter-of-fact way, agreed.

* * *

In June 1985, when Sw Arun from Nepal was on his way to the Fourth Annual World Celebration, he visited Laxmi.

He found her lying on her bed. She was passing through another death. She had been expelled from the commune; she had been expelled from America; she was weakened from her cancer surgery. Maltreatment by the US Immigration Service had added injury to insult. It was midsummer in sweltering south Delhi; all sweat and pollution, noise and weariness. Kul Bhushan and his family were away. Monsoon muttered from the Bay of Bengal.

Arun said he was shocked at the reduced condition in which he found her. He told her, 'You should not be living like this, it is not right. You who looked after Osho, who have devoted your life to him, you should be living like a queen. Please pen a letter to the master. He needs to know of your poor state of health, your expulsion from *sannyas*; explain everything to him. I will find a secret way to convey your message to him personally. Here's a pen and writing paper.'

He went out to buy a few necessities. On returning, he was surprised to find that pen and paper lay untouched beside her. 'Please! Write to him. You have to tell him,' he pleaded with her. 'You deserve much more than this Laxmi. Put everything in writing?'

There was a gravid silence. Laxmi looked at him with those bright brown eyes. 'Writing to HIM would be a violence. It means you do not trust.'

Arun was lost for words. Then, after a long silence she

looked at him with such a tender smile, she said, as if for his clarification, 'He knows everything. So what is happening is exactly for Laxmi's rebirth and growth. You give Him *pranaam* from Laxmi—you bow down to him twice: once from you and once from Laxmi.'

* * *

Rajneeshpuram was by now a living blueprint of sustainable community life, a flower blooming in America's Western semi-desert. The canker at its crimson heart was yet to reveal itself.

Now Arun, after his visit to Laxmi, stopped off for a week in London to stay with friends. He travelled with a sense of longing and of dread. Like Laxmi, he had had no direct communication with Osho for two years: that was his longing. His dread was that Sheela had ostracised him from the commune. On the plane, he wondered if he too had been reported, or mis-reported, for rebellious activities and for linking up with Laxmi. He regretted he had not been able to help her. All she had asked was, 'You bow down to him twice.'

At Rajneeshpuram, Arun stood beside the road where Osho was to drive by. He was with his Nepalese friends. The red and orange ribbon of *sannyasins* stretched out for miles on either side of him. Osho's car moved slower than a strolling walk so he could see and greet each one of more than fifteen thousand friends gathered for the celebration. Arun was jet-lagged, fearful and excited.

He held his hands in n*amaste* and bowed once and then again; the two *pranaams*. Osho's smile illuminated the dark recesses of Arun's mind. The all-devouring worries that encircled him melted away like wolves at the break of day. After the drive-by, he went to his tent for a well-earned and mollified sleep.

He was awakened by a resident of Rajneeshpuram. 'Be at Jesus Grove, the home and office complex of Sheela, at six o'clock. Wear clean clothes.'

Arun's worst fears returned. 'I need to sleep. Please let me alone.'

'No. You must be there. A car will collect you.'

His mind went into spin. *I have been reported. I too will be outlawed. If this is paranoia, then I'm only picking up an odour that is blowing in the air these days.*

The car came early. The driver would neither affirm nor refute his fears. Jesus Grove was seething with people having business of all sorts to discuss with Sheela and her cabal. Arun was directed towards a sitting room to wait.

Entering the room, he stopped dead in his tracks. There on a sofa sat a smiling Laxmi.

'I could not believe my eyes. I was speechless. And then we had a long, long silent hug. Sheela broke the moment entering. "I bring you to a private interview with Him. No one should know. If you tell anyone we will deny and kick you out."'

* * *

Osho was sitting in his chair in the corner of a large room. Laxmi and Arun kneeled at his feet. After two years in the wilderness, both were in tears. Osho touched their heads and then drew them close to his knees.

Osho asked Laxmi about herself, her health, her operation, her work and her experience with the INS. Arun said, 'Like a waterfall, he poured his love on her.'

It is as impossible to write about this event as it was for Arun to describe it thirty years later. A master's love causes time to condense to a pinhead, it is a drowning in bliss,

Their *darshan* continued for over an hour or the duration of a lightening flash. Then Osho requested Sheela, who had remained seated in a far corner by the door, to provide Laxmi with an air-conditioned home with a kitchen, to make a car, a driver and a carer available to her. Now she should rest and take care of her body. 'What work shall Laxmi do?' asked Laxmi.

'Live here like a queen. You have nothing to do.'

Arun says that that was the time when Laxmi attained enlightenment. He says he also was with a silent mind for weeks thereafter.

* * *

Sheela put Laxmi and Dassano in a double A-frame house in a valley named after Alan Watts, the English philosopher, writer and Western pioneer of self-realisation. Anasha again took care of all Laxmi's material needs, including cooking, cleaning, laundry and ironing. She was not the one, however to make Laxmi's afternoon *chai*. Laxmi herself had to do that.

Thirty years later, Anasha apologised to the writer for not remembering any facts such as dates, times or conversations that a writer needs; but what was forcibly brought home was the enduring love and admiration that flowed through Anasha's wordlessness; her struggle to remember was suffused with gratitude.

The A-frame house in Alan Watts had been bugged for special visitors. What did Sheela fear? What did she want— or not want—to hear? One of Sheela's secret techno-squad operatives was enlisted to spy on her. 'Dassano works for the FBI,' he was told.

For the long hot months of that summer tingeing into autumn, he lay on the sweaty sheets of a bed in the next-door house with his headphones on, listening to Laxmi and Dassano banter back and forth, singing the non-stop praises of their master. He was bored to death, he wrote. 'Nothing for Sheela there; Laxmi was just so dammed [sic] cheerful.'

* * *

Laxmi invited Yatri to visit her when she had a brief stay in the commune hospital. She was still not fully recovered from her cancer operation. He has written about that time:

'After some preliminary questions about how I liked it on the Ranch, she suddenly came out with her fears over the power games Sheela was playing and how many of them were wrong and could damage the vision of Osho in the USA.

'She then asked outright that if she made a move to return as his secretary and replace Sheela and her court, would I support such an action.

'What I did not know at the time was that upon re-entering the USA she had been warned by the INS that key people in power at Rajneeshpuram would be arrested shortly. The authorities wanted her cooperation and in exchange for information, they would help handing over authority to her when Sheela and her group would be jailed. She refused to cooperate but obviously wanted to ensure the commune would continue if these arrests happened, so she was now tentatively sounding out some of her old trusted friends to find if they would support her.

'Without knowing that background at the time I could

only suggest some of the seemingly impossible hurdles ahead for an Indian totally unused to the American system. Little did I know she had already tasted the horrors of a Western interrogation and had previously had her visa denied.

'Laxmi lay back and considered what had been said. She looked so frail and ill yet still had a feisty look in her eyes. She was obviously prepared to fight for what she saw was right for Osho. But this was not India and all the rules and politics she was used to no longer applied.'

Yatri recalls further:

'She must have looked back to the time when she was his very first disciple who organised his camps and lectures and cleaned up his whole travelling circus before settling in Bombay. It was she who had organised the great gatherings in that city. It was she who looked after Osho's health, his diabetic tendencies and his increased sensitivities and allergies. It was she who ran the day-to-day business. It was Laxmi who was the first contact with Western disciples. It was she who kept the ink flowing on the presses to ensure the books were printed and sent around the world. She was continually beset by a chronic lack of funds. Nevertheless she still managed to have the Ashram's players perform Shakespeare to great acclaim in Bombay and New Delhi. Her intent was always to spread awareness of the commune's high calibre of innovation and creativity.

'She managed to hold this whole enterprise together with a tireless energy on less than a banana and two cups of tea a day. She wore that little red headscarf and was crazy enough to think it would prevent the wild energy from her crown *chakra* shooting up to the sky. Her *lungi* and *kurta* in dark orange was the hallmark of the Commune in India...

'Through her family's role in the independence movement, she had powerful political connections that enabled her to hold talks with prime ministers and leaders of the various state governments at the time when Osho was considered a major political irritant. She tried for two years to find some place to materialise Osho's vision of a paradise-commune in India.

'Yet the caravanserai eventually moved West without her. In a way Sheela was far more suited to the new, aggressive nature of the American way of life.

'And in the hospital she just smiled and held my hand. Somehow I felt she recognised the loss of any real place for herself in this new world order yet remained totally true to a strangely new Osho...

'The golden age of Poona One that she had worked so tirelessly to create had passed and with it the architect who, more than any other of the master's disciples, epitomizes for me the simplicity and courage of that pioneering era. She embodied India and a spiritual world that got lost in the translation to America. In her own words she calls the story of her life "The Journey of the Heart" and that was the deepest offering she possessed...the heart.'

* * *

The Fourth World Celebration in Rajneeshpuram in 1985 was the beginning of the end of one of the world's most courageous and extraordinary experiments. In four short years a few thousand people with no particular standing or skills had created a sustainable paradise in the semi-desert of Central Oregon. This community of individuals were the prototypes of Osho's New Man and Woman. They built an exemplary city that interwove respect for the environment with celebration, efficient infrastructure with love and a crime-free society with creativity. Almost! The most radiant and fragrant of roses can be crushed by any blunt rock. This commune was destroyed by the invisible worm of corruption in the hearts of a few and by the blunt boot of the US Government.

During a morning *satsang* Sheela's lieutenant tried to murder Osho's doctor by injecting him with poison. Luckily he had the presence of mind to have himself flown to the nearest hospital, out of harm's way. This episode is described in Maneesha James's book, *Bhagwan: The Buddha of the Future.*

It is on record that the United States government of Ronald Reagan had decided to destroy the commune experiment. Sheela and her crooked crew were granting them a foot in the door. Osho said:

The commune is the lifestyle of the future. The family is gone and the commune is going to take its place. Much depends on the success of commune life, and we have to make the commune life such a celebration that it spreads like wildfire; that other communes start of their own accord. We just have to prove that life in a commune is much richer, much livelier, much more meditative; that there is a possibility of living in a different way, different from the way humanity has lived up to now. We have proved it in Rajneeshpuram. It was our success that forced America to destroy the commune. If we were not successful nobody would have bothered about us. Remember this: it was not a failure that we were destroyed; it was our success which could not be tolerated.

[Osho, *Beyond Enlightenment*, Ch. 30, Q. 4]

* * *

In that fateful autumn of 1985 Laxmi would have known little of the climactic events unfolding under her nose. These events were to endanger the life of Osho, his *sannyasins* and the very commune itself. Now it becomes clear why Laxmi had been searching the Himalayas for property. Osho must have clearly sensed the troubled state of Sheela and her close associates and guessed its causes and its likely outcome. He never made suggestions unless asked; he just awaited the unravelling of events.

Sheela and six or eight of her cohort found they were increasingly unable to maintain the sort of power and control over the commune and its neighbours that they felt they needed. They were, contrary to the vision of Osho, emphasising the old ethos of separation, hierarchy and conflict; they were trampling on his vision of connectivity and cooperation. They squeezed meditation out of their lives and out of the life of the commune. That was their core blunder.

They resorted to various forms of criminal activity: wiretapping, bugging rooms, arson and attempting to poison their perceived enemies. Gradually they spiralled down into a morass of guilt, fear of retribution and an increasing haze of Prozac and other chemical panaceas. In this way, they further alienated themselves from Osho's vision and his people. It is certain that Osho had, from early on, perceived the instability of their discipleship. But, as we have seen, he never interfered with what existence brought his way. Only when consulted would he offer a view.

On 14 September 1985 paranoia drove Sheela and her gang to flight. Suddenly they were all gone, fled to various hidey-holes across the world. Sheela's last act on the Ranch was to send her sister to Laxmi's rooms with a beaker full of freshly squeezed fruit juice: it was laced with poison.

Laxmi was violently sick but she survived.

Osho invited the police to investigate the crimes that became apparent upon her departure. The US Government had previously mandated thirty-two government agencies to work on the legal or illegal destruction of the commune. They now had enough ammunition—though not any evidence—to attain their primary objective: the expulsion of Osho and the dispersal of his *sannyasins*. In its four years of existence, Rajneeshpuram had become a beacon, a real and pragmatic model for the future of civilisation; it had avoided the utopian idealism of the sixties and the archaic nostalgia of the seventies. It combined high numinous values with practical realism. To the fundamentalist Christian government and the vested interests of institutional America it presented a profound threat. Encampments of the National Guard had already surrounded the area some time previously.

On 28 October 1985 Osho was arrested without warrant and on trumped-up charges. That story is best told in *A Passage to America* by Max Brecher.

* * *

For the first time in nearly four years Laxmi had a clear-cut role helping to secure her imprisoned master's well-being. From Rajneeshpuram she spoke daily by telephone with Delhi.

She gives clear instructions to *sannyasins* there that they were to contact key figures in the Indian administration and public life. They included Prime Minister Rajiv Gandhi,

JG Krishnamurti and the Bollywood mega-star Amitabh Bachchan. She was galvanising protest at the abuse of one of India's greatest avatars. Demonstrations, she urged, should be peaceful and non-aggressive at all times. The friends were to put out real information to oppose the negative propaganda of the American counter-information services and their press. Daily meetings were also be held for meditation and to keep friends informed. Her willing friends in Delhi worked round the clock.

As soon as Osho was released on bail to Rajneeshpuram, Laxmi and Ma Anando, a lawyer from New Zealand, flew out to Delhi to arrange for Osho's inevitable return to India.

On 14 November 1985, a deportation order was made by a judge in Portland and Osho left America the very same evening, a sage returning to his true home.

13. THEY WILL KILL HIM

When Osho's plane touched down in Delhi, Laxmi was there to meet him along with Swami Vinod Bharti Khanna—the celebrated Bollywood superstar—along with half the world's press, hundreds of *sannyasins* and thousands of cheering supporters. In a Delhi hotel, the next morning, Osho gave a press conference and then left for the mountains.

Laxmi had rented for Osho and his party a section of the expensive, yet stunningly beautiful, property known as Span Resort in the Kullu–Manali valley. It consisted of five acres with a series of chalets, a kitchen and a community hall. The beautiful river Beas bound it on one side; behind it were the Himalayas.

There were dark clouds looming, however. Now began what some have described as an East–West split amongst the disciples. Perhaps it would be more accurate to describe it as an opposing alignment of individuals because actually race or nationality was never the issue: for many years Osho's disciples had not seen themselves as national but as global citizens.

Four concerns immediately arose for Laxmi. Firstly, the Western caretakers and administrators who had arrived with Osho had been given visas only valid for twenty-one days.

The Indian way in all negotiation with bureaucracy is

subtle dance of pulling rank. It rarely involves legality or rightness. The name of the game is 'Who has the Highest Status?' Laxmi assumed the responsibility of having the visas renewed; she might have had the ear of Prime Minister Rajiv Gandhi. But the rituals had to be observed, faces saved and appearances maintained.

The Western way with bureaucracy is to call in the big lawyers firing from the hip and to demand citizen rights. This the Westerners did, complaining that Laxmi was not moving fast enough.

Laxmi's method might have worked; the Western way— never. The requests for visa extensions were rejected.

The Westerners blamed Laxmi for either not trying hard enough or, far worse, for deliberately ensuring that they were not renewed. The accusation was that Laxmi had given the names of all the Westerners to the Indian authorities. They communicated to Osho their belief that she was sabotaging his work.

What neither party had yet realised was the amount of pressure that the Americans were exerting on that rather fragile government by their threats of economic, diplomatic and political sanctions. The situation was complex.

Ma Prem Shunyo for many years took care of Osho's laundry and sometimes his living arrangements. Her book, *Diamond Days with Osho*, is up there along with Ma Dharm Jyoti's *One Hundred Tales for Ten Thousand Buddhas* as an offering to the great canon of intimate, devotional literature—the literature of those close to the rare event of an awakened master. In her chapter describing Osho's return to India and the difficulties Western disciples had with their visas Shunyo writes this:

Hasya (the new international secretary to Osho) and Anando
had been busy in Delhi making appointments to see officials
there. Arun Nehru was the Minister for Internal Security
then, the man at the root of the visa problems, but their
appointments with him were continually cancelled. When
they did see an official they were told "confidentially" that
we should look within our group to see from where the
trouble came. It appeared that Laxmi had written to the
Home Office giving full details of all foreign disciples
and her words were to be repeated to us that "it was not
necessary that Osho needs foreigners to see to His welfare."
It was necessary actually, because more important to Osho
than life itself was His work, and Westerners were needed
for that. Osho was to say, "My Indian disciples meditate, but
will not do anything for me. My Western disciples will do
anything for me but will not meditate."

This serious accusation against Laxmi was repeated by
Swami Avesh, Osho's driver and the keeper of the Rolls
Royce cars. He too had been called to Kullu. In Poona One
he had been Laxmi's interim driver after Veetmoha was
transferred to the Publications Department. He said, 'I was
totally in love with Laxmi and Laxmi loved me. For me she
was like the perfect disciple.' Nevertheless he felt that Laxmi,
after four years in the American wilderness and having
been sent to India ahead of Osho, was expecting to be back
in her former seat of power. 'But the Westerners, Hasya,
Jayesh, Anando and Amrito now occupied that seat. Her role
was to find a property for Osho and his people. If she was
longing to be reinstated and if she had serious doubts about
the medical treatment Osho was asking for and receiving
from his doctor, then why would she not ensure their
removal?'

'Laxmi would never have sabotaged Osho's work,' was Atul's response. 'I was helping her at the time. She understood that Westerners and Indians were both important for his work. I know she tried her utmost to obtain the visas. Her paramount concern was always for Osho's health and his work.'

Osho forever had to deal with the unconsciousness of his people. With a master's skill, he allowed everyone enough rope to hang out their egos to dry. But we humans are a laggardly bunch. We have built high walls to prevent others seeing what we don't want to see in ourselves. Beneath our front rooms of efficiency or holiness or happiness or helpfulness we all have our unconsciousness; our cellar full of toxic, rusting junk.

Over the years, Osho laid bare every aspect of the human psyche. He spoke often of the Indian mind because it raised so much dust in India. We remember his words quoted earlier after he had Laxmi purchase an expensive car. 'Indians have become really materialistic, far more materialistic than any country in the world.'

Here is another such quote about Indian materialism.

I speak against the Italian mind, I speak against the German mind, I speak against the Jewish mind, but nobody makes any objection to it. But if I speak against the Indian mind, immediately somebody is there to object. Indians have become very touchy; deep down they feel some kind of inferiority, and on the surface they pretend superiority. Particularly as far as religion and spirituality is concerned, they feel that they are the spiritual guides of the world, that God has chosen them as messengers, that they are the source of religion, that they are holier than everybody else.

[Osho, *The Dhammapada: The Way of the Buddha*, Vol. 8, Ch. 11]

On another occasion Osho asserted:

*The Indian mind has a schizophrenic quality: on the surface
very holy; and deep inside very unholy. It is bound to be so
because of the thousands of years of repression, the repression of
everything that is natural.*

[Osho, *Zen, Zest, Zip, Zap and Zing*, Ch. 6, Q. 1]

* * *

Laxmi saw that to be a meditator was to be free of saint-
and sinner-hood, free of nationality and gender. Such
labels were at best meaningless, at worst obstacles along
the path. Furthermore she did not promote her nation as a
paragon of right living. She saw how we distort the past to
bathe ourselves in shining light. India has one story about
itself—a nation of holy beings. Britain, after plundering
the continent for two hundred years, has another story—a
nation of incompetents. We use such hollow labels to absolve
ourselves; to duck responsibility for our actions past and
present.

Laxmi, the meditator, had experienced that she was
not her body-mind. But how patent to her was her deep
unconscious? How detached was she from her desires?

Perhaps then Laxmi remembered the second talk
she heard from Osho long ago at the All India Women's
Congress. He had talked about Meera's blessed love for
Krishna. So great, so intense was her devotion for him that
she could face her family's murderous hostility with a smile
and generous gratitude.

What we know of Laxmi so far, her loyalty to people and
her integrity, suggest that these accusations are very unlikely

to be true. Even though Laxmi and Osho's care-giver, Vivek had, on occasions, been in dispute, Laxmi never questioned Vivek's importance for Osho's well-being. Would she have threatened Osho's welfare by having Vivek expelled from the country? Would it even have been necessary to name names considering the Security Services knew to whom they had given short visas, presumably forewarned by the CIA?

* * *

The Westerners have left, mostly for Nepal, and Laxmi inherits her second worry—Osho's health. Both issues were connected and they generated a cloud of misunderstanding between individuals around him.

Osho, then aged fifty-five, had been in a unique and subtle relationship with his body for over thirty years. One could roughly describe him as living in a permanent 'out of body state'.

In Span Resort it appeared that, in order to suppress Osho's allergic symptoms, he was prescribed by his physician a Corticosteroid drug. The problem was that he was given doses well over and above the normal safety limits. A problem with the drug is that it also suppresses the immune system, leaving the patient increasingly open to casual infections. On top of that, Osho was diabetic so the medication interfered with the metabolising of his blood sugars. Over a relatively short time, according to experts, there are serious side effects that include unusual fatigue and weakness, severe joint pain and over-sensitive teeth.

Laxmi fiercely contested whether Osho should be prescribed such drugs and was in favour of trying traditional Ayurvedic treatment. She consulted a number of medical authorities, including Osho's brother who was a doctor, all of whom were adamant that such doses should not be administered. Some of the Westerners were also said to have questioned the physician, Doctor Amrito, for prescribing such high doses. But they did not interfere. It was generally understood that Osho had a special relationship with his body, one that no medical consultant could envisage and that only he himself knew what was best for it. Amrito was quoted as saying before he left, 'I am a disciple first and a doctor second.'

Laxmi consulted with Ma Neelam, now looking after Osho as well as being his newly appointed secretary for Indian affairs. She asked her to put all the facts before him and obtain a second opinion. Osho's response to Neelam was clear, 'Good you have told me this. I appreciate your care. I know my body. Tell Laxmi to relax and not worry.'

Laxmi couldn't relax and she did worry. Some ten years later, shortly before her death, she spoke about her alarm concerning Osho's medication.

'Osho had poor health ever since his enlightenment and that was greatly aggravated by twenty years of travelling throughout India. Therefore, he had a doctor to look after his body. But that doctor did not do a proper job. He said, "I am a disciple first and a doctor second." In Laxmi's view, as far as Osho's body was concerned, he should have been a doctor first. It is no good talking about surrender while treating a master's ailments. That is the time to be professional and intelligent. Osho's body was frequently in pain. Perhaps he asked for anything that relieved the pain. But he wasn't a doctor! The doctor himself should have taken responsibility for the drugs he was prescribing with all their various harmful short and long-term side-effects; things that Osho could not know about. Laxmi's feeling was that Osho's death was not a natural death. He was an innocent man amongst cunning ones. Laxmi was not present when he departed but her heart has grave doubts about his death.'

Laxmi's retrospective advice to Neelam was 'We should have acted first and taken permission later.' She told Neelam of a story that she had heard from Osho, perhaps in a Hindi discourse, about Mahatma Gandhi, whose life was often under threat. Sardar Vallabhbhai Patel, the then home minister, was given the responsibility for providing his security. Gandhi told Patel that he did not need bodyguards. Osho said that Patel should nevertheless have provided the security because that had been his responsibility. His failure to do so led to tragic consequences.

Anuragi and others around Laxmi at this time saw that every breath of her body, every beat of her heart was devoted to Osho and his work and yet...'She would not listen to anyone. She acted like she could not trust anyone with the care of Osho. We told her, "He knows you are getting too much involved." She would not listen.'

* * *

A third worry for Laxmi was the purchasing of land. This had been put on hold for about six months. Ma Yoga Neelam had taken over the day-to-day care of Osho and was dealing with all Osho's Indian matters. This allowed Laxmi to devote her time and effort to the laborious, ongoing search for the 'New Commune'.

The clock was ticking, however. Huge bills were mounting at the Span Resort. Hasya had told Osho that six million US dollars were in hand with Jayesh. He, however, was reluctant to hand them over to Laxmi. Naturally Laxmi was forced to eliminate some of the hopeful properties which, with time, might have come to fruition.

'We will find a place,' was a phrase frequently on her lips Yet, at this time she was described as being unrealistic, blinded by her own over-optimism. Vivek said to Neelam, 'Laxmi lies. Her reports are never factual.'

Neelam said, 'Laxmi was completely reliable and quick in obtaining everything needed. Except property.'

* * *

Laxmi's fourth worry proceeded from the other three; that is, if concern for her own standing was a worry. Laxmi was once the voice and hands of Osho. The blessings and weight of that role was taken from her by Sheela's sleight of hand and the move to America. Now Osho was back in his own land and Laxmi was again at his side. Did she still want the status and intimacy of her previous role? Would her physical health support such a role again?

Of the people who were close to her at that time, most said no—she was not after status or power. Ma Neelam, his secretary for Indian affairs, said she never for a moment felt that Laxmi was jealous of her.

Confusion arose because Laxmi was Laxmi and she would fight fiercely for what she cared about—Osho's health and the propagation of his work. Often this placed her in opposition to his current staff, in this case, Jayesh Hasya, Anando and Amrito. They were irritated by her and wanted to bypass her, 'to put Laxmi aside'. So we had not so much a struggle for power, but more a struggle for values.

But was it as simple as that?

Neelam said, 'I was inexperienced in these things. Laxmi always gave helpful practical guidance. She was always reliable.'

So it probably was as simple as that.

* * *

Osho often spoke of his love of the Himalayas and the silence of its eternal snows. He liked the Span Resort and its adjacent mountains. Was the Span Resort a suitable site for the new commune? Was it for sale, even?

Some say two *crore* rupees or just over 300,000 US dollars would have bought it. Laxmi and some Delhi *sannyasins* did indeed meet the owner but Jayesh and Hasya, who had inherited the purse and debts from Rajneeshpuram, wanted to do the deal themselves. They had cash in hand from the sale of a fleet of Rolls Royces. When they met the Span Resort owner he, not surprisingly, jacked up the price and they, despite their vaunted negotiating skills, were unable to close a deal.

In all her property dealings, Laxmi had to face a myth that the Rajneesh Foundation was made of money. If Laxmi or any Indian *sannyasins* appeared with a Westerner or with a *mala* and a hint of red or orange clothing, the vendor doubled the asking price, then doubled it again. On one occasion, Laxmi sent Atul and Anuragi, dressed in blue jeans and white *kurtas*, to discuss the sale of a palace near Dalhousie. They met the Raja who owned it: he rose to meet them, laying aside a magazine featuring prominent photographs of Osho, Laxmi and Atul himself; so there was not much leverage for them in that deal.

On another occasion, Laxmi and Om Prakash Saraswati presented Osho with video footage of an empty school property in Himachal Pradesh that could accommodate 3,000 people and was available. The Westerners, when they had seen it, dismissed such a prospect because there was no drinkable water on the site. Osho rebuked them, 'See how these friends work from the heart. That is what is important: their love. Water can always be found.'

A final straw for Laxmi's burden was when Osho decided to go to Kathmandu where Sw Arun had rallied extensive royal, political and economic support for him and the possibility of space for a large commune. The Span bills, that included substantial amounts for personal drinks and international telephone calls, were left unpaid by Jayesh. Laxmi saw Osho off to Kathmandu via the Delhi Sheraton. Then and there, she told him of her mistrust of Jayesh, Anando and Hasya.

Atul saw Osho in his hotel at this time and he told him, 'You find a place and send me the message. I will come back.'

The owner of Span Resort held Laxmi as a security chip until the friends at Rajyoga Meditation Centre had collected the money owed that Laxmi was released.

* * *

In Nepal, the king, as a condition of his support, asked Osho to undertake never to speak against Hinduism. Trying to impose a condition on Osho was like asking a lion not to roar.

* * *

Sw Anand Maitreya was a long-time disciple of Osho. He had once been an able politician, about to take up the post of chief minister of the state of Bihar when he had a momentous encounter with Osho; in the blink of an eye his plans and ambitions were dissolved. He had come to see Osho at the house of a well-known Delhi publisher. Osho said to him, 'Between entering the room and sitting down here, some deep transformation has happened.'

Maitreya had felt it. Osho had said it. He bowed in wordless acknowledgment. He became a profound meditator. He never went back to politics.

Years later when Osho mischievously put out a list of those who had attained high spiritual status, with Maitreya's name included, it was only he who rumbled the joke. He said, 'You guys don't understand what a Master of Pranks he is. That Osho is such a rascal.'

Now in Kathmandu, Maitreya brought to Osho's attention that Laxmi's concern for his health and well-being had been too forcefully expressed in a meeting of *sannyasins* at the Delhi Meditation Centre, Rajyoga. 'His life is in danger; they will kill him,' she had declared.

Osho called all his administrators together in Kathmandu, including Laxmi and Arun and his oldest and most trusted Indian disciples, Sw Om Prakash Saraswati, Sw Maitreya, Sw Narendra, Sw Chinmaya Ananda and Ma Neelam along with Ma Hasya and Sw Jayesh, Ma Vivek and Sw Rafia, Ma Anando and Sw Amrito and others.

Laxmi, still with short hair, Western jeans and a white Indian *kurta* placed both hands on her navel. She looked at Jayesh, Hasya and Anando and the doctor unwaveringly. Then she restated her recrimination: 'Yes, Osho, I have this gut feeling, these people will kill you.'

A feather falling to the floor would have been audible in the silence. Osho looked tenderly at Laxmi, his calmness oil on a troubled sea. 'When I agree to someone having a certain role, I take the responsibility for that. From then on, I do not interfere. Neither should anyone else. I choose certain people to get the work done. Everyone needs to support them. In my *sannyas* there is no division. You are all one. Division will not help.'

* * *

Within days of this meeting, Osho flew out to Greece and was soon giving daily discourses to his disciples again. Laxmi was not amongst those with him. Under the blue skies of the island of Crete his people appeared suddenly in their hundreds, along with a bounty of spring flowers and almond blossoms. Twice a day, Osho sat beneath a spreading carob tree beside the wine dark Mediterranean sharing his wisdom and insights. The CIA and the Greek police mobilised rapidly to eject him; from the house, from the island, from Greece. Meanwhile Osho continued on what was to become known as his world tour.

Laxmi stayed behind in south Delhi and then later returned to Bombay, not however to Vatcha Villas but to the house of Sw Manu in Juhu. 'We used to see her from time to time,' said her sister. 'She was always consistently persistent. I remember she had a red chair sent from America—It took her two years to get it through the customs. Then she would not let anyone sit on it without a cover. She didn't say anything against the people looking after Osho but one knew she worried.'

* * *

From February until the end of July 1986 Osho was being harried and defamed across the world by a host of politicians not yet willing to hear of a rational, more wholesome vision to that which gives them their short-lived place in the public eye. Osho was either barred from entering—or forced out of—twenty-one countries. The American administration had a long arm and many dirty tricks up its long dirty sleeve.

Osho returned to India, the one country that could not exclude him. He stayed in Bombay as the guest of a *sannyasin* family. His concept for the present was to buy a sufficiently large house in Bombay where he could live with his staff and receive about a hundred of his *sannyasins* at a time. The old Poona Ashram buildings would again house his vital and enterprising community.

He invited Laxmi to resume being his secretary. Despite her poor health, she had an inexhaustible spirit with which to realise the master's vision. Neelam was also his secretary at this time. Osho told Neelam, 'Laxmi has done a really good job publishing the books. I would like them again to be published in the beautiful formats as before. On the Ranch, Sheela was never interested in books. She did them in a very bad way. We should put our energy in books. We used to get design awards.'

Both secretaries became involved in searching all over Bombay for a large property. They faced huge obstacles: few such extensive buildings were available, high prices were rising higher and now there was very little Vitamin M available. Laxmi was also concerned about the generally polluted and humid climate of the city. Nevertheless, she went about her mission with her usual ebullience and characteristic optimism.

For five months the search was continuous; many properties were seen. Sometimes the secretaries viewed them independently, sometimes together. Neelam said that she often felt Laxmi was still excessively over-optimistic. She was unrealistically hopeful and positive to the point of untruth. Neelam gave the example of a large residence that Laxmi felt was suitable. Neelam discovered that it was partially owned by many members of an extended family who were mostly at loggerheads, a few of whom were in residence with no inclination to move. Neelam challenged Laxmi with this predicament. 'You leave it to Laxmi. One will manage,' she responded.

A decision to leave Bombay was made when the daughter of Osho's host was to be married and the house could no longer support his presence and the hundreds of *sannyasins* coming for his daily discourses. Osho was never one to repeat himself yet, almost certainly aware that his days were numbered, he decided to return to Poona.

* * *

The message to Laxmi was: 'Drop searching for a property, come and live in the Ashram. He knows you don't have much time. So work on yourself.'

She came, she stayed for a few weeks and then left. The expectation among friends was that Laxmi again would be Osho's secretary because Neelam was still inexperienced in such matters. Laxmi never created any problem in the Ashram but did not feel right there.

'During this period known as Poona Two, Laxmi had an intuition that certain Westerners did not have Osho's best interests paramount in their minds. She conveyed this to

A again. HE told her, Laxmi you have said this once,
*e*ver say it again because Westerners and Indians are the
same to me.' [Sohan Ma]

Neelam asked her on one occasion, 'Why are you so
against the Westerners?' Laxmi responded, 'Laxmi is not
against Westerners. Laxmi has no trust of Jayesh, Amrito
and Hasyo only.'

Osho had told Laxmi to let go of organising things and
to turn her attention inwards during the early days of the
Ranch. Now five years later, back in the old Ashram for the
Poona Two era, he had repeated the message.

Laxmi was a person too motivated, too charged with
energy for her mission to heed his words. Her stated
objective was, on each occasion, to find a place where
Osho's work and his health would most prosper. She had
good reasons and a vindication for her intended actions.
Osho had said:

*People were trained that obedience is the greatest virtue. It is
not! Sometimes it is disobedience that is the greatest virtue.
Sometimes, of course, it is obedience. But the choice has to be
yours: you have consciously to choose whether to obey or not to
obey. That means you have consciously to remain the master in
every situation, whether you obey or you disobey.*

[*A Sudden Clash of Thunder*]

There were many savours and spices at play in Laxmi's cook-
pot now. The clearly expressed one was of concern for Osho's
health. Were there other unexpressed or invisible impulses?
To wrest him away from those whom she perceived as giving
him the wrong care? To remove him from a place where
he had once lived but that had now fallen into disrepair?

To regain her former position as Osho's right hand and spokesperson? To better further Osho's work elsewhere?

Laxmi was both a subtle and a simple character. She was complex in her admixture of esoterica and materialism and yet she was single-minded and thorough in action. She was a deeply devoted and surrendered disciple and she had her own blinkered views.

There can be no absolute truth in the relative world of human behaviour. The fact is Laxmi moved back to the family home of Vatcha Villas and made regular visits to Poona to sit in discourse and on one occasion cook a kedgeree or *khichdi* called for by Osho. Neelam remembered, 'Laxmi came early in the morning with both a cooking pot and all the ingredients. She spent the whole day preparing the dish. She cooked with so much love. And Osho enjoyed. Afterwards she shared it with me too.' During visits to Poona she stayed with the couple Bafnaji and Sohan Ma, much loved and respected long-time devotees of Osho.

She told a friend, 'Laxmi has the gut feeling that these people will kill Him. One hopes one is wrong. Laxmi feels it so strongly in the belly. One knows that Osho's work has to be done by practical and materialist people. They are more efficient and political than people like us. But Laxmi fears for his life. For that reason one cannot rest. One must continue to look for a better situation.'

* * *

Here is a hypothetical question for you, dear reader. It is also a real question. Your master—your ineffably wise, compassionate and beloved *guru*—is informed that in the audience tonight there is a man carrying a hand gun intent on killing him. The master has beside him armed guards who are his disciples specially trained to protect him in just such an eventuality. He tells the guards that his work is complete and he is ready to die. His life is in the hands of existence. The guards should put down their weapons and not interfere with the course that existence would follow. This actually happened in the last days of Sheela's time in Rajneeshpuram.

Readers of these words, you are the guard, what would you do? Obey your master or your instinct and your training?

Disciplehood is the laying down of the calculating mind at the feet of higher consciousness; the enlightened one. At no time does the master ask us to abandon responsibility for ourselves.

The Christian Church in the Middle Ages was torn apart by a theological dispute concerning the number of angels that could fit on the head of a pin. That debate could be solved at one blow. The angels are as small or as large as you imagine them to be.

We have this actual event of the gunman in the audience. Would you put down your gun or would you defend your master?

We have another story of a qualified doctor prescribing drugs for a chronic condition; drugs that are known to have long-term fatal consequences. Now we have the account of Laxmi being told to drop her concerns for both Osho's health and for a new property and to deepen her meditation.

These dilemmas, like the argument of the angels on the head of a pin, might be resolved in one cut of the master's sword.

'Should a disciple ever disobey his or her master?' Ma Jyoti was asked.

'The master looks after the things of the spirit,' she replied. 'The disciple looks after things of the world.' She went on to illustrate this with a story.

'In Woodlands once I was sitting beside Osho when a recently married woman came to see him. Her question concerned what she should do or not do about a previous boyfriend who was still in love with her and still writing love letters to her.

'Osho told her to show the letters to her husband and explain the situation to him. I spontaneously interrupted. "But Osho! If she does that, her husband will disown her! Then she'll be a social outcast rejected by everyone."

'Osho turned back to the woman, "Okay, you get together with Jyoti afterwards. She will advise you."

'Jesus said render unto Caesar the things which are Caesar's and unto God the things which are God's.

'The unarmed guards of Poona One and Two who were asked to stay alert during discourses following various threats to Osho's life were all, without question, ready to interpose their bodies between Osho and any potential threat. For the rational mind, hypothetical questions suggest obvious answers: for the heart of the devotee there are no set answers, only the vast mystery of a master at work.

'For the reader's peace of mind, it should be added that the gunman in the audience at Rajneeshpuram never materialised. Perhaps he was a figment of Sheela's disorder.'

* * *

Laxmi's decision to follow her gut feeling required courage and a fair smattering of self-delusion. She continued to look for land more favourable to Osho's health.

Her search centred on Lonavala, the small hill station poised exactly where the great Deccan Plain crumples into the Western Ghats which then drop down to the steaming levels of Bombay. It was the self-same area she had rejected fourteen years earlier on account of its high humidity during monsoon. At this time she had few financial resources but with her usual compulsive optimism, she showed friends videos of various properties that might or might not be available and suitable. And she asked who amongst them would offer financial support.

'We tried to tell her, we tried to explain that Osho wanted a new way to work with his people. But Laxmi is Laxmi. She never listens,' said one friend.

When questioned if this search was at Osho's request Laxmi replied, 'If Laxmi buys the right place and invites Osho, HE will accept.'

Such an assumption of compliance is especially dangerous when referring to a master. A master follows no logic but the meta-logic of existence. Osho never interfered with people; his way was the unpredictable way of the white cloud that moves according to any breeze, any updraft, any stirring of the air. We saw how Sheela had used this quality to establish herself as his secretary and take him to New Jersey and then Oregon. Laxmi perhaps hoped, in all sincerity, to use the same tactic.

It was brought to Osho's attention that while money was being raised to repair and expand the old Poona Ashram, Laxmi, they said, was canvassing the same *sannyasins* for money for a different site. Laxmi later said of these reports. 'These people do not give the true information to Osho.'

However, a master also works with that which underlies

prevailing information. He is cooking something bigger more subtle than mere facts reveal. Osho immediately told Neelam to say to Laxmi, 'You are not dropping the search for another property. You are dividing the energy of my people. You are therefore not welcome in the commune anymore.'

'What I feel is that Laxmi failed the inner test of power,' commented Swami Avesh concerning this ultimatum. 'The facts are so clear. She was banned after he has forgiven her for following him to America against his express wishes, been divisive in her behaviour prior to the world tour and even after he has given her a special invitation to live in the Ashram. Enough is enough; there is no excuse for this last thing she has done. He would not have banned her otherwise.'

* * *

But are the facts clear? Are facts ever clear? And anyway, who can say why a master acts as he does?

The crucial and irrevocable night came in April 1989 when Laxmi, sitting like a marble buddha in the marble Buddha Hall, was escorted from her front row seat moments before Osho arrived for his evening discourse. This is the story that starts this story. And this is her death before her death. Those who knew her and saw the event were profoundly shocked. How had things come to this? How had a powerful, high-spirited, devoted and cherished disciple of Osho come to such a place of indignity and exclusion?

Swami Tathagat, who was then Ashram-in-Charge or manager, tells of the event as he saw it.

'A few weeks after I heard she had been banned, I saw Laxmi sitting in the front row. I'd just brought in Osho's chair. I hurried back to Lao Tzu House to inform Neelam. Neelam and I went back to Buddha hall. Laxmi was in meditation but Neelam gently asked her to step outside with us. I told a guard to bring her cushion. We stood there in the carport behind Osho's podium and told her that she was not allowed in the Ashram. She burst out in a rage, albeit hushed. Then Neelam told her, "This message comes from Osho. You are not welcome in the commune anymore." For a moment Laxmi was speechless, looking from face to face. You could see she was in shock.

'Neelam continued, "Did Bafnaji not tell you?"

'"Tell Laxmi what?"

'"Osho's message."

'"Laxmi has received no message from Osho."

'Now we were walking on the gravel path towards the front gate. Inside Buddha Hall the musicians had started playing for the arrival of Osho. It dawned on all of us there had been some awful misunderstanding. Osho's direction to Laxmi had been given some five or six weeks before. Neelam had conveyed this message to Bafnaji. He was to tell Laxmi that she was no longer welcome in the Ashram. Laxmi had been in Mumbai: she had not received that message.

'When this was explained Laxmi said "This is the Master's Zen stick. This is for Laxmi's transformation. Laxmi trusts what you are saying and is sorry the anger came on you." We were at the main gate now. Laxmi had sent her car away. So Premgeet took her to Bafnaji and Sohan Ma's house in my car.

'Apparently, she did not speak much on the journey but she told him, "Life is a therapy with Osho. HE is working on us. This is HIS device. There is nothing bad in being expelled. This is between me and my master."

'On arrival at Bafnaji's she stepped out lightly. As Premgeet prepared to drive off she put her head again through the car window, "This is the Master's grace; This is the Master's Zen stick. *Lakdi lag gayi.*"'

* * *

Why had Laxmi not received Osho's message? Why did she have to receive what many people saw as such a public shaming? Neelam spoke about it years later with a disarming candour. 'I did not dare tell her. I could not bring myself to give the message directly. I passed the job to Bafnaji. I had called him because he was Laxmi's host. He also did not want to be the one. As it happened, weeks passed, Laxmi was in Mumbai. We sort of forgot about it.'

* * *

Jyoti Ma, Laxmi's long-time colleague, was shocked and upset. She went to see her that very evening after discourse. 'It is His Grace,' she was told.

In the following day many other friends visited Laxmi in tears, to console her and commiserate. 'Why you are crying? This is between Laxmi and her master. *Lakdi lag gayi!* This is the Master's Zen stick. There is no drama, no tragedy. Laxmi has no blame or doubts. This is the Master's work. This is His gift for Laxmi's growth.'

Still her body was shaking; still her mind was in shock. Her trust and her courage were now on call as never before. At a time like this, devotion either flowers into immortality or collapses into embittered grievance.

A master delivers his hits in a time and a mode for the optimum strike. Something in Laxmi was unresolved. She knew it: he knew it. She was clinging to an idea, albeit a lofty idea. She thought she knew best what was needed for Osho and his work. She would, if she could, override his decision to go with the flow of those around him.

Over the minutes and days that followed her expulsion, Laxmi let her meditation open up. She began to accommodate a new and deeper understanding. She feared that they would kill him. This was Laxmi's fear, not Osho's fear. Her trust had been imperfect—dangerously imperfect. Laxmi let a larger awareness subsume that fear. It dawned on her that the radical changes Osho offers to the world must happen, indeed can only happen, through the energy and efficacy of that mainly Western group.

She remembered the story of a famous samurai who visited the Zen master Hakuin, head monk at the Shoin-ji monastery. The old man was seated on a mat under a tree in the garden surrounded by a small circle of disciples. Without ceremony or respect, the samurai interrupted the talk and demanded of Hakuin, 'Is there a heaven, is there a hell? Can you prove it to me?'

'And who are you?' enquired Hakuin.

'I'm a samurai. Nobushige by name.'

'You a samurai? I can hardly believe it. When did you last wash? And who would employ you with such an idiot look on your face? You seem more like a beggar to me.'

Enraged, Nobushige started to draw his sword.

'Oh, you've got a toy sword, have you?' Hakuin remained motionless. 'How rusty is the blade? Too blunt to cut my head off, I expect.'

Even as the samurai stood over Hakuin, his sword drawn back to strike, the monk remarked, 'Ha! Here open the gates of Hell.'

At these quiet words, the samurai understood the master's self-discipline and courage. He re-sheathed his blade and bowed.

'And here open the gates of Heaven.'

Laxmi perceived that just as the monk had offered his life for the illumination of his disciples and a passing samurai, so too did Osho offer his life and entrust the care of his body to those whose understanding and meditation was nugatory but whose reach into the contemporary world would be considerable. He himself had no attachment to the continuation of his life. To him the bidding of existence was paramount. His words would live by themselves. Laxmi's attachment to his body was her last barrier. This hit was her chance to surmount it, her chance to return to the source.

14. THE FINAL MASTERPIECE

To change the world we must change ourselves; find inside ourselves that which never changes.

Not everyone will. Fortunately for future generations, what Carl Jung called the 'Collective Unconscious' and Teillard de Chardin called the 'Noosphere' and contemporary scientists call 'Morphic Resonance', not everyone has to change. When enough individuals transform themselves, a domino effect occurs and the whole behavioural environment is changed. With meditation and growing awareness, the global balance would be tipped towards a more conscious way of living. This is easily possible.

Indeed, more and more neuroscientists and psycho-physiologists are asserting that humans are actually hard-wired for cooperation and harmony rather than the competition and aggression to which we are conditioned. On top of that, they are discovering areas of the brain that are rarely activated in everyday life but which, when mobilised in either sex or meditation, trigger a human propensity for connection to others, to nature and to all that is. To see and understand the rising spiral pathway of Laxmi's life is to see a way out of the current social, spiritual, political, religious and environmental entanglements of our age.

Laxmi did the work just as we and future generations

must. She herself had no particular concern for the environment or politics or religions. Her focus was the vision of her master, which included her own self-realisation and the evolutionary leap humanity must take for its survival.

Global warming was recognised as problematic back in the 1980s. Nations have made half-hearted, largely unsuccessful attempts to reverse its effects. We see this and all the manifold problems of our time. We will not properly address them until we address the structural flaws in ourselves.

We first have to change ourselves.

* * *

Now Laxmi stayed steadfast in the old family home in Bombay, but Vatcha Villas was a sadder place that echoed with the memories of another life. She had few financial resources. Hitherto her life insurance and social security were always her trust in her *guru*. She had never had a bank account. A Delhi friend who loved Osho and saw Laxmi as part of Osho's great family had been supporting her in a modest way for some years.

Laxmi's lifestyle was always congruent to her situation. When travelling on the business of Osho, nothing but the best would do; when living on her own account, her requirements were simple and unpretentious.

She had learned from Osho that disciples have to walk their own uniquely personal way; the master cannot walk it for you. A year earlier she had teamed up with her younger sister Shobana and together they started a *tiffin*-filling business for lunches. A *tiffin* is a tiered collection of stainless steel vessels that fit tightly together and are held in place by a metal strap that is also a handle. Filling *tiffins* is a well-established profession in India, where commuters like to eat a proper lunch but not in a restaurant or cafeteria. Either they will bring their *tiffin* from home or they will have one filled near their place of work.

The Kuruwa wealth had diminished so now Laxmi's enjoyment of cooking was again married to her desire to raise her Vitamin M intake. She had leaflets designed, printed and distributed. She and her sister undertook to serve a daily lunch of high quality, well-cooked rice, dal and vegetables with two *chapatis* for six days a week.

As it happened, there was a hospital in their vicinity. Many of the young, unmarried doctors there took up her services. During the years from 1988 the business grew. Laxmi said, 'See what happens when you have good food prepared with love in a hygienic kitchen and presented beautifully? You have wealth!'

Gradually more and more members of the family were co-opted into the process and they remember the fun and the labour of rolling out hundreds of *chapatis* by hand every day.

Laxmi still made occasional visits to Poona to see Bafnaji and Sohan Ma. The latter said, shortly before she herself passed away, 'Laxmi was always very loving and simple with us; always unassuming. I never saw her in pain or misery about what happened with her. She used that opportunity for her growth.'

* * *

In these last years, living in the family home, Laxmi would open the house for a *satsang* every week or two. Twenty or thirty seekers after truth would gather; they were mostly local residents of Bombay but with a scattering of Westerners and Japanese. Laxmi made brownies beforehand. Musicians on sitar, guitar and tablas played with intervals of silence before all listened to a recorded discourse. Then there was an hour or two of stories, conversation and laughter. Laxmi never lectured, never presumed to interpret the words of Osho, she only shared her own experience.

When her cancer symptoms reappeared, Laxmi continued the *satsangs*, reminding friends that meditation is the most efficient and most rapid route to self-realisation. 'That is the real freedom, the real release from the treadmill of hope, fear, pleasure and pain. But Laxmi is a slow learner, that's why the master, in his tenderness, had to dole out so many hits.'

* * *

To read and write of Laxmi's faults and shortcomings is not to cut her down to size; it is to see her as an ordinary, therefore courageous, fearful and egoic, individual struggling towards the light. Thus, she remains accessible to all who face their own life struggles. All around we see the greed, incompetence and self-importance of our global leaders. They cannot solve our global problems.

The world we all want needs our love and courage purified by meditation. Everyone with ears to hear and eyes to see will make a difference. Everyone's gift is important now. Laxmi's journey of the heart is the journey all of us are on

* * *

In the afternoon of 19 January 1990 Osho left his poor distressed and damaged body. The news was instant

headlines all around the world. There in the Poona Ashram
his vacated body was laid on a litter covered with flowers
and placed upon the podium in Buddha Hall, the very same
podium from which he had delivered so many momentous
discourses. Musicians played and the hall was filled with
the sounds of singing and weeping.

After a short while the body was carried through
darkened streets to the Poona Burning Ghats beside the
Mullah-Mutha River; in its wake there walked and danced
many thousand white robed *sannyasin*s. Osho's brothers
and his old-time disciples built, log by log, the pyre around
his body. While that was being done, the heartfelt tributes
of his people were their singing and their sobbing and their
silences. The fire was lit and underneath a vault of tar-black
night a great white bird of love arose, its wings assuring all
his people everywhere that love is deathless.

* * *

As soon as she heard the news, Laxmi travelled to Poona
for the last time. She arrived well before midnight when the
flames were still burning high. Around the pyre, *sannyasin*s
were a sea of grief and celebration. Laxmi sat far back from
the throng, closed her eyes and turned her attention inwards.
Tears were coursing down her cheeks yet joy and gratitude
were blooming in her heart. For many years she had been
assayed in the furnace of her master's physicality. The
Zen stick of his compassion had broken her attachments
to it. Now she clearly saw how Osho's transition from
embodiment to disembodiment was a very small move,
indeed was no move at all. Laxmi knew it now not just as
mental understanding; she knew it from the depths of her

experience. Osho was still perfectly present to her. He ha~ talked many times of the great blessing and massive release of energy occurring when a buddha leaves the body. It is an energy that can transform lives.

If you have loved me and trusted me you will feel me in a thousand ways once I am unembodied: my consciousness is universal. Right now you have to come to me. Then, you will not need to seek and search for me. Wherever you are...your thirst, your love...and you will find me in your very heart, in your very heartbeat.

Now Laxmi, sitting silently at the edge of darkness, heard him in the rhythm of her heartbeat.

* * *

Osho was never a teacher yet people learn from him. He was an ordinary man transmitting an extraordinary experience, the magnitude of which most people rarely perceive. Now his lovers celebrated his life and death in the manner they have learned from him. They surrounded the incandescent pyre, singing, crying and laughing, mourning and sitting silently in the dark Indian night. When finally, gradually, fitfully, the flames died down and the embers were a pale grey ash and the dawn a pale grey luminescence over the river, they started to wend their way home to their beds. The inconspicuous figure of a small Indian lady that they passed was noted by some, recognised by few.

In her heart she heard his words, 'Right now I am available to you only embodied, imprisoned in a certain shape and form. When I am gone, where can I go? I will be here in the winds, in the ocean; and if you have loved me, if you have trusted *me*, you will feel me in a thousand

and one ways. In your silent moments you will suddenly feel my presence.'

She remained alone by the ashes of her beloved master a long, long time. She remembered so much of her life with HIM. The memories were not memories, they were knowings in her breast, vivid actualities, wordless. They were who she was. His final gift to her had seen to that. Each moment was a death. And a rebirth.

When the ashes were cold, she retired to the home of Bafnaji and Sohan Ma. Later she sent a message that she would like to visit the Ashram.

Her request was refused. *Unki anukampa hai.* Laxmi smiled, the Master's grace.

* * *

Laxmi's health was declining. She and her sisters decided to wind down the *tiffin* business. Members of the family rallied around and cared for her; half a dozen of her relatives were *sannyasins*. She felt weak and she could not swallow. As yet she was not in pain. She continued to have streams of visitors both Western and Indian even as the Ashram started its morph into a resort and its slow decline from global hub of spiritual endeavour to a husk of Osho's seed.

When the pain started, it was constant and often excruciating. With the visitors gone, Laxmi sat immobile in her chair for hours on end. At night she slept on a massage table also brought back from the States. She had lived her life intensely and with bright intelligence. She had watched the passing parade of wealth and poverty, fame and infamy, success and failure, pleasure and pain. She had seen they are but transient events not bearing on one's own essential being. She had understood that freedom and bliss do not come cheap nor can they be obtained from anyone else: each must do the work on him- or herself.

What did she think of death? She had understood that every moment is a death and a rebirth—and that is the only real life. Osho was her pathfinder and inspiration on this lone journey to Selfhood, but death, when it comes, is done alone. Meditation was her vehicle to transcendence and she had brought it to each and every aspect of her life. According to her master, to die beautifully one has to live beautifully. To die amazingly and in excitement, in ecstasy, one has to prepare one's whole life for ecstasy, excitement, amazement. Death is simply the culmination point, the crescendo of your life.

Laxmi wrote to a friend in Oregon.

Beloved Seeta,
Love.

Earlier had received your letter and some photos of your oil-paintings. Had replied to that.

Now it seems this old Rolls-Royce engine has started giving trouble. Old junk needs to be changed for a better model. Isn't that the style in America?

Here let-go is the way...so the body is in let-go—when, how, where, cannot be predicted by anyone.

The goose is out. Cancer has appeared in the pulmonary artery so enjoying is happening every moment.

The bell is ringing; any moment the bird may fly from the cage.

Love to all the friends there.

Ma Yoga Laxmi

* * *

Friends received the news that Laxmi's time was running out; that they should come to say goodbye. Small gatherings took place.

'Laxmi Ma, you often tell us meditation is the fast track to living life more consciously. What do you mean by that? And what is the slow track?'

'Laxmi speaks of what she learned from HIM and now experiences for herself. When we search outside ourselves, our life appears as meaningless. Yes meaningless! When we search inside ourselves, our life appears to be full of meaning. And significance. We meet what is enduring. This body, this bed, the world in its turmoil, this bright blue sky, are all passing ripples, all you can see of the *leela*, the play of existence. None of it endures.

'Everyone thinks that they are their bodies and their minds. We think we own the world. We all must mend our ways. Osho points the way. The fast track to consciousness is deliberate meditation. Meditation is nothing but peeling the onion. When nothing is left, you have arrived. Isn't that amazing? Who we are is nothingness! A vast, conscious nothingness! A witnessing.

'There have been tears, but now there is clarity. Meditation is not therapy but it is therapeutic, It has allowed Laxmi to step back from her conditioned mind and painful body into unchanging consciousness. Ma Yoga Laxmi is just a passing cloud, neither a heretic nor a saviour.

'She is a tiny part of Osho's work to wake up the world to its real potential. Once upon a time Laxmi was on the slow track with Gandhiji, thinking things could be improved by changing society from outside. But look at the poverty and misuse of power in India today. The West thinks psychotherapy will get them a heaven on earth. And look at them now!

'Yes, certain things can help. A humble work-life that will not feed the ego; serving nature, the community, a friend in need; these things help. Eating vegetarian, creativity, celebration, dance and music, laughter, they all bring us closer to higher consciousness. Laxmi says that the fast track is meditation. And our master has given us the most modern, most efficient, tools for transformation to this higher consciousness: Dynamic meditation, *Kundalini*, Mystic Rose and a hundred and one others.

'Laxmi understands also that now, more than ever, we need meditation as life becomes more complex and people become more specialised. We are marching briskly into a state of ever deepening crisis. Meditation is the only way we disparate individuals can really come together.'

"Would you not like to be in Poona near the Ashram for your death?'

'Poona Ashram, all of *sannyas* and His *samadhi* are in these body cells. He is with Laxmi wherever she is. Laxmi is free of desires and fears, free of pleasure and pain.'

'So you don't feel any pain?'

'Laxmi did not say that! Pain is there; always there. She is free of it. You must understand two things she has learned from HIM. First thing is—twenty-four years ago Laxmi saw she was not the body. She was the awareness of it. Awareness is not confined to the life of this body-mind. Second thing is—acceptance is HIS message! If one wants the pain to not be there, then problems happen. To fight with "what is" causes pain. Acceptance is Laxmi's anaesthetic. That and this *mala*.' Laxmi touched it, now wrapped around the turban holding her hair.

'Have you any complaints or wishes?' asked another friend.

'Laxmi has no complaints but a non-serious observation and one wish only. Laxmi has understood that Osho is clearing away old musty furniture in order to make place for the new. Laxmi is a devotee but in India we make devotion a ritual. Why? We make ourselves appear devoted in order to avoid the true work.'

'And the true work is...?'

'Laxmi knows you are kidding her. The true work is what has brought you here. Self-enquiry. To find out who you really are. To find freedom. To become not separate from all that is. So Laxmi is saying, don't get stuck in past beliefs, old rituals, warmed up religious left-overs. Make a fresh meal.'

'And Laxmi's wish...?'

'Laxmi's wish is that His work be properly archived and protected, tapes that are missing be searched for and found. He once told Laxmi, "I only have my words." His words are the work, the only life that Laxmi has. Oh yes! Another wish, *khichdi* for lunch.'

'What is your message to friends, Laxmi?'

'Laxmi has known the greatest gift that life can give; to find a master, to fall in love with Him, to receive His hits and drink His overflowing silence. Laxmi says, Friends! Open your eyes! The world needs people who can see. We are pioneers. When we are gone, you youngsters will grow in the soil of our making. We are the compost for you to flower. Now fill the world with a riot of colour and beautiful perfume.'

'Oh Laxmi, we will miss you. You somehow...' the sentence dissolved in the tears of a young Brazilian *sannyasin*.

'Don't cry for Laxmi. Laxmi remembers the story of a Zen monk who was given a beautiful glass goblet by the participants of a meditation camp. Before the camp dispersed, a woman who had not spoken much all week burst into voice. She was desperate; she was feeling that the camp had been a waste of time. She said that for the whole week her mind had been filled with the death of her son. He had been murdered in New York two years before. The monk listened attentively to her tearful outburst. Then he held up the engraved goblet and said, "When you gave me this precious gift I understood that it is already broken. What comes into form dissolves again into formlessness. It is useless and it is painful to resist that. Everything that has a beginning has an ending. Our opportunity in this body is to find in ourselves that awareness, that consciousness which is never born and never dies; that within us which is eternal." Laxmi reminds you that from the very moment we are born, we start to die.

'Some years ago, when Laxmi was in Washington she realised she was still clinging to the past, to an old idea of herself as Osho's carer. That all had to be dropped. That garbage had to be thrown out.'

'Do you have any regrets Laxmi Ma?'

'Regrets? Regrets are garbage!' Laxmi laughed. 'Laxmi has gratitude only. She has received more gifts from life than anyone could expect. One never liked being barred from the Ashram. However, it served its purpose. It handed Laxmi her freedom. One has no regrets.'

After a long introspective pause she concluded, 'Laxmi is happy. Death is nothing but a small bubble on the surface of the water that dissolves back into the stream. The stream

The Only Life

is flowing to the river and the river dissolves in the ocean. For all ills, meditation is the medicine. Shall we play a tape? And who will make *masala chai?*'

* * *

Friends spoke of her beauty at this time, her radiance, her care for visitors and distant friends. Despite the pain she laughed a lot, was always vibrant, always a joy to be with.

Death itself has no existence. What actually happens is the transformation of consciousness from one form into another form, or, finally and ultimately, into formlessness. It is not against life. It does not destroy life. That's why I said death does not exist as conceived. It really gives the body another chance to grow. And if you have grown fully then there is no need for another chance; then your being moves into the ultimate being. You are no more a separate small dewdrop, but the whole ocean of existence.

* * *

At this time Laxmi was recorded on video speaking in Hindi with Sw Atul from Delhi. He put to her a number of questions.

Q: 'What are your feelings and thoughts on these newly introduced meditations?'

A: 'Osho's meditation techniques are complete and timeless. They should not be meddled with. New techniques are certainly appropriate for therapies but not for meditations. Osho gave many, many talks on techniques. Indeed, he revitalised the *Vigyan Bhairav Tantra* and evolved meditations for the modern mind. We do not have the depth of insight to invent new meditations. And Osho would *never* have suggested techniques to a few people to be used at some future date after his death. He once told Laxmi years ago in Mumbai that, after his death, there would be floods of followers claiming special knowledge. Laxmi is sharing this with you, Atul, because his presence and his showering of love for many years have blessed her. Friends can hear Laxmi's words and then decide to value them or to bin them.'

Q: 'You met nearly all those who became *sannyasins* from the mid-sixties onwards. We know about a few who died enlightened; how many living enlightened ones are there?'

A: 'There are enlightened ones. In Laxmi's understanding, Osho saw how people would so easily turn them into gods and saints as crutches for their own egos. So he did not announce their transcendence. Enlightened ones give off a fragrance that will be detected by anyone who is open. There are uncountable people on this earth; those who are seeking truth will find an enlightened one. Just as false seekers will find false teachers. This process is inevitable.

'And there is another dimension to it. Things don't stop with enlightenment. Osho did not want his people to become complacent lest their growth stopped. This was an example of his compassion, as Laxmi understands it.'

Q: 'Can one fall back from enlightenment?'

A: 'Indeed one can. Osho has explained that there are seven stages in the process of full self-realisation or enlightenment; we call them chakras. At the fourth stage, there is an awakening that can come and go. At the fifth stage, awareness is deeper but it is still mixed with unawareness. From the sixth stage, it is not possible to fall back. About the seventh step...Laxmi will tell you when she gets there.

'Laxmi would certainly have fallen back without Osho's continual hits and his love. Actually, from the outside, He appeared to be hitting Laxmi, but from the inside He was taking the most tender care. He knew Laxmi might fall back when He gave her the hit in Poona and banned her from the commune. She had to focus all her energy then. "Be single pointed", He once told her. But Laxmi is Laxmi. She had to do it her way. And get the big Zen stick.

'His compassion is overflowing. Laxmi is ecstatic. That is on the front page. The physical pain with this cancer doesn't make any difference. Some people think that an enlightened being doesn't feel pain, but in my experience the pain is more not less. The painkillers don't help. However the awareness is foremost. The body is in pain, but not Laxmi. There is sheer ecstasy and bliss, and His blessing always there. HE takes care of everybody's journey.

'Every situation can be used for the growth of awareness. That is our responsibility. And if awakening can happen to someone as ordinary as me, it can happen to anyone. Trust the master and be aware!'

Q: 'How did Vivek, his care-giver for so many years, miss her opportunity?'

A: 'She lost her inner focus. She became more and more diverted towards worldly things. In Poona One her responsibility had been within Lao Tzu House only. On the Ranch she became involved with the politics of the administration. Her awareness faltered. She gradually closed down her windows and doors. When that happens what can the sun do? For a master no one is special. And everyone is special.'

Q: 'How did Sheela take over from you?'

A: 'Osho did not appoint Sheela. She just told him that all heads of departments wanted a change, that Laxmi was too old fashioned and slow and Indian. She said we should move out of India to America. Osho asked her to get signatures from the heads. She did get some. Then Sheela's brother came up with the land in Oregon.'

* * *

The family home of the Kuruwas was no longer what it used to be. The patriarchs of old India were fading away. The house may have seemed a poorer place, yet Laxmi was richer, more joyous, more free and luminous that ever she might have expected in her adolescent dreams of Gandhi and the Independence Movement.

Laxmi was loved. In those final months a box of six apples arrived every day from somewhere in the Himalayas where apples grow. The devotee is worthy of devotion.

All who saw Laxmi in those final days saw that she was afloat on a tranquil sea. Frail though her body was, her hair seemed more black and glossy than ever, her eyes more a-sparkle, her voice always vibrant with life. Anuragi, her driver from the Delhi days, visited her at the end of November in 1994. He said, 'You could feel the fire and the force in her. She told stories but she never preached. She never ever presented herself as a priestess of Osho. She had her master's antipathy for such pundits. Yet she could still express herself with force.'

'The Westerners have prevailed,' she said on one occasion. That was an observation, not an expression of despondency or criticism. She had long before stopped judging the Ashram administration. To a friend Manju, she said about the banning, 'Laxmi has understood. It was futile what Laxmi was doing, searching property.'

Her body grew progressively weaker, her spirit never. When visitors came she greeted them with a surge of energy. 'Laxmi is happy to see those friends who tasted His honey. You are welcome here.'

To one visitor she said, 'There are no instant cures for cancer or any of the problems that we have. The only cure is awareness. Then the problem isn't a problem. Awareness brings resolution. What Osho has been telling us is all that coming generations need to know.'

She said more than once, 'We have so much to be grateful for, we could be thanking existence all day and night for the trees, the sunrise, the birds that sing at dawn.' She made it known she would like her body to be cremated and her passing celebrated with a *kirtan*.

* * *

As the final days of 1994 slid into 1995, Laxmi withdrew into the spacious realms within herself. She sometimes listened to tapes of musicians that Osho had loved and to tapes of Osho himself.

Very few people die consciously, hence the fear; because very few people live consciously, hence the fear. Whatever you want your death to be, let first your life be exactly the same—because death is not separate from life, it is not an end to life, but only a change. Life continues, has continued, will always continue. But forms become old. Death is a blessing; it is not a curse.

Sometimes she slept, sometimes made feeble efforts to clean her room. When a doctor came to drain fluid from her she said, 'This body does not feel pain anymore.' She had never forgotten the lesson she learned in Nargol; it is only the body that dies. Laxmi had fully lived this life.

Her youngest sister Azadi spent the nights with her. She was with her when the end came on the 6 January. 'So much changed in my life because of her,' said Azadi with a tender sigh some twenty years after the event. 'It was not what she said but how she was. She was a satisfied soul. She looked so beautiful when dying. So peaceful.'

There is nobody who can punish you, and there is nobody who can reward you. You are part of the whole; you are not doing anything. The whole is doing through you, whether you know it or not. The moment you know that it is the whole which is functioning through you, you become absolutely free of all responsibility. Yes my context is vast—but it is not my context, it is the context of the whole. It is functioning perfectly well— nothing ever goes wrong. But if you take yourself separately, then you are unnecessarily becoming burdened. My whole teaching is: drop all the burden on the whole, be free of all burden, and live spontaneously and totally and without any guilt.

* * *

Even from her mother's womb, Laxmi brought a memory and a purpose to her life. She sought for truth. She carried in her genes the incorruptible wealth of ancient India; the sages of the *Upanishads,* the merchants of the spice trade and the warriors of Shivaji Bhonsle. Laxmi was colourful like the wings of the kingfisher and the purple clouds of monsoon. She was generous, hard-headed and light-hearted. In her genes too was devotion to the *guru,* patience and acceptance, a teasing humour and a deep immersion in the inner, hidden world. She could take the long view and the short view, the *karmic* and the pragmatic. She had to immerse herself in meditation, feel the horrors and the wonders of the new world of America and sustain two big hits to her ego in order to fully realise her purpose and her truth.

Laxmi was the New Woman in her simplicity and her respect for people and nature. Her life was a journey of purification just as later generations will purify themselves to regain for humanity the health of this long abused planet. Osho pointed the way...Laxmi walked it.

The End

EPILOGUE

Was Laxmi enlightened? Had full self-realisation happened to her? Laxmi's nephew, a self-proclaimed sceptic said, 'I think Laxmi found what she was looking for. She was the one person I ever saw who was not there. She was so happy. Winning and losing meant nothing to her.'

Another relative of hers declared that Laxmi lived like there was no personal self—only a universal Self. She recounted this example. Little Sanjay, one of the great-nephews living in Vatcha Villas, spilled a pot of *chai* across the table onto the floor.

'I didn't do it!' he proclaimed. 'It happened.'

In the silence Laxmi's voice rang out, 'Listen to him!'

* * *

During the July monsoon of 1995 a young schoolboy arrived at the Ashram in Poona, found his way to the office and enquired about taking *sannyas*.

'Have you meditated?' he was asked.

'No. But I would like to meditate.'

'Have you been reading Osho then?'

'No. But I would like to read him.'

'Then how do you know of him?'

'I have a friend at school. I often go to his house. We

would see his aunt. She was an Osho *sannyasin*. She was dying and in pain. She looked so beautiful: she shone. When we arrived she always tried to sit up and always joked with us. She said "Laxmi's body is not good, Laxmi is very good."'

Here the boy paused a moment looking shy. 'She was so loving. I always felt happy with her. We went to see her every day. The way she lived, I want to live like that. If Osho teaches one to be so beautiful when pain and death are there, then I want to be his disciple.'

The End

APPENDIX

THREE IMPORTANT MEDITATIONS

Dynamic Meditation

Osho devised this meditation for our restless modern world. It is a fast, intense and thorough way to break up ingrained and unproductive patterns in our body-minds. In the past people could sit still naturally, now we need to exert ourselves first in order to achieve stillness.

Dynamic is best done in early mornings, when the whole of nature becomes alive. There are five stages, the first three of ten minutes each, the last two of fifteen minutes each. During all of them, remain a witness. Watch all the thoughts and feelings and sensations that arise. Just be a neutral observer.

In the first stage, to a background of boisterous music, breathe chaotically out through the nose. Let it be intense, deep, fast yet with no pattern. Use your natural body movements to help yourself build up energy. You will become the breathing.

In the second stage—explode! Let go of everything that needs to be cleaned out. Express whatever feelings need expression: scream, shout, cry, jump, kick, shake, dance, sing, laugh. A little acting sometimes helps to get you started. Watch everything that happens.

In the third stage, with arms raised above your head, jump up and down shouting the mantra, 'Hoo! Hoo! Hoo!' The music now is rhythmic. Each time your heels touch the ground, let the sound Hoo hammer deep into the body. It will awaken dormant energies.Give it all you have!

For the fourth stage—STOP! Freeze! The music stops abruptly. Now be the silent watcher on the hill, watching all the traffic of your thoughts below. Don't re-arrange the body.

The final stage is dance and celebrate; you will often feel a high that can be carried through the day.

For many, many people this meditation has been a life-changing gift.

Kundalini Meditation

An evening meditation called *Kundalini* meditation is an equally powerful practice. This has four, fifteen-minute stages. We start in a relaxed standing position and let the body shake or vibrate vigorously with the music. When it changes we move to the next stage of dance. The third stage is to sit silently watching thoughts and sensations. The fourth stage is to sit or lie in total relaxation.

Mystic Rose

Mystic Rose meditation is another dynamic, healing and life-changing process. It is utterly simple and deeply transformative. It happens for three hours a day over a three-week period. The first week participants immerse themselves in laughter; the second week in just crying, and; the third week they sit silently as Watchers on the Hill. It is an extraordinarily powerful and enduring meditation.

A CLOSING THOUGHT

We hope that having read this book, you have found it affecting and significant.

Laxmi was my bridge to Osho before I had learned to swim. I learned by watching her—absorbing her intelligent devotion. Writing this appreciation of her life has hugely helped me on my odyssey returning to the source. If it transmits to you a sense of the only life, the life of love and consciousness that Osho was enabling, then love and consciousness have done their work. What we who sat with Osho have received is so extraordinary, so precious and so deep—it feels vital that we pass it on in one form or another.

Swami Deva Rashid

OSHO WORLD FOUNDATION

OSHO
DHAM

A MEDITATION CAMPUS FOR INNER GROWTH

ओशो वर्ल्ड
मासिक पत्रिका

www.oshoworld.com

OSHO CHAIR
PATH FOR MEDITATION AND HOLISTIC GROWTH
VEER NARMAD SOUTH GUJARAT UNIVERSITY

OSHO
RAJYOGA
MEDITATION CENTRE

C-5/44, Safdarjung Development Area, New Delhi-110016
Phone: +91-11-26964533, 26862898, 9717490340
Email: contact@oshoworld.com

ACKNOWLEDGEMENTS

Implicit in the making of this book is the freely given offering of those who were interviewed and those who gave support, but also all of those who have, in one way or another, swayed my life. This book is indicating the interconnectedness of all things, that everyone is part of everyone else, so the list of people who I want to thank is multitudinous. Some of the people, alive and dead, I list below.

My first bow of gratitude is to Osho, a crazy luminous man who baffled or incensed many but lit up the way for millions more. He helped me to accept, love and honour both the mundane and the inexplicable supernal.

My thanks then go to Laxmi's friends and family and those who helped this story to evolve. In the first place to Atul, an inspiration and a mighty force of love and care, and then to Anuragi, Alpana, Mamta, Veetmoha, Veena, Yatri, Azadhi, Jyoti, Prachi, Naina, Max Brecher, Avesh, Satya Vedant, Neelam, Sohanma, Kul Bushan and his family, Kirti, Pragya, Sneh, Sangeet, Krishna Prem Allanach, Sakshi, Urvashi, Vishwanath, Sunshine, Isabelle, Bhagawati, Tathaghat, Shunyo, Savita, Dhanyam, Madhura and Madhuro, Amit, Devyani. Also to the friends at Simon and Schuster; Bharti, Dharini, Namrata, Rahul, Sayantan.

Then too I thank my family and friends; Nisheetha,

Arabella, Beatrice, Melita, Noa, Joseph, Puja, Becalelis, Julian, Paul, Luca, Orla, Anne: the grandchildren Jordy, Sam, Laurie, Joseph ll, Tom and Alex, Jessica, Tequan, Zyrell, Josh, Elia, Sofia, Caspar, Ciara, Inigo, Freya, Solomon ll, Amaya, Solomon l and Gabriel, Hilda, Lawrence Margery and the mothers of my children, Nicky and Naomi. Such friends I thank as Agama, Robin, Christo, Erach, Gyanrani, Roddy, Alice, Michael W, Michael Z, Michael D, Tony who just died and another beekeeping one still living, Premgit and Sandiya, Smita, Sunshine, Isabelle, Mahima, Nishok, Punya, Mukti, Divya, Pulak, Mara, Prabhat, Devopama, Stuart, Eileen, Blom, Candida, Dhanyam, Chetna, Mira, Anneke, Tarisha, Swaram, Kensho, Srajan, Abhiti, Pankaja l & ll, Atulya, Vani, Manchar, Anasha, Yama, Khoji, Roger, Sangeeta, Luma, Nishant, Anselm, Andrew, Chandan, Alima, Somesh, Sarasi, Manohar, Meriel, Bhagwati, Dhanyam, Punya, Prasad, Amrit, Moumina, Satish, Paula, Madhupran, Kensho, Jivan, Gopa, Veetam, Greek Mukta, Agneya, Satgyana, Anuragi I & ll, Krishna Gopa, Vinod, Graham G. Tarshita, Lucie, Alanka, Vivek, Aradhana, Phoebe and Premgeet.

Many enlightened ones have helped in the creation of this book; Ramana and Ramakrishna, Jesus and Siddartha Gautama, Meyer Baba, Neem Karoli, Rumi, Ikkyu and Hafiz plus all those whom Osho talked about like Patanjali and the Bauls, Socrates, Nanak, LaoTsu, Lieh Tzu, Chuang Tzu, Heraclitus, Pythagoras, Hakuin, Bodhidharma, Gurdjieff, Krishna, Meister Eckhart, Pythagoras, Nansen, Dogen, Naropa, Tilopa, Shankara, Baal Shem, Moses, Omar Khayyam, Mansoor, Bahaudin, Hakim Sanai, Zeno, plus those I have had the honour to meet; Poonjaji, Gangaji,

Kiran, Pamela, Eckhart, Neelam, Ramesh, Amma, Mooji, John de Ruiter, Radha, Rupert, Francis, Tony, Douglas, Mother Mira, and others.

Really important it is too, to acknowledge the poets, painters, scientists, musicians and other creative ones who have greatly touched me in one way or another; Cezanne, Michelangelo, Botticelli, Rothko, Piero della Francesca, Caravaggio, Goya, Cotman, Vermeer, Giotto, Bonnard, Titian, Rembrandt, Matisse, Van Gogh, Monet, Renoir, Auerbach, De Kooning, Malevitch, Giacometti, Twombly, Munch, Soutine, Kiefer, Nolde, Bomberg, Dumas, Shakespeare, Blake, Tolstoy, Nabokov, Tagore, Dostoevsky, Bronte, Borges, Basho, Rilke, Bly, Galway, Kerouac, Delillo, Li Po, Kabir, Whitman, Hopkins, Yeats, Eliot, Cummings, Dickinson, Teresa of Avila, B.Collins, Renais, Robbe-Grillet, Fowles, Huxley, Einstein, Newton, Tesla, Maxwell, Darwin, Schrodinger, Freud, Jung Heisenberg, Feynman, Capra, Chomsky, Margulis, Lovelock, Eisenstein, Truffaut, Bresson, Satyajit Ray, Renoir, Chaplin, Kurosowa, Godard, Bergman, Allen, Stone, Welles, Fellini, Antonioni, Visconti, Beethoven, Bach, Mozart, Purcell, Presley, Dillon, Ali Akbar Khan, Hari Prasad, Ravi Shankar, Ghulam Ali, Gundecha Bros... oh where does it stop?

Yes all these people and many more, met by chance or from long involvement, I thank for enriching this life and this work.